SWARM LEADERSHIP AND THE COLLECTIVE MIND

Using Collaborative Innovation Networks to Build a Better Business

SWARM LEADERSHIP AND THE COLLECTIVE MIND

Using Collaborative Innovation Networks to Build a Better Business

BY

PETER A. GLOOR
MIT Center for Collective Intelligence, Massachusetts Institute of Technology, Cambridge, MA, USA

United Kingdom — North America — Japan
India — Malaysia — China

Emerald Publishing Limited
Howard House, Wagon Lane, Bingley BD16 1WA, UK

First edition 2017

Reprints and permissions service
Contact: permissions@emeraldinsight.com

British Library Cataloguing in Publication Data
A catalogue record for this book is available from the British Library

ISBN: 978-1-78714-201-5 (Print)
ISBN: 978-1-78714-200-8 (Online)
ISBN: 978-1-78714-726-3 (Epub)

ISOQAR certified
Management System,
awarded to Emerald
for adherence to
Environmental
standard
ISO 14001:2004.

ISOQAR
REGISTERED

Certificate Number 1985
ISO 14001

INVESTOR IN PEOPLE

CONTENTS

ACKNOWLEDGMENTS

Isaac Newton famously said, "If I see farther, it is only because I have been standing on the shoulders of giants." While I am by no means claiming to see as far ahead as Isaac Newton, I have definitively been standing on the shoulders of many giants.

First of all I would like to thank my children Sarah and David for many long discussions deep into the night, critically tearing apart and reassembling my ideas. My friend and colleague Hauke Fuehres has also been a constant critic and contributor of crucial ideas all along the way. In particular Hauke came up with the term "homo collaborensis."

The members of my own COINs have been role models and inspiration for how to build the creative swarm. I am deeply indebted to Ken Riopelle and Julia Gluesing for reading early drafts and giving excellent feedback. Gianni Giacomelli, Vinit Verma, and George Dellal are all former industrial research sponsors who joined the COIN and commented on early versions of the manuscript. Andrea Fronzetti Colladon and Francesca Grippa are long-time academic collaborators, we have been jointly developing many of the ideas described in this book. Collaboration with Casper Lassenius, Maria Paasivaara, Cristobal Garcia, Christine Z. Miller,

Takashi Iba, and Keiichi Nemoto goes back decades, they have been core members of our COIN significantly contributing to the concepts described here. Peter Margolis, Michael Seid, and George Dellal have been fearless leaders and role models of the C3N "poster" COIN described in this book, which greatly shaped my understanding of the inner workings of COINs.

Detlef Schoder, Kai Fischbach, Daniel Oster, Gloria Volkmann, Matthaeus P. Zylka, Oliver Posegga, Karin Frick, Detlef Guertler, Yang Song, Stephanie Woerner, Ornit Raz, Arlette Maurer, Daniel Olguin Olguin, and Ben Waber are all long-time collaborators and friends who contributed to projects described in the book.

Finally I am deeply indebted to Thomas W. Malone, Rob Laubacher, Alex (Sandy) Pentland, and Thomas J. Allen for being inspiring mentors and friends at MIT for the last 14 years.

1

INTRODUCTION

CHAPTER CONTENTS

- Swarm leadership means listening first.

- Swarms practice competitive collaboration, not collaborative competition.

- The five-layer model of collaboration for individuals, organizations, and society.

Steve Jobs did *not* create Apple! Of course, Steve Jobs started Apple — together with Steve Wozniak! But he did not create it. He could never have done it on his own. Steve Jobs created the swarm that created Apple. From the very first day on, he was relying on untold legions of engineers, scientists, technicians, accountants, and janitors — not to speak of 4000 years of accumulated wisdom, and scientific and technological expertise accumulated from Chinese, Indian, Mesoamerican, Greek, Roman, German, English, French, and American philosophers, scientists, engineers, and entrepreneurs.

One human on its own is as useful as a single ant in creating the next Tesla, Apple, Google, or Facebook. However, just like the ants or the bees, a swarm of humans can do amazing things. And just like a swarm of ants or bees, the human swarm needs a queen bee, which is where Steve Jobs, Larry Page, Mark Zuckerberg, or Elon Musk comes in. The key, however, to their endeavor is communication! Only by communicating their goals, and channeling the accumulated energy and wisdom of their swarm can they set out to create the next big thing changing the world.

The goal of this book is to describe how to communicate to bring together groups of people to innovate. Better communication leads to better collaboration, which leads to more innovation. The information stored in a single neuron in the brain only becomes meaningful through the massively parallel network of connecting axons and synapses. This is no different for thousands of human brains, which can only work together to innovate by communicating with each other in the best possible way.

The future of business is swarm business — whether it's at Uber, Airbnb, Tesla, or Apple, it's not about being a fearless leader, but about creating a swarm that works together in collective consciousness to create great things that change the world. This book helps you to become the leader of your own swarm by building its collective consciousness. A successful swarm channels the competitive energies of all stakeholders toward collaboration, demonstrated by exemplary swarm leaders such as Steve Jobs or Elon Musk, and exemplary swarm businesses such as Airbnb and Uber. The art is to select, grow, and nurture the right swarm. The overlooked secret of swarm businesses like Airbnb or Uber is not the genius of Uber and Airbnb's CEOs, but the pride *all* Airbnb landlords take in their apartments, and Uber drivers in their cars, forming a cohesive swarm delivering a superb experience to the customer.

This book takes you on a journey from *homo competitivus* to *homo collaborensis*. It explains how you as an individual, as a member of an organization, and as part of society can become more collaborative, and why this is good not just for society and the organization, but also for you. In a parallel to quantum physics, this book introduces social quantum physics, defining *four key principles of social quantum physics: empathy* leading to *entanglement*, and *reflection* leading to *reboot* and refocus. Collaborative organizations combine these four principles to build collective consciousness: deep empathy that builds an entangled team, and self-reflection that leads to constant self-criticism and refocus. Once the team is operational, its collaboration can be tracked and boosted using the "six honest signals of collaboration," patterns of collaboration which will further increase the performance of the swarm. The six honest signals are central leadership, rotating leadership, balanced contribution, responsiveness, honest sentiment, and shared context. In their way of working together, team members apply the five ethical laws of collaboration: transparency, fairness, honesty, forgiveness, and listening. By operating according to these laws of collaborative ethics, such groups work together as collaborative teams, entangled in collective consciousness. Their journey starts with recruiting and building an intrinsically motivated group of early enthusiasts, the Collaborative Innovation Network (COIN). The fundamental concepts are illustrated with a wealth of examples from leading organizations based on decades of research by our team at MIT, ranging from Uber and

Airbnb over open source communities to Fortune 500 high-tech firms and healthcare. These examples will tell you, as an individual, how becoming more collaborative will give more meaning and satisfaction to your professional life. They will also tell the managers of an organization how they can leverage their teams' creative energies to increase organizational performance. And finally, they will lay out a way forward for society, toward a more collaborative and less competitive future.

1.1. SWARM BUSINESS IS COMPETITIVE COLLABORATION, NOT COLLABORATIVE COMPETITION

Humans have always been torn between competition and collaboration. This apparent contradiction of the benefits of collaboration puzzled Charles Darwin, as evolutionary survival of the fittest should favor the most competitive at the expense of the most collaborative. Research of the last 50 years indicates the opposite. Super-social species like ants, bees, and humans have been spectacularly successful at the expense of more solitary and competitive species. The conclusion is that humans need to channel their competitive energies toward supporting collaboration — a process I call *competitive* **collaboration**. This is in contrast to *collaborative* **competition**, where humans collaborate to compete more effectively. Musicians in an orchestra are competitive collaborators; they collaborate to play the most beautiful music. Orchestra and audience are all elated and happy after the concert, with individual competition between the musicians channeled toward a superior collaborative experience. A soccer game demonstrates the opposite process of collaborative competition. The two soccer teams play against each other with each team internally collaborating to compete for victory, with one team ending up as the winner, leaving the other, unhappy team in the dust, together with its disappointed fans.

We can find similar examples in industry, where more collaborative companies leave the most competitive ones behind. Texas energy company Enron was hailed the most innovative company six years in a row by *Fortune* magazine. CEO and former McKinsey consultant Jeffrey Skilling had introduced an up-or-out process where the least performing 15% of the workforce were yanked out every year, leading to a culture of backstabbing and mutual denigration. In 2002, Enron went bankrupt, when its large-scale corporate fraud was exposed. Compare this with company W. L. Gore & Associates, inventors and manufacturers of waterproof fabric Gore-Tex. In contrast to Enron's short rise and demise, Gore & Associates has been consistently successful since 1958, when Bill Gore left his position at Du Pont to start a company in the basement of his house. With over 10,000 employees in 2015, Gore & Associates still lives by the core principles of its founder, which he described as freedom, fairness, commitment, and waterline. Associates have the freedom to help others grow in knowledge, skill, and responsibility. They should be fair against everybody they get in contact with. Associates are in a position to make their own commitments. Before engaging in a situation that might impact the waterline of the company by "sinking the ship," they should engage in consultation with other associates. In combination, these four principles result in a uniquely collaborative culture with highly engaged employees putting the long-term interest of the firm before their own individual interests.

While it is the communication among swarm members, which is key for the uniquely collaborative and innovative climate, it is the leaders who put it into place. Steve Jobs was not the first charismatic leader to start something radically new. Qin Shi Huang, the first Emperor of China, unified his country with an iron fist. Whoever incurred his wrath was put to death, together with their relatives up to the third degree. In one instance, 460 scholars owning forbidden books were buried alive. Qin Shi Huang was so much afraid of the afterlife that he had an army of 6000 terracotta warriors built to protect him. Leaders have come a long way since Qin Shi Huang, but even today there are still adherents of Qin Shi Huang's approach. When I worked in 2001 as a consultant for the ill-fated merger between Daimler and Chrysler, Juergen Schrempp, the CEO of DaimlerChrysler and main architect of the merger, was commanding his enterprise from his war room outside Stuttgart, Germany, surrounded by triple rows of computer monitors manned not by Terracotta warriors, but by scores of assistants attending to all his whims. Or take Donald Trump, who loves to fire people, and loathes losers.

It is time for a new type of leader. Linus Torvalds, the creator of Linux, Tim Berners-Lee, who created the World Wide Web, and Jimmy Wales, the founder of Wikipedia, are exemplars of this new style of collaborative leadership. They are the undisputed queen bees of swarms of thousands of open source developers and Wikipedia editors. And yet neither Linus, Tim, nor Jimmy have the authority to fire any of their subordinates. Rather they lead by example and conviction, by carrying the responsibility for their respective projects. They constantly worry about the success of their innovations, and are themselves the chief creators, designers, and builders of their products. They are also evangelists and teachers, the flag bearers of their innovation, incessantly singing the praises of the merits of their "labor of love." They are also entrepreneurs, securing funding and engineering the growth of their enterprise. They are a new species of leaders, moving from Donald Trump-style "home competitivus" toward "homo collaborensis," rechanneling innate human competitive energy toward collaboration.

Creative swarms are the main carriers of change. They move us from a world driven by competition toward altruistic collaboration. This new style of swarm-based collaborative leadership leads to intrinsically motivated groups where there are only winners, no losers. Swarm-based leadership moves from collaborative *competition* to competitive *collaboration*: Two soccer teams playing against each other collaborate to *compete*, while within the team the players compete to *collaborate*. Today's society and economy demonstrate more and more examples of competitive collaboration. For example, on the Stack Overflow website, millions of highly skilled programmers assist novices solving software problems, developing an invaluable resource of programming skills along the way — all without being paid a dime. All these exemplars of swarm-based leadership follow the framework of Collaborative Innovation Networks (COINs), progressing from COIN to Collaborative Learning Network (CLN) to Collaborative Interest Network (see Chapter 4). Collaboration in COINs is based on social quantum physics, most prominently entanglement between two people over long distance, and the Heisenberg uncertainty principle — a system that is measured will change its behavior. Entanglement in quantum physics means that if two geographically separated particles are entangled, if one particle changes, for example, its spin angle, the other will change it the same way at the same time, independent of location (see Section 3.7). The Heisenberg uncertainty principle states that the more accurately one property of a particle is measured, the less accurately other complementary properties of the particle can be measured (see Section 3.8). Collaboration in human networks follows the same two principles of entanglement and reflection. Just as entangled particles will move in parallel, entangled people will too; for example, look at a Jazz band grooving in synch. Just like with Heisenberg uncertainty, reflecting on one's behavior will change the behavior. Self-organizing swarms apply the five laws of collaboration: transparency, fairness, honesty, forgiveness, and listening. Six honest signals of collaboration developed over 10 years of research by our team at MIT show how everybody can communicate to collaborate in small teams, measuring interpersonal interaction through social networking: strong leadership, balanced contribution, rotating leadership, responsiveness, honest sentiment, and shared context (see Chapter 5).

1.2. THE FIVE-LAYER MODEL OF COLLABORATION

I propose a five-layer model of communication applied to building creative swarms. Protocol stacks composed of layered models of communication levels are popular for describing physical communication networks, most prominently the Internet. The idea is that when computers talk to each other, the software that does the talking between computers can be modeled on different layers of abstraction. For instance, when you read a Wikipedia article on your Web browser, your browser — independent of whether it is Firefox, Internet Explorer, Safari, or Chrome — talks with the Wikipedia Web server to load the entire page. On a lower level, the Wikipedia article page is broken up into pieces of text described in a language called HTML. On the next lower level, these HTML text pieces are decomposed into a sequence of bits by the Wikipedia Web server and sent over the Internet to your browser, where your computer reassembles the bit stream into HTML text fragments, which are then shown to you as the Wikipedia article page. In this book, I introduce a similar protocol stack of five layers of communication among humans. **Figure 1** (see page 11) shows these five layers of human communication. This five-layer model extends my earlier work on COINs with four additional layers that govern and control how humans communicate to work together. The lowest layer, the physical layer, describes how humans exchange bits of information using social quantum physics. The second layer, the network layer, defines network structure and topology. The third layer, the signal layer, tracks the "honest signals" that people exchange to achieve their task in differing degrees of collective consciousness. Each element of this interpersonal network is an individual human. The fourth layer, the ethical layer, describes the ethical laws, the basic rules that people adhere to or not while working together. The highest layer, the collaboration layer, finally decides if people collaborate or compete against each other while working together toward reaching their goals.

Just as with a computer networking protocol stacks, we can track and study communication between the members of a social system on each different layer. On the physical layer, groups of humans work together with differing degrees of collective consciousness — a well-functioning team has some degree of collective consciousness; if it does not, it is not a real team. On the networking layer, groups of humans are connected in many different ways, forming networks of different structures and dynamics. In innovation networks, these communication structures are COINs. On the signal layer, humans signal their intent subconsciously to each other, using a simple repertory of six "honest signals" that tell other people about their goals. On the ethical layer, collaborative people treat each other according to moral and ethical standards; if they don't, they will not work together well. On the highest layer, the collaboration layer, members of a group choose either to compete with each other, or they decide to collaborate on the given task. Whether people are collaborating or competing is controlled by their adherence to the ethical laws, the honest signals they exchange, the amount of collective consciousness they achieve through social quantum physics, and the way in which they network with each other.

Figure 1 shows the "five layers of collaboration," which also correspond to five book chapters. It puts the usual hierarchy with the leader at the top on its head, as swarm leadership is defined not through hierarchy, but through responsibility. Just like in Greek mythology where Hercules set up two pillars in the strait of Gibraltar between Spain and Morocco to secure the entry

Figure 1: Five-Layer Model of Collaboration.

into the Mediterranean, the leader of a swarm is literally carrying the weight of the swarm on his shoulders. The fundamentals of swarm leadership are explained in the next chapter. Each layer in the five-layer model of collaboration is then discussed in a subsequent chapter. The final three chapters lay out how this new style of swarm leadership can be applied by the individual, by the organization, and by society.

The next chapter on the foundations of swarm leadership describes why contributing to the greater good is not just good for others, but also for the contributor. A key reason for this is that behaving less selfishly makes us more emphatic to the needs of others, thanks to mirror neurons. This is crucial for our own well-being and happiness.

Chapter 3 discusses how the four principles of social quantum physics empower and create collective consciousness. It describes how social entanglement is created through the theory of mind. The theory of mind, enabled by mirror neurons, corresponds to the quantum physics wave-particle duality. By nurturing empathy, the theory of mind gets us to collaborate more closely, leading to entanglement. Social quantum physics also explains how the future redefines the past, by applying the Heisenberg uncertainty principle: if a social system is measured, and the measurements are mirrored back to the participants, it triggers their self-reflection; the participants will change through reinterpretation of the past, leading to an internal reboot.

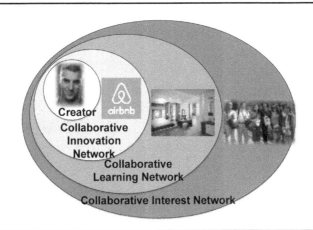

Chapter 4 introduces the three phases of building your swarm, starting out with the Collaborative Innovation Networks (COINs), small groups of self-organizing, emergent team members collaborating over the Internet. COINs are leading to larger groups of people, the Collaborative Learning Network (CLN), whose members are testing the prototypes of the COIN, and the Collaborative Interest Network (CIN) whose members are spreading the word about the cool products of the COIN. The concept of COINs has been introduced in my earlier book *Swarm Creativity*; this chapter gives a brief overview of the core ideas.

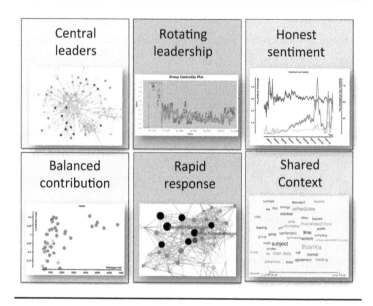

Chapter 5 discusses the six honest signals of collaboration. They are calculated by mining all sorts of communication archives such as e-mail, phone logs, Twitter, and blogs, or tracking direct interaction though sociometric badges worn on the body. Strong leadership, balanced contribution, rotating leadership, responsiveness, honest sentiment, and shared context make collaboration effectiveness and efficiency measurable.

Chapter 6 introduces the five laws of ethical collaboration. Transparency, fairness, honesty, forgiveness, and listening are the five key axioms that will lead to more collaborative teams, where self-motivated team members work together on the issues they really are passionate about.

Chapter 7 shows how we move from competition toward collaboration, both of them inseparably linked like yin and yang. It describes how competitive and collaborative behaviors can be combined to channel our competitive energies toward better collaboration. It discusses the concepts of

competitive collaboration — think musical orchestra —
and collaborative competition — think two sports teams
competing-illustrating it with practical examples.

Chapter 8 illustrates what this means for the individual. It
shows how each of us can apply the principles described in
this book to become a happier, more creative, and successful instigator of our own swarm. It explains how transactive memory allows each individual to access the
accumulated knowledge of humankind through the
Internet, educating collaborative and creative "renaissance
humans." It also introduces a first version of a course to
educate "renaissance humans," the COINs seminar that
brings together global virtual teams of students to solve
complex collaborative tasks, providing a blueprint for
becoming a member of a collaboratively creative swarm.

Chapter 9 discusses what this means for organizations. It introduces a wealth of business examples from my own research done at MIT and elsewhere. These examples illustrate how building COINs leads to innovation that sticks, because they are based on competitive collaboration, not collaborative competition. Numerous case studies from different industries ranging from high-tech to process outsourcing illustrate how companies can leverage competitive collaboration to increase innovation by improving collaboration. The chapter also introduces Collaborative Chronic Care Networks (C3Ns), a novel healthcare paradigm. C3Ns are intrinsically motivated communities of patients, doctors, and researchers of chronic diseases who collaborate to develop a better life and cure for their disease.

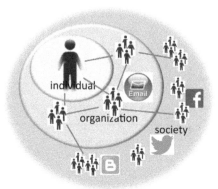

Chapter 10 discusses implications for society. It brings up consequences of social capital for personal happiness, the key role of transparency to build trust, and the satisfaction we draw from helping others, leading to a society where the community takes care of the basic needs of the individual.

MAIN LESSONS LEARNED

- Swarm leaders succeed in creating collective consciousness of their swarm through building a shared context.

- Swarms practice competitive collaboration — in an orchestra, musicians compete to collaborate. This is different from collaborative competition — two soccer teams collaborate to compete.

- The five-layer model of collaboration defines a framework for individuals, organizations, and society; the five layers are the physical, the networking, the signal, the ethical, and the collaborative layer.

2

FOUNDATIONS OF SWARM LEADERSHIP

CHAPTER CONTENTS

- Empathy is more than emotional intelligence.

- The best managers are creators and connectors.

- Money, power, and glory are bad motivators; love is better.

The age of imperial CEOs is over. The future belongs to collaborative leaders of the type of Alan Mulally, former CEO of Ford. My friends Julia and Ken have been teaching in the Engineering Management Masters Program at

Ford to high-potential managers for many years. In their courses, the Ford CEOs regularly gave a speech at some time during the semester. They told me how Jacques Nasser, the previous CEO of Ford, arrived with an entourage of a half dozen people to their class, with assistants sweeping in before and preparing the stage, others carrying Nasser's notes and briefing materials, and yet others ensuring uninterrupted reachability. When Nasser was giving his talk, it was mostly about himself, and about "creating value" using financial engineering to increase the profits of Ford. The students asked a couple of questions, but Nasser's responses made it clear that he didn't know who the students were and what they needed to know. While Nasser's conduct as a CEO was imperial, his performance was abysmal.[1] When Nasser had taken over Ford, it was the most profitable car company. During Nasser's tenure, Ford spent billions acquiring Volvo and Land Rover, companies which it then tried to integrate with its Ford, Jaguar, and Aston Martin brands, as well as attempting integration with Mazda (partially owned by Ford), in pursuit of creating a "global car." He also introduced a personnel review system modeled after Jack Welch's General Electric (GE) system to force out the bottom 5% of all Ford employees every year, which led to a slate of lawsuits and huge employee dissatisfaction. When he was forced out, Ford was in deep problems. It was left to his successors Bill Ford and Alan Mulally as Ford's next CEOs to clean up the mess. Bill Ford recruited Alan Mulally to really turn things around. His style could not have been more different than Jacques

---

[1]http://www.economist.com/node/842705

Nasser's. When Mulally gave his presentation in Julia and Ken's class, Mulally arranged the visit himself by exchanging a few e-mails with my friends. When he came to the classroom, it was just himself, and one assistant who was carrying a large box of just-released *Ford Annual Reports*. Before coming to class, he had thoroughly prepared by asking for the class syllabus and a roster with pictures of the students so he would know as much about them as possible. He engaged with the students by beginning with asking them what questions they had and what concerned them about technology, cars, and the future of Ford. Mulally sat on the edge of a desk and just conversed with the students for over an hour and half. At the end of his talk, he personally distributed a copy of the Annual Report to each student, shaking their hands and thanking them for their dedication to Ford. Under his leadership, Ford got through the 2000s recession without bankruptcy and returned to be highly profitable. Mulally shows all attributes of the leader of the future, combining deep knowledge, emotional intelligence, and empathy.

2.1. FROM EMOTIONAL INTELLIGENCE TO EMPATHY

As evolution pits individuals against each other in relentless competition, with the winner getting to transfer his genes to the next generation as the big prize, the question arises why people should be motivated at all to collaborate. While many people, such as Wall Street bankers and contenders for the top job in politics or industry show the expected "rational" behavior, competing against each other with the winner getting it all, there are many others who voluntarily forgo their chance to beat others by placing collaboration before competition. Whether it is monks in a monastery, teachers in primary school, or orchestra musicians, they are all renouncing competition and choosing collaboration instead.

In order to win a competition, it pays to outguess and outsmart your competitors. Popularized by Daniel Goleman in his book of the same name, the value of "emotional intelligence" or EQ has been widely recognized as being at least as important for professional success as intelligence. However, Josef Mengele was a highly trained scientist with doctorates both in anthropology and medicine. When he took over his post in Nazi Germany as a concentration camp doctor in Auschwitz, he was also assigned to evaluate which inmates would directly go to the gas chamber, and which ones would go to slave labor. While most other physicians dreaded this task, Mengele was enjoying it, frequently whistling a tune. He was obviously highly emotionally intelligent, as for his horrible experiments with identical twins, he would first comfort them and give them sweets, but — totally devoid of empathy — the next day intentionally infect them with typhus.

Fortunately, people like Mengele are exceedingly rare. Most of us suffer also when we see somebody else suffer, and are able to enjoy the pleasure of somebody else.

The psychologies of competition and collaboration exhibit fundamental differences. On the psychological and social level, competition imposes huge costs on individuals and groups. As Donald Trump in his 2015 presidential campaign said about John McCain, "He's not a war hero. He's a war hero because he was captured. I like people who weren't captured." This basically means whoever is captured is a loser, and only winners are good. In the medieval days, winning a competition took mostly brawn; today it takes mostly brains, not just as IQ, but even more in the form of emotional intelligence. As in the example with John McCain, war is the ultimate competition, where both opponents try to destroy each other. Usually, there is nothing collaborative in this competition, although even among warring adversaries, collaboration occasionally comes up. For instance, in the First World War in the trenches of the Western Front, the Germans and the Allies had unspoken rules about not shooting into each other's most exposed areas, or to hold off killing each other altogether on Christmas Day.

We find collaborative competition in sports too. In group games like soccer or baseball, it's not the most competitive individual who wins, but the team that collaborates best. However, on the psychological level, competitive sport is basically ritualized warfare. Winners draw energy from beating losers. The Greeks already realized this in classic antiquity, interrupting wars during the Olympics, to let athletes of warring city-states continue their fights through athletic competition. This has not much changed since then. While it is exhilarating to win the Soccer World Cup, there are always many more losing teams than the winning one, with the losers traveling home drained of energy, and extremely disappointed. For a recent example, it's enough to look at the 2014 World Soccer championship semifinals, where Germany beat host Brazil 7 to 1. This utter humiliation of the World Cup hosts led to a national trauma, with tears of the Brazilian spectators flowing like water in the later parts of the game and subsequent national mourning for weeks.

This is why I like collaboration much better. Collaboration is a win—win situation. Just look at the audience in a concert, where both musicians and listeners are elated, and go home extremely satisfied and happy. Collaborating individuals draw energy from helping each other. Wikipedia and open source software development projects are prime examples of this process, with Wikipedians and open source developers being generous with praise for each other's work, frequently giving each other a virtual hug or pat on the back. Whoever wants to honestly collaborate is welcome to contribute with the best ideas to be combined into the best possible solution. In rare cases, even competition can lead to such collaboration. For example, when in 2006 Netflix announced a one million dollar prize for the best collaborative filtering algorithm to predict ratings of movies, researchers from the two best teams decided to work together and combined their different approaches to jointly win the prize in 2009.

Researchers speculate that there is a neurological foundation to collaboration by empathy triggered through the mirror neurons in our brain. Mirror neurons have been discovered in the 1980s and 1990s by researchers working with primates, who found that the same neurons in a monkey's brain were firing when a monkey observed another monkey doing an action, as when the original monkey was doing the same action. This has been shown to be true also for humans. For example, when you see somebody getting hurt, you might immediately feel the pain of the other person as if it were in your own body. V. S. Ramachandran, one of the main proponents of mirror neurons, calls them the "basis of civilization." According to V. S. Ramachandran, "the extraordinary implication of this is that my brain is hooked up to your brain directly." Mirror neurons are one of the keys to collective intelligence, and to social collaboration.

2.2. INTRINSIC AND EXTRINSIC MOTIVATION: CREATORS AND EXECUTORS

Why is it that some people are motivated to compete, while others are motivated to collaborate? It seems that competition and collaboration are based on fundamentally different triggers in our brain. On the lowest, neurological level, mirror neurons as the major cause of empathy give a plausible explanation for collaboration: two people helping each other should make both happy. If your neurons tell you that you are happy, my brain will mirror your happiness and will tell me that I am happy too. If I help you to become happy, the neurons in your brain will start producing dopamine, making you happy. This will trigger the mirror neurons in my brain to start producing dopamine, making me happy also. Mirror neurons and empathy leading to collaboration thus question Darwin's evolutionary theory of survival of the fittest. Darwinist evolution motivates the prevalence of competition over collaboration, with the prize being the opportunity for the winners to pass on their genes to the next generation.

Winning a competition will make me happy also, as I will bask in the admiration and envy of others. However, this is a shaky type of gratification, which can be easily destroyed by somebody else beating me in my own game, and taking over my admired and envied position. Finding gratification through collaboration is far more sustainable. It basically means building up and nurturing a network of give-and-take relationships within my environment. Whether it is monkeys grooming each other, or musicians playing together in the same orchestra or jazz band, it is being together with "people like me" that makes one happy. Called "homophily" in sociology, it is also known as "birds of a feather flock together." Simply put, I am motivated by wanting to be with people like myself and look for company which resembles me as much as possible. The only problem is that if I am a very competitive person, and I am getting together with other very competitive people, we will invariably start competing against each other, which will reduce the happiness of the loser. It is much better if I am a very collaborative person, and select other collaborative people as my friends. Our desire will be to collaborate with each other, something we should very easily be capable of. Research on homophily among Hadza Stone Age hunter-gatherers in Tanzania[2] has indeed shown that generous people tend to select other generous people, while stingy people select other stingy people as friends. The same effect has been observed among Nobel Prize winners,[3] who — compared with similarly accomplished scholars — tend to collaborate with other future Nobel Prize winners at a young age, well before being nominated for the Nobel Prize.

A key question is what motivates leaders to become leaders. My theory is that true leaders are creators. Successful role models like Steve Jobs, Elon Musk, Larry

---

[2] Apicella, Marlowe, Fowler, and Christakis (2012).
[3] Wagner, Horlings, Whetsell, Mattsson, and Nordqvist (2015).

Page, Linus Torvalds, Bill Gates, Tim Berners-Lee, and Mark Zuckerberg are not managers in the conventional sense. They lead by personal example, by superior skills, by width and breadth of their vision, by educating the people working with them, and by creating something radically new. Larry Page, cofounder of Google, stepped down as CEO of Google for the second time in 2015, passing the baton to Sundar Pichai. According to a profile in the *New York Times*, rather than CEO, Page is innovator-in-chief.[4]

There are many different types of leaders, motivated by different forces. In this book, I propose a grouping of leaders into four stereotypes. Note however that these are just stereotypes; exemplary leaders like the ones listed earlier combine traits from all four. These four types of leaders, vastly differing in skill set and motivation, are (1) managers, (2) entrepreneurs, (3) teachers, and (4) artists and scientists (**Figure 2**). They differ along two dimensions, creative versus execution-oriented activities, and intrinsic versus extrinsic motivation. Intrinsically motivated people

Figure 2: Categories of Leaders and Their Motivation.

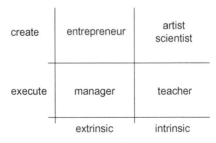

---

[4]*New York Times* (2016).

do something for the sake and pleasure of doing it, while extrinsically motivated people do something for external reasons such as money, power, or glory.

The key objective of a *manager* is to facilitate an environment where the members of the organization they are leading can deliver top performance. The main motivation of managers, as stipulated by proponents of agency theory, is to increase the revenue of their organization in a way that will also optimize their own paycheck. For an example of an extrinsically motivated manager, look at Bill Ackman, billionaire hedge fund manager and owner of hedge fund Pershing Square Capital Management. With two degrees from Harvard, Ackman is on a personal crusade against nutritional supplement vendor Herbalife — on the pretense of saving the world from predatory vendor Herbalife — while shorting its stock price. At the same time he invests into predatory "pharmaceutical" company Valeant, which buys old heart drugs, and increases their prices by 200–500% while slashing research and development. He clearly puts his money where his mouth is, not his heart.

Entrepreneurs want to not just create a new product, but also an organization that will produce and market the new product. While both Bill Gates and Steve Jobs were driven to create the best possible personal computer, smartphone, and tablet computer, they also wanted to win, and get immensely wealthy along the way. There is a story told of Bill Gates being taught a new game by a new manager at Microsoft; Bill initially lost it every time. They did not meet for a few months. Next time, however, when the manager and Bill Gates played the game again, Bill was beating the other manager every time. Highly competitive

Bill had practiced the game until he had cracked it, to win it consistently in the future. In the same vein, in spite of his philanthropy, donating billions of dollars each year to alleviate poverty and human suffering, Bill Gates keeps enough money to still be the richest person in the world.

Teachers want to impart knowledge to their students. They want their pupils to understand, to become lifelong learners, and to be self-sustaining members of society. The creativity of teachers consists of developing new ways and methods of conveying and transferring knowledge, going back to Greek philosopher Socrates, who came up with the teaching method of the Socratic Dialog described by his disciple Plato, which guides the student to learn a new subject through masterful questioning of the teacher.

Artists and *scientists* both create something new. Artists want to create something original and beautiful, to touch the lives of people interacting with their art. Whether it is painters, sculptors, actors, singers, or orchestra musicians, they do what they do mostly not because they are paid to do it, but because they love what they do. Artists have no choice but to be intrinsically motivated, as the chance to become rich and famous as an artist is minuscule. Scientists identify new patterns of how nature works. At their best, they are driven by their desire to discover something new, to further the state of the art in their chosen field of science. Whether it is pure science like physics or astronomy, or applied science like medicine or engineering, their goal is to create something new by taking what is there, and combining it in new, innovative ways.

While entrepreneurs and artists and scientists want to create something new, either a new product, a new piece of art, or a new scientific insight, managers and teachers are mostly users of existing systems and processes. Most of the time they do not really excel in creating new things, but in carrying out project plans, or executing curricula. Artists do what they do because they love it. They are the most intrinsically motivated by the four stereotypes — followed by the scientists and the teachers, who are scientists and teachers because that's what they like, with little chance to ever get rich. This is very different for the managers, who frequently choose their profession to be rich and powerful. They expect their success to be rewarded by fat paychecks and high status in society. The income of artists, on the other hand, shows a definitively long-tail distribution, meaning that there are very few Picassos and Andrew Lloyd Webbers getting rich and famous. Rather, the vast majority of artists can expect to make very little money over the course of their careers. A musician today is still as likely to end like Mozart (although probably not as famous) dying relatively young and poor, as a painter is more likely to end like Van Gogh than like Picasso. Salaries of scientists and teachers show a more favorable distribution with most of them living off quite modest salaries, although somewhat more comfortable than musicians and painters. Income distribution of managers, on the other hand, shows a fat tail, meaning that many can expect to make a substantial income, and a still sizeable number can expect to make a lot of money. The most popular way for scientists, artists, and teachers to increase the size of their salaries is to accept "managerial" roles.

The key difference, therefore, between managers and entrepreneur stereotypes on the one hand, and artists, scientists, and teachers on the other hand, is that stereo-typical artists, scientists, and teachers are more intrinsi-cally motivated — they love what they do — while managers are mostly extrinsically motivated — they love money, power, and glory. Of course, this motivational framework is an oversimplification, as there are as many great managers and nurturers of talent, as there are greedy and selfish artists and scientists. The perfect leader combines all four stereotypes, creating new inventions as an artist and scientist, making the new ideas sustainable and self-maintaining as an entrepreneur, telling about the invention to others as a teacher, and organizing the idea implementation process as a manager.

2.3. WHY MONEY, POWER, AND GLORY ARE BAD MOTIVATORS

Figure 3 shows the motivational pyramid that drives our life. It maps right to the extrinsic and intrinsic motiva-tions described in **Figure 2** for the four leadership stereo-types. Money, power, and glory are extrinsic motivators;

Figure 3: Motivation Pyramid.

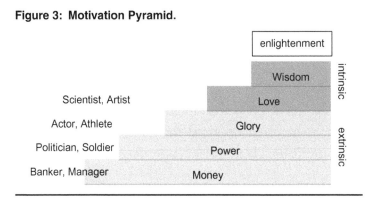

stereotypical managers, bankers, politicians, and entrepreneurs do what they do to become as rich, famous, and
powerful as possible. Love and wisdom are intrinsic motivators; stereotypical artists and scientists — at least in
theory — do what they do because they love what they
do and want to gain more insight and wisdom.

If all we want is money, power, and glory, the world
becomes a sad spot to live on. Academic research provides solid evidence that the single-minded pursuit of
these three things makes the world a more miserable
place. For instance, it appears that students of management and economics, who make the pursuit of money
and power their life's goal, are more greedy even before
they start their studies, and that they become even more
so over the course of their education. In behavioral
research, first year economics students have been shown
to be more likely to free-ride in public goods games. In
one experiment,[5] students could deposit money into a
public account where it was multiplied and distributed to
all participants, or keep their money in a private account,
and still participate in the distribution of the public pool.
First year graduate students in economics kept 80% of the
money for themselves, and only put 20% into the public
pool, compared to all other participants in the game who
put 50% of their money into the public pool. In a follow-
up survey, the researchers asked the students about their
understanding of fairness. While for all other students the
concept of fairness was an important one, a large part of
the economics students either refused to answer this question or were unable to give an understandable answer.

---

[5]Frank, Gilovich, and Regan (1993).

In another experiment, when the students got the opportunity to play the prisoner's dilemma game, which rewards participants for cheating, economics majors were almost twice as likely to cheat on their teammates as students with other majors.

The researchers also explored if economics students became even more selfish over the course of their studies. This seems indeed to be the case, documented by having the students play the prisoner's dilemma game over extended periods of time. Normally, participants become more collaborative over time, cheating less on their teammates. This effect of increasing collaboration over time was conspicuously absent for the economics students. In an experiment[6] comparing economics students and students from other majors in the first and second years, economists were significantly less fair, and more selfish than their peers, and this effect became stronger in the second year. It seems that economists start out more selfish than others, and that their selfish behavior gets reinforced over time in daily interaction with other economists.

The researchers also found that economics professors are more stingy as charitable givers than professors in other disciplines. In a survey answered by 576 academics, there were almost 10 times as many nongivers among the economics professors than in all other disciplines. In another natural experiment, Bruno Frey, a professor of economics at the University of Zurich, and his colleagues investigated[7] the charitable behavior of 28,586 students at the University of Zurich. Each semester students could decide

---

[6]Carter and Irons (1991).
[7]Frey and Meier (2003).

if they wanted to contribute a small amount of money toward a fund for needy students. Frey and his colleague found that in particular students of business economics were significantly less generous than students from other majors, and this effect stayed over the entire duration of their studies. Frey even found that the effect goes back to high school, as students from high schools with emphasis on business economics were stingier than their peers. The late Stanford professor Hal Leavitt put it succinctly,[8] stating that business education transforms students into "critters with lopsided brains, icy hearts, and shrunken souls."

Power corrupts — behavioral economists have demonstrated[9] this folk wisdom in a series of ingenious experiments. In a research project in Boston and New York, researchers manipulated the feeling of power of study participants by inviting them to stand in either an impressive posture, or in a more humble and modest way. They then gave the participants the opportunity to cheat on them by "accidentally" overpaying them after the "official" experiment was over. People in the humble posture were more than twice as likely to return the overpayment than people standing in the power position. In a second experiment, the feeling of power was manipulated by either seating participants at a wide and expansive desk, or giving them a small table and chair. When study participants got an opportunity to grade their own tests, the likelihood of cheating by correcting their own answers was again more than twice as high for participants experiencing the "feeling of power" sitting at the wide

---

[8]Leavitt (1989).
[9]Yap, Wazlawek, Lucas, Cuddy, and Carney (2013).

and expansive desk. In two further experiments, the researchers compared the driving behavior of car drivers with the size of their car. In a car simulator, if participants got a large car seat, they drove more recklessly than when sitting on a small and cramped car seat. In the final experiment, the researchers counted the instances of double parking in New York, which is illegal, and encumbers other traffic participants. They found that the larger the car, the more likely it was that drivers were willing to double park in the streets of New York.

In addition, researchers also found[10] that people of higher social classes, having more power and glory, behaved less ethically. For example, when driving on the streets, drivers of upper-class cars were more willing to cut off other vehicles on a busy four-way intersection, and to cut off pedestrians at a crosswalk. In further studies, participants were asked about their socioeconomic status, as well as their willingness to lie to job applicants to entice them to accept a job. It turned out that people with higher socioeconomic status and thus more power were more willing to cheat and to lie. In another experiment, a feeling of power was established through psychological manipulation, by asking participants to compare themselves against people with the least money, least education, and least respected jobs. This put them in a mind-set of power, which made them more willing to behave unethical by taking away more candy which would otherwise have gone to small children.

More powerful people are also more willing to cheat on their spouses.[11] Conducting a survey with 1561 participants,

---

[10]Piff, Stancato, Côté, Mendoza-Denton, and Keltner (2012).
[11]Lammers, Stoker, Jordan, Pollmann, and Stapel (2011).

researchers found that the higher the socioeconomic status of a person was, the higher was both their willingness to cheat on their partner and their actual infidelity. This was independent of gender; more powerful women were as willing to cheat as more powerful men. In another project,[12] the same researchers found that power increased hypocrisy. The powerful were stricter with others' moral transgressions while being more willing to misbehave themselves. The feeling of power was again induced by priming participants to recall experiences of low or high power. More powerful participants were quick in condemning the cheating of others while cheating more themselves when playing lottery games. It seems that a position of power goes along with a sense of entitlement.

Glory also has a dark side, as famous people have been shown to be more narcissistic than ordinary people. In a research project,[13] the degree of narcissism of celebrities was measured and compared against the narcissism scores of regular people. While narcissism also has some good aspects — for example, it seems that narcissistic people are less depressed — narcissists crave attention, are overconfident, and frequently lack empathy. For this project, the researchers recruited 200 actors, comedians, musicians, and reality television personalities to fill out a survey. The celebrities had participated in a national radio show that gives advice about drugs, sex, and relationships. They had been invited to this show because they all appeared frequently in the entertainment media and because of their ability to draw an audience. These

---

[12]Lammers, Stapel, and Galinsky (2010).
[13]Young and Pinsky (2006).

celebrities were compared against a similarly sized sample of MBA students. The survey that was used breaks narcissism down into seven sub-properties: authority, exhibitionism, superiority, entitlement, exploitativeness, self-sufficiency, and vanity. Different from the normal population, where men are more narcissistic than women, female celebrities were even more narcissistic than men. In particular, female celebrities excelled in exhibitionism, superiority, and vanity. Among the different types of celebrities, reality television personalities were the most narcissistic, while musicians were the least narcissistic. The researchers also wanted to know if naturally narcissistic people were drawn to the entertainment industry, or if long years in the entertainment industry made less narcissistic participants more narcissistic. Their conclusion was that the length of being in the entertainment industry has no influence on the degree of narcissism; it rather seems that more narcissistic people are drawn to work in entertainment.

On a side note, the researchers also compared the average narcissism of their MBA students with the overall US population. They also found that the MBA students were more narcissistic than the rest of the population, but much less so than the celebrities.

At the lowest level in the motivational pyramid in **Figure 3** is the quest for getting as much money as possible. This is why most Wall Street bankers and hedge fund managers choose their career; for them happiness is directly correlated with the number of zeros being added to their bank account.

The next motivational level is power. This is what motivates politicians and soldiers. Becoming the president of the United States will give the holder of that office a lot of power. Somebody who has a lot of money can — to some extent — use money to buy power, although in a transparent democratic society buying power is somewhat restricted. Nevertheless, as the conferences for prospective Republican presidential candidates organized by the billionaire Koch brothers show, their money buys them a direct way into the innermost circles of power.

On the next motivational level comes glory, this is what motivates actors and artists. George Clooney and Roger Federer are nowhere as rich as the Koch brothers, nevertheless their fame gives them at least as much clout as the billionaires. The downside of the hunt for glory is that for an aspiring musician, painter, or sculptor, the chances to become the next David Bowie, Pablo Picasso, or Damien Hirst are quite low. Another problem with the chase for fame is that many of the artists who become famous too young end up leading a troubled life. For instance, the chances for Justin Bieber to follow his role model Michael Jackson in all regards of rise and demise are unfortunately quite high.

The next motivational level is "love." In an ideal world, we do what we do because we love doing it. However, most people who "love" making money love it because the money they make buys them prestige, power, and fame. People motivated by money, power, and glory try to use these to buy love; Tiger Wood's excesses of marital infidelity provide a brazen example of using money, power, and glory to buy love.

For somebody who is truly intrinsically motivated, the activity of the task is the reward in itself. Mother Teresa worked in the slums of Kolkata (formerly Calcutta) because she wanted to help the underprivileged in the slums, not to get rich, powerful, or famous. Her reward was the gratitude of the poor; in return for her help she got the love of the people she helped. As Mother Teresa helped others to become happier, this made her happier too, thanks to her empathy triggered by her mirror neurons. This is very similar to members of the Salvation Army, who also provide unconditional help to the poor, but in return get a network of love from their fellow soldiers and the poor; they feel good by doing good to others. As we have seen before, thanks to mirror neurons and empathy, doing good to others is a reward in itself, as it makes us feel good too.

On the highest motivational level is the search for wisdom. Of course, it is an oversimplification to position scientists exclusively on this level, because they are also motivated by money, trying to commercialize their knowledge by consulting for companies and gaining power and influence by sitting on the boards of companies. They jostle for power by climbing the academic career ladder or acquiring a position as editor-in-chief at a prestigious academic journal. They strive for glory, trying to get publications into top scientific journals and vying for the Nobel Prize. As we all are only humans, even visionary leaders like Mark Zuckerberg and Linus Torvalds are motivated by all levels of the motivation pyramid. The goal though is that the motivator on the step below is the enabler of the motivator on the next higher level in the pyramid. Money allows us to buy power, power allows one to gain fame and glory, glory allows one to do what one loves, and by doing what we love we hopefully will gain insight and wisdom.

There might be an even higher level, enlightenment, derived from the Buddhist term "Bodhi," which also means awakening. Enlightenment in the Buddhist context means reaching the level of "Nirvana," unquestioning acceptance of the current state, and being free of sensual desire, craving for material existence, conceit, and restlessness. According to Buddhist teaching, though, it is near to impossible for mere mortals to reach this level of insight and wisdom.

Wikipedia editors and Stack Overflow contributors are individuals who have no money to gain, no power to acquire, and no glory to get. When asked what motivates them, it's primarily the vision to contribute to the creation of a global repository of knowledge by sharing what they know. Of course, Wikipedia editors are also human; status, power, and hierarchy do matter, and so they engage in occasional bickering. Some Wikipedia editors aspire to move up the hierarchy, from sporadic contributor to the highest level, "Wikipedia steward," who has the power to exclude others for manipulative editing and lock pages in case of so-called editing wars. However, even stewards have to play by the rules; in fact, it seems Wikipedia has a rule for everything, described on numerous pages of policies and guidelines. These rules can sound frightening to newcomers; however, they establish a shared context, which, whether it is formalized or informal, is essential for successful collaboration. In the next chapter, we will look at the importance of shared context and its generalization, collective consciousness, which are an essential part of the first, social, quantum physics layer of the five-layer model of collaboration.

MAIN LESSONS LEARNED

- Ideal leaders are not just emotionally intelligent, but also empathic to the needs of the people working with them.

- Ideal leaders are managers, entrepreneurs, teachers, artists, and scientists rolled into one.

- One can either be motivated to accumulate as much money, power, and glory as possible to buy love, or skip the first three, and do what one loves.

3

THE PHYSICAL LAYER: COLLECTIVE CONSCIOUSNESS

CHAPTER CONTENTS

- Social quantum physics enables the collective mind.

- Shared context can be created through spoken language, music, painting, or cooking.

- The collective mind is established through four parts:
  1. each person is characterized through a particle/ wave duality;

  2. entanglement between people;

  3. the Heisenberg uncertainty principle; and

  4. the future redefining the past.

Just like quantum physics explains how matter on the level of atoms and subatomic particles operates through space and time, social quantum physics provides a useful framework for describing how humans form bonds and build collective consciousness over long distance and over time. Among humans, a key way to trigger attractive and repulsive forces is through language. The *Oxford English Dictionary* defines "language" in three ways. First, as "the method of human communication, either spoken or written, consisting of the use of words in a structured and conventional way," which it extends by "any nonverbal method of expression or communication." Second, it also defines language as "the system of communication used by a particular community or country." Third, it is defined as "the manner or style of a piece of writing or speech." This extended definition of culture-specific language is what motivates this chapter. The six honest signals of collaboration described in Chapter 4 are the basic building blocks of human interaction that, applied consistently, help to measure and improve collective consciousness.

Language consists of more than just text. We communicate with much more than words. Sometimes we cannot stand the odor of a person, or we love the way a little baby smells. With our eyes, we continuously track and interpret the body language of our communication partners. Our brain is sending electrical signals, which can be measured through brainwave reading, potentially giving additional cues to self and others. In the animal and plant kingdoms, nonverbal communication is key. Grooming among monkeys, the waggle dance of the bees, and the pheromone trail of the ants permit them to collectively accomplish phenomenal tasks. Trees communicate through sending pheromones through their leaves, and through electricity exchanged through their roots.

Wikipedia provides a great example of how language provides the key glue for building collective consciousness. Wikipedia has a rule for everything, described on numerous pages of its policies and guidelines. These rules can sound frightening to newbies; however, they establish a shared context, which, whether it is formalized or informal, is essential for successful collaboration. To define this shared context, we need some sort of language, for example, made up of words, music, or pictures.

3.1. SHARED LANGUAGE CREATES SHARED CONTEXT CREATES SHARED AWARENESS

According to Oxford anthropologist Robin Dunbar, the acquisition of language has been the main driver of human civilization. In his book *Grooming, Gossip, and the Evolution of Language*, Dunbar makes the argument that language is the glue keeping groups together, just like grooming is essential for the bonding of monkeys. He found that we are spending the major part of our speaking time, more than 80%, just gossiping about other people. We only use a minuscule fraction of time talking about, for example, black holes and understanding theories of relativity. Dunbar also suggests that women in ancestral times had to talk more than men, because they had to collaborate and coordinate childcare, while men spent the time hunting, which required much less talking. Collaboration, however, needs a lot of coordination, which is greatly assisted by language.

The more time a collaborating team needs to spend on coordination, the less time it has to get the real work done. A highly functioning team will thus develop a shared language to efficiently coordinate its collaboration. This shared language consists of much more than just sequences of words. It can be unspoken rules, but also code words and abbreviations, and implicit and explicit rules, just like syntax and semantics define a spoken language.

3.2. THE LANGUAGE OF MUSIC TO CREATE SHARED AWARENESS

Jazz musicians improvising together talk to each other through music the same way as two people speaking with words do. This has been shown by Charles Limb, a neurosurgeon at Johns Hopkins, who is also a jazz musician.[1] He put a jazz musician inside an fMRI scanner, and let him jam with a colleague. He found that the same brain regions that we use for processing language were also activated when the musician was jamming with his partner. However, it was the regions needed for syntax, and not for semantics, that were activated. This means that while the rules of how jazz has to be played are similar to spoken language, the content is not clear, and the specificity of meaning is missing. When you listen to a piece of music, your emotions are moved, but you cannot readily associate it with precise meaning. You only know that the four parts of Vivaldi's Four Seasons represent winter, spring, summer, and autumn because

---

[1]https://www.ted.com/talks/charles_limb_your_brain_on_improv?language=en

the composer said so. Once you know, you can hear the sadness of winter, the birds singing in spring, the summer afternoon, and the fall celebrations after the successful harvest. Just like any English speaker knows when to say "nice to meet you," a jazz musician knows when to play a certain rhythm. This means that the subconscious takes over, just like in spoken language, and responds in the "correct" way to an external cue. According to Limb, "in jazz, there is no lying and very little misunderstanding."

3.3. THE LANGUAGE OF PAINTING, AND OTHER LANGUAGES

It's not just jazz musicians communicating in their own language. When Picasso, Braque, and half a dozen other painters developed cubism in Paris, they started inventing a new language of painting, where artworks are broken up, and assembled again in geometric forms. This is no different for architects; for instance, the Bauhaus school founded by Walter Gropius in Weimar who combined architecture with all aspects of art in a modernist style with radically simplified forms, rationality and functionality. Or take the language of cooking, for instance, nouvelle cuisine developed by Paul Bocuse and his team in Lyon. The unifying theme of all these artists of cooking, architecture, and painting is their collaborative spirit. Paul Bocuse is famous not only for his cooking, but also for the success of his students who went on to create their own Michelin three star restaurants all over the world. Walter Gropius not only developed a new architectural style, but also founded the Bauhaus School in Weimar where he was joined by other famous architects such as Ludwig Mies van der Rohe and painters such as Paul Klee and Wassily Kandinsky. The same is true for cubism, which was not invented by Picasso alone, but by an entire group of painters. In order to innovate, each of these groups developed their own vocabulary and syntax, consisting of text, form, and function.

The way words are used conveys subtle cues about the characteristics of a community. For example, word usage in specific languages tells about the nature of the speakers. Germans are known to be blunt and outspoken; German workers also tend to easily strike to settle work disputes. Swiss on the other hand are known to be overly polite; there is the joke of two Swiss to be stuck forever in the elevator because each wanted to be more polite and kept the door open for the other. Swiss workers also almost never strike; in fact the only strike I can remember was in a small factory in the Swiss Jura mountains which had gotten a new boss from Germany who did not employ the consensus-based negotiation style of the Swiss. While Swiss German is a dialect of German, the Swiss have re(de)fined word usage. The Swiss German dialect split off from mainstream German in the seclusion of the Swiss mountains and valleys during the Middle Ages. In those times, close physical proximity was a key for developing a shared context leading to a separate language. Back then, the Swiss peasants were fearsome warriors, repeatedly defeating the Habsburg emperors and their Germanic knights to win their independence. But it seems they did not think it was necessary to wage a war to get a gift, rather their dialect stresses the voluntary nature of receiving the gift. In German, "getting a gift" means "kriegen." "Krieg," however, is the German word for war, suggesting that the recipient of the gift is waging a war to get the present. On the other hand, the word "kriegen" does not exist in the Swiss German dialect in this context, rather Swiss German speakers use "uebercho," which means "coming over"; in other words, "something is coming my way" — two very different words describing the same activity, but conveying a totally different context.

Another example of the subtle meaning of language is the translation of "lazy" as in "the quick brown fox jumps over the lazy dog" from English to German. "Lazy," according to some etymological dictionaries, has the same roots as "slacker," which is sort of cool. The corresponding word in German is "faul," which is definitively uncool, as it means rotten or putrid. So while in the Anglo-Saxon culture, lazy people get grudging admiration making a living as free-riders, there is definitively no such admiration for laziness in German culture, where every upright citizen is expected to contribute their days' work to society. This illustrates that language is very much context dependent, and reflects collective awareness of the local culture. On a side note, this also gives rise to a great deal of unintentional misunderstandings, because people assume sameness when in fact it is not as in the examples above of "getting a gift" and "laziness."

That shared language defines shared context is also true for creative innovators like Picasso, Gropius, and Bocuse, who were all collaborating and creating their shared language within co-located teams in Paris, Weimar, and Lyon. The rise of the Internet is greatly speeding up this process, enabling the fast creation of virtual tribes and collaborative groups working together over long distance. Virtual tribes are developing their shared awareness through shared language. As noted earlier, German identity is different from Swiss German identity, English identity is different from German identity, and the master chef, master painter, and master musician create their own shared identity and shared awareness for their own virtual tribe.

3.4. THE RISE OF COLLECTIVE CONSCIOUSNESS

News of the 2012 Sandy Hook shooting in Newtown, Connecticut, or the Hajj stampede in Mecca in 2015 that left thousands of people dead, spread in hours around the world. Social media, Twitter, and Facebook have surpassed conventional TV and other mass media's capabilities to broadcast news and rumors not in days but minutes around the globe. This almost instantaneous propagation of information exponentially increases the level of global collective awareness. Moments of collective awareness existed in pre-Twitter and Facebook times, for example, with the mass broadcast of the wedding between Princess Diana and Prince Charles, or the global mourning on the day when Princess Diana died in a car crash. Since then, Twitter, Facebook, and other social media channels have increased ever more in breadth, depth, and scope. For instance, on September 2, 2015, the picture of dead toddler Alan Kurdi laying on the beach in Turkey went viral around the world in a few hours, retweeted and reposted on Facebook a zillion times, putting a human face on the Syrian refugee crisis and making it a major issue in the Western world.

Self-consciousness is defined as the individual ability to introspect and recognize oneself as an individual separate from the environment and other individuals. Collective consciousness can thus be characterized as the individual ability to recognize oneself as part of a collective identity. Collective consciousness requires team members to create and nurture a climate of reciprocity with regard to information exchange. Intense interaction plays a key role in the creation and maintenance of collective consciousness and in the development of shared consciousness. Thanks to the Internet and other mass media, mirror neurons of large groups of people can be activated over long distance, leading to global collective awareness. For instance, the "7:1" breakdown of the Brazil soccer team against the German national team at the 2014 World Soccer championship semifinals was experienced simultaneously by billions of TV spectators around the world. Everybody I spoke to right after the game told me how sad they felt for the losing Brazilians; even my German friends expressed their discomfort. In such moments, we are experiencing collective awareness, we are part of one global tribe sharing the same emotions. Google, Twitter, and Wikipedia are the drivers of this global phenomenon.

I experienced this firsthand during the Boston Marathon in 2013, when I was sitting in my home in Cambridge, Massachusetts, on Sunday morning April 15, when the Boston marathon bomber struck. In the frantic and panic-filled hours after 14.49 local time when the bombs went off, Twitter became the main source of information, much faster and more encompassing than the official news from CNN, ABC, and other news channels. At 19.27 on April 15, 2013, the Wikipedia page for the corresponding article was created, and subsequently became one of the most complete sources of the rapidly evolving events.

Similarly, the Paris terrorist attacks on the evening of November 13, 2015, triggered collective consciousness on social media. Minutes after the attacks, Twitter was already buzzing with tweets about the Stade de France, the Bataclan Theatre, and the Restaurant Le Petit Cambodge.

Social media provides the perfect platform to measure and analyze collective consciousness.

Figure 4 shows a screenshot of our real-time Twitter-, Wikipedia-, and Blog-based trend monitoring system "Swarmpulse." It shows the most active Twitter topics on November 14, 2015. The Paris terrorist attacks dominate

Figure 4: Most Active Tweets on News Subjects, November 14, 2015: Paris Terrorist Attacks Dominate (swarmpulse.galaxy advisors.com).

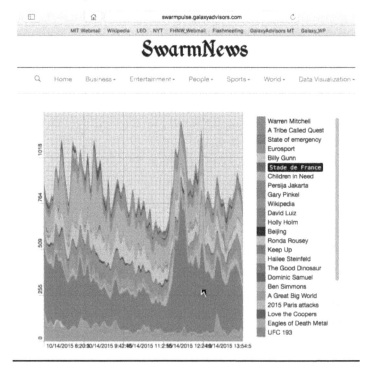

collective awareness. Similarly to the human brain, where individual neurons combine to individual consciousness, individual tweeters combined to form collective consciousness of the terroristic events in Paris playing out during November 2015.

While analyzing Twitter provides access to the crowd, analyzing the collaborative processes of Wikipedia gives excellent insights into more focused collective consciousness. Wikipedia editors are one global tribe, an intrinsically motivated community self-organizing to reach their shared goal. Wikipedians are developing collective consciousness by developing a shared language — made up of policies and guidelines — including the final guideline "ignore all rules." But while they form a global tribe, this tribe still has local clans for each different language, reflecting the cultural characteristics of the corresponding national culture. Each language version of Wikipedia tells us about the cultural particularities of the countries speaking that language. For example, the Japanese Wikipedia editors are the most hierarchical, with the proportionally smallest number of top-level administrators. The consensus-minded Swedish and Finnish Wikipedia editors on the other hand are able to resolve their editing conflicts without the need for a formal conflict resolution process.[2] This means that even if collaborative people form a global tribe, it will still include characteristics of the local culture. The key is the shared language leading to shared context — the policies and guidelines in the case of the Wikipedia editors — which enables all of them to collaborate on the global level to reach their shared goal.

---

[2]Nemoto and Gloor (2010).

3.5. COLLECTIVE CONSCIOUSNESS DRIVES INNOVATION

Examples of collective consciousness are everywhere. Fashion is an example of collective consciousness. Whether it is fashionable first names of children, the latest clothing trends from Paris or Milan, the latest trends in hairstyles, or the Gangnam Style video, instances of collective consciousness abound. The same parallel discovery of breakthrough ideas can also be found in science. Sociologist Robert K. Merton called them "multiple discoveries," alluding to the fact that frequently Nobel Prize winners independently make the same discovery. This phenomenon is not new. There are numerous scientific inventions made at the same time, in parallel. In the 17th century, calculus was invented in parallel by Isaac Newton and Gottfried Wilhelm Leibniz. While later in their lives disputes arose about who had first described it, initially the two scientists exchanged descriptions of their innovation and corresponded with each other. Although toward the end of his life, Newton claimed to have invented calculus first, today's historians of science tend to give equal credit to both Leibniz and Newton. About a century later, Charles Darwin was working in London on his seminal book *On the Origin of Species* when fellow naturalist Alfred Russell Wallace sent him his paper "On the Law Which Has Regulated the Introduction of New Species." As Darwin immediately realized that Wallace had independently invented the theory of evolution, he arranged for a joint presentation of his and Wallace's idea in front of the Linnaean Society. Again two different giants of biology inventing this breakthrough idea of science at the same time!

The development of electric power about 50 years later was also driven independently by different innovators. Other than Russell and Darwin, Nikolas Tesla and Thomas Alva Edison were engaged in a bitter "war of currents." Coming from today's Croatia, Tesla initially worked for Edison developing a new DC power generator. When, instead of the promised 50,000 dollars for his invention, Edison offered him a 10-dollar pay rise, Tesla immediately resigned, and started work on the AC system, teaming up with George Westinghouse. Edison then started touring the United States, electrocuting animals in his presentations to show the dangers of AC power, and cynically promoting the first electric chair to illustrate the risks of high voltage. Nevertheless, both Tesla and Edison were tackling the same problem, initially independently, triggered through the same type of collective awareness that electrical power might be tamed for the good of humanity.

In another instance of parallel development at the beginning of the 20th century, the Wright brothers and Glenn Curtiss competed on who would first be airborne in an aircraft. In their first flight of 12 seconds in 1903, the Wright brother piloted an aircraft that was basically uncontrollable by anybody except themselves. Glenn Curtiss started producing aircraft engines in 1904, taking his experience producing and racing motorbikes to airplane manufacturing. In 1909, the Wright brothers' airplane manufacturing company engaged in a long-lasting patent dispute with Curtiss' company, although ultimately, in 1929, just before Curtiss' death, the two companies merged into the Curtiss-Wright company.

In yet another example of parallel innovation, when in 1977 Steve Jobs launched the Apple II computer, Bill

Gates had just brought Microsoft Basic for the Altair computer to the market. Mostly competing, and occasionally collaborating, Jobs and Gates drove development of the personal computer industry through mutual lawsuits, antitrust litigation, and near bankruptcy of Apple.

All of these parallel innovations, sometimes in competitive collaboration, more often in collaborative competition, are manifestations of collective consciousness. While Gates, Jobs, Curtiss, Wright, Tesla, Edison, Russell, Darwin, Leibniz, and Newton are all men — no women — of undoubtedly high intelligence, imagination, courage, and persistence, they were all products of their time. They invented or contributed toward the discovery of calculus, evolution, electric power, powered flight, and the personal computer by standing, in Newton's words, on the shoulders of giants, leveraging the aggregated knowledge of previous scientists and engineers.

The big question is why there was always more than one innovator? Why did the same ideas come up simultaneously in Germany and the United Kingdom, in the United States and the Habsburg empire, or at the east and west coast of the United States? Is there a way to understand, measure, and analyze this phenomenon of global collective consciousness? Brain and cognitive researchers have defined individual consciousness in different ways, most famously through Rene Descartes exclaiming, "I think therefore I am." Individual consciousness has been described as "… our awareness that we exist, and that consciously existing and having sensory experience is … to be alive, to have a body and to experience the color red and the numerous other sensory inputs. Put another way, we have a subjective experience

of the external world, our bodies, our emotions and preferences and our thoughts."[3] This definition of individual
consciousness can be extended to collective consciousness. Collective consciousness is our awareness that we
are part of a group, that we share our subjective experiences, our emotions, preferences, and thoughts with
others of the same collective.

One way of explaining individual consciousness is
based on the quantum mind. The concept of the quantum
mind explains individual consciousness by modeling the
brain as a quantum computer. It has been described by
Alexander Wendt in his 2015 book *Quantum Mind and
Social Science* where he bases his analysis on research by
physicists Roger Penrose, Stuart Hameroff, Henry Stapp,
and David Bohm, all leading proponents of the quantum
mind theory. He identifies four principles of quantum
physics: the wave-particle duality, the uncertainty principle, entanglement, and the future changing the past.
These are also key elements of the quantum mind,
explaining how collective consciousness works.

3.6. EMPATHY: WAVE-PARTICLE DUALITY AND THE "THEORY OF MIND"

The wave-particle duality in quantum physics tries to
explain the puzzling behavior of elementary particles,
which exhibit properties of both waves and particles.
Numerous experiments have tried to answer the question
if light consists of waves or particles, coming to the

---

[3]http://quantum-mind.co.uk

conclusion that light consists of both. There is a similar duality in our understanding of other people whom we perceive both as particles — bodies — and waves — projections of ourselves.

With our eyes, we clearly recognize others as consisting of a unique body; however, when interacting with them, we are constantly employing the "theory of mind." "Theory of mind" is the name given by psychologists to the incessant reading of the mind of others, where we are trying to adjust our response to our interpretation of the mind of our interaction partner. This view of others is based on our perception of the other person's body and behavior. We therefore have the same duality between other people's bodily presence and the likelihood of other people to behave according to our own experiences and expectations (Figure 5).

Theory of mind, or mind reading, is a function of empathy and of mirror neurons. For most people — except

---

Figure 5: Theory of Mind and Particle-Wave Duality.

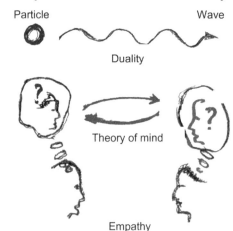

Particle   Wave

Duality

Theory of mind

Empathy

psychopaths — seeing somebody enjoying a pleasurable experience gives them pleasure also, seeing somebody suffer makes them suffer also; this behavior is explained by the mirror neurons. On the other hand, somebody can be an expert in emotional intelligence without being empathic. A master car salesperson who tells prospective customers precisely what they want to hear, although she knows that the customer is not really able to afford the car, is engaging in the "theory of mind" and using her emotional intelligence. However, convincing a poor customer to take out a car loan for a luxurious car might be good for the car salesperson, but not for the customer. The car salesperson is emotionally intelligent, but not empathic. In psychology, the capability to tailor one's own behavior according to the expectations of their opposites is called self-monitoring. People who score high on self-monitoring blend easily in social situations, knowing what to say. They will change their behavior so they are perceived more positively, while a low self-monitoring person will act more consistently. High self-monitoring people thus engage into the theory of mind for their own benefit.

The "body/wave duality" studies interaction among humans by measuring them both as "bodies" and as "waves" or likelihoods. When studying what honest signal of communication exchanged among a group of people will lead to what outcome, there are only probabilities, no firm black or white conclusions. When measuring patterns of behavior and mapping them to the desired outcome, we can never be 100% certain that the outcome is the final consequence of the behavior. For example, rotating leadership might be an indicator of creativity (see discussion in Section 5.3), but it could also be that the rotation in leadership was caused by the illness of the main leader. When studying the interaction between two humans, we define a pattern language of communication that tracks interaction through words, pictures, smell, and even brainwaves. Words measure honesty and emotionality, but also novelty of word usage. Pictures give social cues through body language, eye contact, and posturing. Smell tells others through pheromones what somebody feels about them. In addition, brainwaves also show through electrical signals if for instance two jazz musicians play in synch.

3.7. ENTANGLEMENT

Quantum entanglement describes the link between elementary particles over long distance. It appears that one particle of an entangled pair "knows" what action has been performed on the other, even though there is no known means for such information to be communicated between the particles, which may be separated by large distances. The same happens between two connected people, for example, between mother and child, or between spouses.

When on Sunday morning at ten in my house in Cambridge my phone rings, I know that this is my mother, because she has the habit of calling me on Sunday mornings at about this time. This is because — through the "theory of mind" — my mother's and my brain are entangled. I know what she thinks even when she is on the other side of the Atlantic and can therefore correctly deduce her actions. People who are close to each other, who are connected through strong ties, are constantly active in each other's subconscious, and a part of their brain thinks about the other person even when their consciousness is busy doing other things. Our capability to be entangled is limited to the people with whom we share a strong tie. According to anthropologist Robin Dunbar, humans are capable of managing at most 15 strong tie relationships at any given time, although most people have less. On the other hand, we have today, thanks to Facebook and Twitter, the capability for weak entanglement with large numbers of people by following their Facebook updates and Twitter feeds. This activity restricts our capacity to manage our strong ties. The challenge thus is to maintain a healthy mix of strong and weak ties, building strong relationships with good friends while monitoring what our casual acquaintances are up to (**Figure 6**).

"Entanglement" is the key mechanism to build and nurture collaborative consciousness. Thanks to the Internet, Wikipedia, and Google, humans might be able for the first time to create *one* single truth. Until now, it has been accepted that each individual is living in his or her individual bubble, and is making up their individual

Figure 6: Entanglement Is the Building Block of Strong Ties.

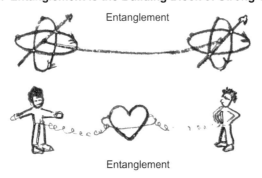

Entanglement

Entanglement

reality based on personal experiences. But as today all information can be easily shared, and unknown bits and pieces be added by everybody from the same global dictionary, for instance Wikipedia and other sources on the Web, global consciousness finally can become truly global. As humans understand the benefits of knowledge sharing in systems such as Wikipedia and Stack Overflow, they will start making collaborative behavior part of their "system 1," not "system 2." "System 1" has been defined by Nobel Prize winner Daniel Kahnemann as being part of human intuition, while "system 2" is responsible for deliberative reasoning.

3.8. REFLECTION: HEISENBERG UNCERTAINTY PRINCIPLE

Heisenberg's uncertainty principle of quantum physics states that the more precise the location of a particle is known, the less precise its movement can be calculated, or to strongly simplify, we cannot know at the same time the location and movement of a particle. The same is true for humans. If we measure the behavior of a group of people, and they become aware of this measurement, they will start changing their behavior, at which point the previous measurements are no longer correct.

Many stock traders are trying to predict the development of stock prices based on buzz on online social media. If the perfect formula to predict stock prices based on online social media would be found, and everybody would start trading using that formula, it would stop working the next day. We can however apply the Heisenberg uncertainty principle to the advantage of groups of people. By measuring their communication behavior, and telling them how each individual is doing, we will get the people to change their behavior for the better. In Section 9.5, such a method for measuring and improving communication behavior to make people more collaborative will be introduced. For instance, we found that rotating leadership, where people take turns leading the group, is good for creativity. Analyzing the e-mail archive of their teams, we have shown leaders that they were non-rotating leaders, which we found is bad for the creativity of their team. Providing them with this virtual mirror got them to change their leadership behavior, and take turns as leaders. In other words, measuring the collaborative behavior of a group and subsequently exposing the group to the measurements will change their collaborative behavior (**Figure 7**).

"Heisenberg uncertainty" comes into play as soon as the social system is measured. Because it is a social system, the

Figure 7: The Uncertainty Principle States That If We Measure a System, We Will Change Its Behavior.

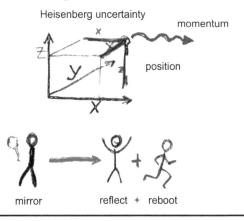

measured components — the humans — learn that they are being measured, and also what is being measured, and what behavior is considered "good" behavior. A system measured this way will thus change for the better, because of the increase in transparency. Virtual mirroring provides consistent feedback of communication and collaboration effectiveness and performance. As improving collaboration is the key objective for introducing such a system, the system will improve its collaborative capabilities by reinforcing key patterns of collaboration.

3.9. REBOOT: THE FUTURE REDEFINES THE PAST

In quantum mechanics, the future can change the past. Before a particle is measured, its state is unknown. The act of measuring the state changes the state of the particle, which then also becomes known in the past. In other words, an action in the future has changed the past. The same is true for historic events.

A soldier in a German tank invading Poland at the beginning of the Second World War did not know he was participating in the Second World War; he only knew he was riding a tank invading Poland. Only the interpretation in the future made this act of the German tanks crossing into Poland the beginning of the Second World War. Today, Wikipedia has a similar influence in rewriting the past. For example, the shooting of black teenager Trayvon Martin by white volunteer neighborhood watchman George Zimmerman was one of the triggers of the "black lives matter" campaign in the United States. Depending on the contrasting types of pictures of Trayvon Martin and George Zimmerman, with Trayvon Martin as a smiling youngster with a mug shot of George Zimmermann, or Trayvon Martin with a snoot, and George Zimmerman smiling in suit and tie, two very different sides of the same story are told. Showing Trayvon Martin in positive light, and George Zimmermann with a negative picture, Wikipedia editors rewrite the past of Trayvon Martin and George Zimmermann — although they explicitly commit to "NPOV," a neutral point of view. On a side note, this illustrates that "absolute truth" never exists, and that we are always filtering new events coming our way based on individual past experiences. Harvard psychologist Daniel Schacter attests a similar function to the human memory, which he claims is made for looking into the future, not remembering the past. He argues that the human memory is built to improve our future performance, thus filtering the past to enhance the future (**Figure 8**).

Figure 8: The Future Changes Interpretation of the Past.

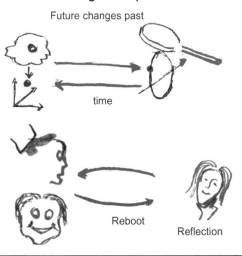

The "future changes the past" extends the well-known premise that we are a product of our past actions. Most of the time, we only know in retrospective if a particular action was foolish or a stroke of genius. Historians constantly rewrite history. For example, Napoleon and the outcome of the Battle of Waterloo are assessed quite differently by British and French historians. This means that past actions are constantly reevaluated based on present interpretations. This leads to our future behavior being influenced by constant reinterpretation of past actions. On the other hand, we tailor today's behavior to what we think will be happening tomorrow. For example, Facebook's stock price today already factors in the growth of Facebook we anticipate for the next year. We are therefore willing to pay a premium because we believe Facebook stock will get even more valuable tomorrow. This means that we reinterpret the price of the stock at the IPO of Facebook, rating the buyer of a Facebook share at the time of the IPO as a farsighted genius. The future has thus changed the past.

Another example of the future changing the past is our response to traumatic childhood experiences, or Adverse Childhood Experiences (ACEs). ACEs have been identified by a path-breaking study[4] by Kaiser Permanente in California from 1995 to 1997, where it was found that many health problems later in life were caused by adverse experiences in the first few childhood years. Physical, sexual, and emotional abuse and neglect, for instance, having to see the mother being treated violently, or parental

---

[4]Felitti et al. (1998).

separation or divorce, lead to adult risky behaviors such as smoking, and alcohol and drug abuse, and to obesity, resulting in ill-health including depression, heart disease, cancer, chronic lung disease, and consequently shorter lifespan. The first treatment as an adult of ACEs is to make the adult aware of the causal link between her or his high-risk behavior today and the traumatic experiences as a young child. Just being made aware of the link, and to reflect on it can lead to a "reboot," to a change in interpretation of the past, and thus to changed future behavior.

These four principles of social quantum physics define collective consciousness. Combining the particle-wave duality as the "theory of mind" with entanglement leads to constantly redefining interpersonal relationships through the long-distance second-guessing of the behaviors of others. The stronger the ties between two people are, and the more frequently this second-guessing and reinterpretation of each other's actions happen, the stronger is the entanglement. The second-guessing is also habitually verified through direct interaction, be it using phone, e-mail, or face-to-face. The more we share a cultural, social, and familial bond with other people, the better we become in this mind guessing game, and the more we consequently will be entangled. Similarly, the uncertainty principle and the future redefining the past are also combined in collective consciousness. When we are measuring a social system as a group of people interacting with each other, exposing the people to the results of the measurement will lead to the social system changing its behavior, which changes our interpretation of the past actions of the social system. These

Figure 9: The Four Components of Social Quantum Physics Creating Collective Consciousness.

basic principles of social quantum physics can be applied both on the level of entire societies, defining collective consciousness, or on the organizational or firm level, where they constitute the main building blocks of organizational consciousness (**Figure 9**).

The four components of social quantum physics — particle-wave, entanglement, uncertainty principle, future defining past — provide the building blocks to enable collective consciousness. They extend "social physics" introduced by Alex (Sandy) Pentland in his book of the same name (Pentland, 2015). The individual human "atoms" are connected with and communicate in different types of network structures and configurations, introduced in the next chapter.

MAIN LESSONS LEARNED

- Humans create shared context through using shared language; this language is not just words, but can also be music, pictures, and smells.

- Shared context leads to collective consciousness.

- Collective consciousness is explained through social quantum physics.

- Social quantum physics consists of four parts:
  1. wave/particle duality, the second-guessing of the behavior of others;

  2. entanglement, the existence of strong ties between people;

  3. Heisenberg uncertainty, inducing behavioral change through mirroring one's interactions; and

  4. the future redefining the past, by reinterpreting past actions in the current context.

4

THE NETWORKING LAYER: COINS

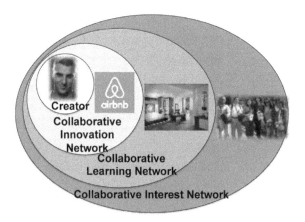

CHAPTER CONTENTS

- Collaborative Innovation Networks (COINs) as core engines of disruptive innovation.

- The 1-9-90 rule.

- Uber and Airbnb as COIN examples.

- Solving the puzzle of the Zika virus by a COIN.

- Coolfarming builds COINs — learning from the bees.

> • COINs lead to Collaborative Learning Networks
> (CLNs) which lead to Collaborative Interest
> Networks (CINs).

In 1727, Benjamin Franklin brought together 12 men in Philadelphia, creating the "Junto" to ponder issues of mutual improvement. Ranging from cabinetmaker, scrivener, and surveyor to printer — Franklin himself — they met every Friday night to discuss questions of morals, politics, and natural philosophy. Over time, the Junto developed the first town library by pooling their members' books, and started promoting concepts such as volunteer firefighters, night watchmen, and a public hospital. By recruiting their friends, and their friends' friends, Junto members made Philadelphia the first town to have volunteer firefighters, a city library, and night watchmen. Benjamin Franklin's Junto was an early example of a Collaborative Innovation Network (COIN), a small team of 3–15 people, who collaborate in emergent self-organization and intrinsic motivation to create something radically new.

The Junto was by no means the first COIN. Founded in 1663 by charter of King Charles II, the Royal Society was a group of physicians and natural philosophers who wanted to advance science and natural philosophy. Just like Benjamin Franklin, the Royal Society's first secretary, Henry Oldenburg, was a great connector with a pan-European network of scientific correspondents. One of his sponsors at the Royal Society was Robert Boyle, the seventh son of the Earl of Cork and a prominent chemist. After his education at Eton, Boyle was sent on a grand

European tour, meeting Galileo Galilei in Florence, and building his own pan-European science network. After inheriting a substantial fortune from his father, Boyle became part of a group of researchers called the Invisible College which was converted in 1663 to the Royal Society of London for Improving Natural Knowledge. Together with Oldenburg they wove a European network of scientists, where researchers like Isaac Newton and Gottfried Wilhelm Leibniz corresponded on developing calculus to jump-start the development of Western sciences.

But we can go back much farther, for example to Plato, who in the fourth century BC founded the Academy of Athens at a sacred grove of olive trees dedicated to Athena, the goddess of wisdom. The Academy was one of the first documented institutions of higher learning and research in the Western world, bringing together Greek philosophers such as mathematician Theaetetus of Sunium, philosopher Archytas of Tarentum, and mathematician Leodamas of Thasos. The group collaborated on many mathematical discoveries and theorems, for example, to find the simplest explanation for the movement of heavenly bodies. Just like the Royal Society in the age of Oldenburg, or Franklin's Junto, Plato's Academy was an early prototype of a COIN, a Collaborative *Innovation* Network where a small group of intrinsically motivated people, usually 3–15, get together to innovate and create something radically new. Just as happened with the Junto, the Royal Society and the Academy, in a "ripple effect" in a second phase the ideas developed in the COIN spread to a larger group, the Collaborative *Learning* Network or CLN, encompassing hundreds of people. In the case of the Junto, the

CLN members were the first users of the town library, or the first volunteer firefighters. In the case of the Royal Society, it was the first few hundred members joining the presentations of the Royal Society; in the case of the Academy, it was the students and teachers participating in the discussions at the Academy. In the third phase, the idea ripples out to society, to the Collaborative *Interest* Network or CIN, with thousands of people interested in the new idea. In the case of the Junto, the CIN was the population of Philadelphia, which was profiting from the inventions of the Junto. In the case of the Royal Society, it was English society which profited from the inventions of the learned members of the Royal Society. In the case of the Academy, the CIN consisted of the free population of Athens, who integrated the knowledge created from the Academy into the collective consciousness of the city.

In today's world, this innovation engine with the COIN at its core, is being turbocharged by the Internet. A creator with a world-changing idea, be it Elon Musk, Mark Zuckerberg, or Malala Yousafzai, can easily reach out to like-minded people anywhere on the world to start their COIN. However, they all share some (un)common characteristics.

4.1. THE ROLE OF LEADERS OF COINS: THE 1-9-90 RULE

When in 1632 Swedish King Gustavus II Adolphus was killed leading a cavalry charge against Sweden's enemies, he was at the peak of his career. Single-handedly he had converted Sweden from a rural backwater to Northern Europe's great power. Through superior generalship and solid training of numerically smaller armies of Swedish soldiers, he had won one battle after the other against the armies of Holy Roman emperor Ferdinand II during the Thirty Years' War. The key point to his success was that he was leading his cavalry charge from the front. In this regard, he was no different from Elon Musk, Mark Zuckerberg, and Malala Yousafzai. By taking great personal risk, by setting an example, and by being a member of the swarm, the swarm gets energized and is willing to join the leaders on their world-changing endeavor.

In her research on how the most efficient teams operate, MIT Sloan professor Deborah Ancona distinguishes between three types of team members. She calls them the "pigs," the "chickens," and the "cows." She takes their differing contribution to breakfast as the metaphor for the team's goal. The pigs — contributing ham, bacon, and sausage — are in it with their lives, giving all they have to give. Those would be the core members of the team, for instance Mark Zuckerberg and the founding team of Facebook, or Malala Yousafzai and her close friends fighting for the right of girls to education in Pakistan. The chickens — contributing the eggs — provide an essential part to breakfast, but can easily move on if their interests change. They would be among the initial employees of Facebook and its first users, or among the girls in Malala's home region, the Swat valley in Pakistan, attending a school in spite of the Taliban's threats. The cows — providing the milk for breakfast — provide a supplementary addition to the breakfast, at small cost to themselves. They would be later Facebook employees or users, or the girls in Pakistan getting an education, profiting from the trailblazer work of Malala and her initial friends.

The X-team structure of Deborah Ancona with pigs, chickens, and cows motivates the 1-9-90 rule: 1% of the people do 90% of the work, 9% of the people do 9% of the work, and 90% of the people do 1% of the work. I stumbled on the 1-9-90 rule when studying the editing behavior of the English Wikipedians. As of end of 2015, Wikipedia is edited about 3 million times per month, by a total of more than 2 million active editors,[1] who are defined as people who made at least 10 edits since they arrived on Wikipedia. A total of 27 million users registered on the English Wikipedia, but only a bit less than 10% of these are active editors. The top 3000 most active Wikipedians, on the other hand, made almost half of all the edits on Wikipedia[2] since its founding in 2001. So, on Wikipedia, the top one-tenth of a percent of all users does almost half of all the edits ever done on Wikipedia. Talk about strong and dedicated leadership!

When picking a random month, for example September 2013, and looking at the top most active 4000 editors at Wikipedia, we find that the most active editor made almost 20,000 edits in that month, while the editor on position 4000 still made a respectable 100 edits in September 2013. For the most active editor, this means that during his waking hours, assuming a 12-hour online day, he made 60 edits every hour, every day, every week. Looking at the 4000 most active editors in September 2013, the top 40 editors made 310,000 edits, with the next 360 adding another 640,000. The remaining 3600 editors made one

---

[1] https://stats.wikimedia.org/EN/TablesWikipediansEditsGt5.htm
[2] 184 million of the 470 million edits https://en.wikipedia.org/wiki/Wikipedia:List_of_Wikipedians_by_number_of_edits

million edits. To put it in other words, the top 10% made as many edits as the other 90% combined. If we factor in the quality of the edits, where we found in earlier work that the most dedicated Wikipedians deliver the most high-quality work,[3] we find that Wikipedians really confirm the 1-9-90 rule: 1% does 90%, 9% does 9%, and 90% does 1% of the work. The call therefore — in adaptation to Occupy Wall Street's slogan "We are the ninety nine percent" — becomes a call to "be the one percent" in dedication and commitment to your cause.

4.2. COINS ARE EVERYWHERE

Crowdsourced businesses like Uber or Airbnb are great exemplars of successful COINs. They follow the same three-step process from the creator to the COIN, followed by the CLN, and finally the CIN. The original group of Uber or Airbnb founders, Joe Gebbia and Brian Chesky from Airbnb and Travis Kalanick and Garrett Camp from Uber, turned their crazy idea into a start-up business, making up the COIN. The CLN consists of the first business partners, the drivers of the cars working for Uber, or the landlords of the apartments who list them on Airbnb. Finally, the first tourists booking an Uber car or renting an Airbnb room are members of the CIN. Over time, the software developers working on the software powering the Uber and Airbnb booking systems become part of the extended COIN, while all Uber drivers and Airbnb landlords join the swarm or CLN. They also follow the 1-9-90 rule, in that a small fraction of

---

[3]Nemoto, Gloor, and Laubacher (2011).

the community — much less than the 1% — consisting of the software developers building the software powering Uber and Airbnb — is responsible for most innovation in the COIN. The 9% are the Uber drivers and Airbnb hosts, who are mostly doing their job as a part-time activity, to supplement their income. The 90% are the guests booking a ride with Uber, or renting a room with Airbnb (Figure 10).

Both Uber drivers and Airbnb landlords are true members of the swarm, or "chicken" in the language of Deborah Ancona, as they have skin in the game as owners of their own car or owners or tenants of their apartments. Not everybody can become a member of the swarm; the entry ticket is owning a well-kept car or a nicely furnished apartment. Each Uber driver is a micro-entrepreneur running his or her own business and turning owning a car into a profitable venture. The same is true for the people renting parts of their apartments through Airbnb. Compared to the original business model of taking a cab or renting a bed and breakfast room, Internet-based crowdsourcing businesses add trust through transparency. When taking a taxi in a foreign city, we can rarely trust the taxi driver to take

---

Figure 10: Uber and Airbnb as COINs.

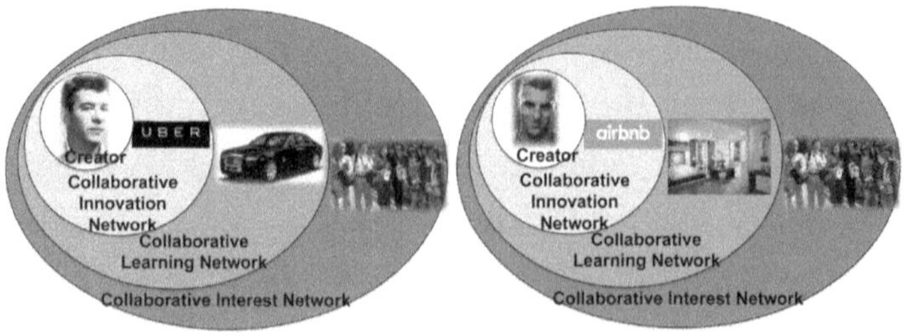

the fastest way to the destination, as he is paid for the distance driven and has every incentive to drive as long and far as possible. There is no such worry with Uber or Lyft, as the price estimate is given in advance. There is even more transparency as both driver and customer are identified before the transaction is conducted. After the ride, driver and customer rate each other, this way building each other's reputation for future transactions. The same is true for Airbnb, where the room is described and ranked by previous travelers, as well as the hospitality of the landlord. But on the flip side of the coin (pun intended) the same is also true of the traveler, who is ranked by the Uber driver or the Airbnb host. A traveler who molested the driver, or left a mess behind in the guest room, will not be accepted by future Uber drivers or Airbnb hosts.

In some regards, leaders of successful crowdsourcing businesses such as Uber's Travis Kalanick, or Airbnb's Brian Chesky, are more similar to Swedish king Gustaphus Adolphus than to leaders of nonprofit open source COINs such as Tim Berners-Lee (creator of the Web), Linus Torvalds (creator of Linux), or Jimmy Wales (creator of Wikipedia), as they show some decidedly not-so-ethical traits. Their behavior stretches the boundaries of moral conduct. For instance, Travis Kalanick, the cofounder of Uber, has a reputation for taking the gloves off and not being squeamish when dealing with competitors. In order to deal a blow to his strongest competitor Lyft, Uber was accused of falsely booking Lyft drivers in New York City to create a scarcity of available Lyft cars and lure potential customers to its own cars. In a comparable incident, Airbnb spammed Craigslist property owners with adverts to also list their property on its own website. While these are creative ways of growing their own business at the expense of competitors, they are more indicative of collaborative competition than of competitive collaboration (see Section 7.5).

4.3. CREATING A MEDICAL COIN: TRACKING DOWN THE ZIKA VIRUS

When in fall 2015 dozens of babies in northern Brazil were born with microcephaly — abnormally small brains — the doctors in the hospitals were shocked and left without an explanation. The Zika virus had reached Brazil earlier, at the end of the Soccer Championship in 2014. But at that time the Brazilian minister of health had declared Zika to be relatively benign, "only" leading to a rash, bloodshot eyes, headache, fever, and joint pain. The way in which medical researchers figured out the link between the Zika virus and the babies born with microcephaly is a great example of competitive collaboration, and COINs. At the beginning of the microcephaly outbreak, Vanessa van der Linden, a neurologist who was testing the first baby born with microcephaly on a variety of causes, was left without an explanation. When more babies with the disease were born, doctors all across Brazil started collaborating, and sharing test results. Vanessa learned that some of the mothers had had Zika infections early in their pregnancies, but a connection could not be established. In October of 2015, another prominent epidemiologist, Celina Turchi, was asked to join the investigation. According to her own words, she was grappling with the problem day and night, at the same time shocked, but also highly motivated to dig down to the root cause of the problem. Celina called all the doctors she knew, bringing together a COIN with members from London and all over Brazil. She called it the MERG, the Microcephaly Epidemic Research Group. Members stayed in Dr. Turchi's apartment, brainstorming and discussing until late at night. When members of her team discovered traces of the Zika virus in brain tissue of stillborn babies, they had some first proof for their suspicion. In order to prove the link, they set up a large-scale experiment, recruiting a thousand expecting mothers who had had Zika symptoms, and comparing them against a control group of mothers giving birth to healthy babies. As the director of the committee of the World Health Organization, which recommended to declare the Zika outbreak a public health emergency, said, "Sorting out a rare event will take a lot of women, and they must be followed for months."[4]

MERG is working as a perfect COIN, intrinsically motivated, working day and night to solve the mystery. The mothers participating in the study make up the CLN, contributing their time and personal experience so other expecting mothers will not have to go through the same ordeal. Any expecting mother in Brazil is part of the CIN, as they all are intimately interested in sparing their children this fate.

4.4. THE COOLFARMING PROCESS

In an earlier book I described how to support the creation of COINs by providing an environment that nurtures and

---

[4]http://www.nytimes.com/2016/02/07/health/zika-virus-brazil-how-it-spread-explained.html

grows COINs into CLNs, a process I call "coolfarming." A group of enthusiasts get together to create something radically new, and to recruit early adapters to try their innovation, thereby turning it into a cool trend. Coolfarming describes the genesis of an emergent trend — something new and fresh, developed by a team of daring individuals who then spread it to the rest of the world. Coolhunting and coolfarming have been described in detail in two earlier books; here I will just give a very brief high-level overview of the coolfarming process.

As a metaphor for how this three-step swarm building process works, bees are great exemplars. The way in which they self-organize with no direct guidance by the bee queen, how they waggle dance to recruit other bees to a honey source, and how they vote to choose a new home for their swarm directly translate to human swarms. For human bees, the Internet offers a great way to reach other like-minded people with laser-like focus. An aspiring queen bee wanting to start a new swarm can easily post her goals, advertising what she wants to do on blogs, Twitter, and Facebook pages. She can put up a mission statement, and also develop a profile of other prospective members of her swarm.

For example,[5] when aspiring software entrepreneur Jon Schlossberg was about to develop a smartphone app that would put a stop to payday lending by taking over cash management for people with highly fluctuating incomes who have a hard time making ends meet, he found a blog post by Quinten Farmer who was describing

---

[5]http://www.nytimes.com/2015/05/03/magazine/want-a-steady-income-theres-an-app-for-that.htm

a similar idea using bitcoin. Schlossberg approached Farmer, and they quickly hit it off, with Farmer deciding to join Schlossberg's start-up.

The second step will be to "coolhunt" for other people on the same wavelength, extending personal networking by using Google and other search tools to find like-minded people on Twitter, Facebook, online forums, and blogs. The queen bee might also initiate a Kickstarter campaign to test the validity of her idea.

The final step will be to nurture and grow her swarm, reaching out to prospective members and try to convince them to buy into her endeavor and start working together to turn the common vision into a first prototype. The key will be to accept the first members as peers, and build collective consciousness as described in the next chapter. Wikipedia volunteers spending hours creating articles on topics close to their heart, LEGO Mindstorm hackers paying for their own tickets to Denmark to tell LEGO about their most recent inventions, and Silicon Valley start-up entrepreneurs all collaborate as creative swarms — they behave in a strikingly similar manner to how bees swarm to a new location. This is the "coolfarming" process — using the beehive as a metaphor to describe how to tap the creative potential of communities of innovators (**Figure 11**).

Coolfarming works by unlocking the creative potential of COINs, introduced informally at the beginning of this chapter at the example of Benjamin Franklin's Junto, the British Royal Society, and Plato's Academy of Athens. COINs are made up of groups of self-motivated individuals linked by the idea of something new and exciting and by the common goal of improving existing business practices, and create new products or services for which

Figure 11: The Coolfarming Process — the Three Phases of Building Your Swarm, with Lessons from the Beehive as a Metaphor.

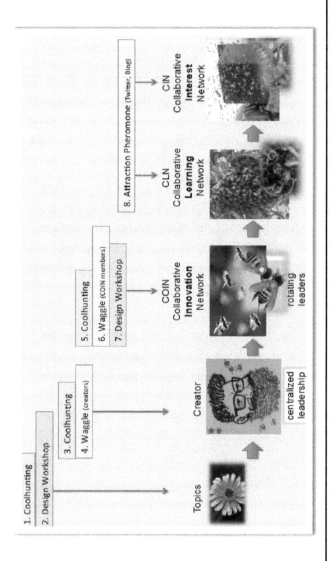

they see a real need. The strength of COINs is based on their ability to activate creative collaboration and knowledge sharing by leveraging social networking mechanisms, affecting positively individual capabilities and organizations' performance. Swarm creativity gets people to work together in a structure that enables a fluid creation and exchange of ideas. Patterns of collaborative innovation follow an identical path, from creator to COIN to CLN to CIN.

Similarly, in the bee world, the queen, corresponding to the creator shaping the vision of a new product, recruits a swarm of dedicated bees, which join her in leaving the old hive to create something radically new (steps 3 and 4 in **Figure 11**). The swarm then sends out the coolhunters, the most experienced bees, to scout for a new location of the hive. These most committed bees, usually just a few dozen, dynamically, and in rotating leadership, check out and vote on each other's proposed new hive settings. Democratically, they agree on a new location, convincing each other and their sisters in the swarm through the intensity of their waggle dance (steps 5−7 of **Figure 11**). This corresponds to the human COIN, developing a new product, and then recruiting their friends and family to the CLN, to fine-tune the product, and recruit the most dedicated beta-testers as COIN members. Among the bees, once the decision for the new hive location has been made, the coolhunter bees heat the swarm by increasing their own body temperature while sitting in the midst of the swarm, until all the bees take off together, following the coolhunters to the new location. This new location has been previously marked by the coolhunter bees with attraction pheromone, so that it becomes an irresistible destination for the swarm (step 8 in **Figure 11**).

The same process as for the bees applies to the human swarm, where the queen bee and her coolhunting core team members convince their friends of the greatness of their new idea. The key challenge for the queen bee, the creator of the COIN, and the core COIN team members will be to create collective consciousness of the swarm. Collective consciousness of COINs can be measured using the six honest signals of collaboration, introduced in Chapter 5.

4.5. THE SIX HONEST SIGNALS MEASURE THE QUALITY OF COINS

The six honest signals will track if a group of people are working together as a COIN. The COIN in the center of the network will have a few key people demonstrating "strong leadership." The more collaborative the team is, the more "rotating leadership" it will show, with the key people taking turns as leaders. The members of the core COIN will show a "balanced contribution index," with different core team members contributing ideas and content. The core COIN members will also show strong passion and respect through "responsiveness," by responding quickly, and by getting fast responses from the other people in the network. The COIN members will use "honest language," saying both what is positive, and what is negative. And finally, they will develop a "shared context," developing their own vernacular to discuss and further develop their ideas.

How well communication functions can be measured using the six "honest signals of collaborations" will be introduced in the next chapter.

MAIN LESSONS LEARNED

- COINs are the key drivers of innovation.

- The way how bees swarm delivers a blueprint for coolfarming of COINs.

- COINs grow to CLNs which extend to CINs.

- Airbnb and Uber are examples of COINs, as is the discovery of the link between the Zika virus and microcephaly.

5

THE SIGNAL LAYER: SIX HONEST SIGNALS OF COLLABORATION

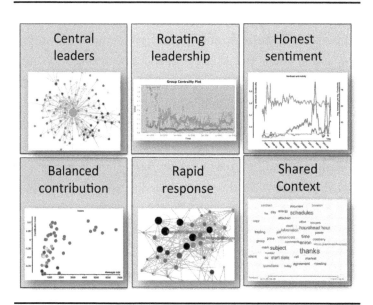

CHAPTER CONTENTS

- Central leadership.
- Balanced contribution.

- Rotating leadership.
- Rapid response.
- Honest sentiment.
- Shared language.

In our research at the MIT Center for Collective Intelligence over the last 14 years, we have studied hundreds of communication archives of organizations to understand what patterns of communication are most supportive of collaboration, creativity, and innovation. We found that the degree of collaboration, and the performance of a team or organization, can be measured and improved through analyzing communication between team members. In our studies of Collaborative Innovation Networks (COINs) we have identified key characteristics of high-performing groups by tracking their communication in Twitter, Facebook, Wikipedia, e-mail, and small group face-to-face networks. Building on work done by Alex (Sandy) Pentland at the MIT Media Lab (Pentland 2008), we identified six communication patterns that are indicative of healthy communication in highly functioning teams, two patterns each based on network structure, network dynamics, and network content (**Figure 12**).

5.1. CENTRAL LEADERSHIP

While I initially expected collaborative swarms to not have any clearly recognizable leaders, I found the opposite: there were strong leaders, clearly dominating the

Figure 12: The Six Honest Signals of Collaboration.

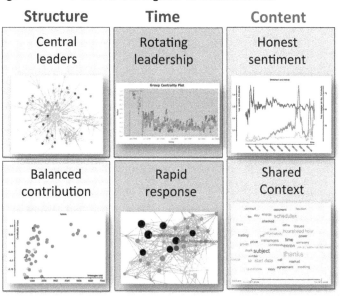

discussion whenever they felt competent. The key was that it was not blind obedience, but a meritocratic style of leadership where the one who was qualified best for a task stepped up to it and assumed the leadership role. For example, when Tim Berners-Lee came to MIT to further develop the World Wide Web, he built up his network with thought leaders, for instance, at the World Economic Forum by connecting with other creative thinkers such as the head of the MIT Lab for Computer Science, Michael Dertouzos. Even Wikipedia, the epitome of creative collaboration, shows this pattern, as we found that articles, where a small group of editors are in charge, become high-quality much faster than articles where a large group of writers are working without clear leaders. In the meantime, we have seen the same patterns whenever we studied creative groups, for example, in teams of medical researchers and shared business process service providers, to name just a few.

5.2. BALANCED CONTRIBUTION

In a team, members can be distinguished by their level of commitment and activity to team goals. In particular, we can differentiate between information consumers and information producers. We call net information producers "contributors." For a team communicating by e-mail this means the contributors are the people who send more than they receive, while information consumers receive more than they send. For instance, when we studied the e-mail archive of the World Wide Web consortium in its early days, its creator Tim Berners-Lee frequently was the most active sender within this community. Over time, others began contributing their ideas, leading to an overall well-balanced contribution index. We found that teams with a low variance in contribution — all members of the core team contributing a similar number of messages — were more creative than teams where one or a few people were contributing most of the messages. On the other hand, for account management teams catering to customers of a global outsourcing services provider, a skewed contribution index, where a few central leaders sent a steady stream of messages to customers, led to more satisfied customers than a pattern where customers were bombarded in scattergun fashion from many different employees of the service provider. Studying global distributed teams in the COINs course over the last 10 years with students from

Aalto University Helsinki, University of Cologne, MIT, and Savannah College of Art and Design (described in Section 8.5), we found that the more similar the ratio of sent to received messages in a team over time was, the higher was its performance. This means that team members are frequently switching roles, from being information producers and active senders to being passive information consumers mostly receiving e-mail. Over the entire duration of the project, however, everybody should contribute about the same amount of messages.

Note that central leadership and balanced contribution are network structure measures. When communication messages are mapped showing who communicates with whom, people who are central become easy to see in a network picture. Likewise, when counting the number of messages that a person sends and receives over time, one can calculate a contribution index which reveals who has a well-balanced sending and receiving pattern. These two measures make visible the structure or pattern of communication among team members over time. The next two metrics — rotating leadership and responsiveness — measure the temporal dynamics of communication. The final two metrics — honest sentiment and shared context — track the content of communication.

5.3. ROTATING LEADERSHIP — OSCILLATING NETWORK POSITION AS AN INDICATOR OF CREATIVITY

In our research where we measured interpersonal interaction through e-mail and sociometric badges — cellphone-sized sensors worn around the neck developed by Sandy

Pentland's team from the MIT Media Lab — we found that if a team communicated in ever changing structures, oscillating between a star and a galaxy structure, this was predictive of high creativity. While strong leaders with the right personality characteristics are essential for successful collaboration, a group of leaders taking turns is even better. We first discovered this studying the e-mail communication among Eclipse[1] open source software developers, where rotating leadership was the best predictor of the most creative teams.[2] It was later confirmed when looking at teams of marketing employees at a bank, and teams of graduate students and medical researchers developing innovations for the care of patients with chronic diseases where teams with different leaders taking turns were most creative.

5.4. RAPID RESPONSE

When I was a young post-doc at MIT, the speed with which Tim Berners-Lee, the creator of the Web, answered his e-mails was an eye-opening experience in a time when people took a few days to answer to e-mail. In the meantime, I have found this pattern many times. The speed of response and the number of "nudges" or "pings" it takes until a prospective communication partner answers e-mails are excellent predictors of employee and customer satisfaction and mutual respect. For example, in a consulting company we calculated the average e-mail response times of

---

[1]Eclipse is a popular Java software development environment developed and maintained by a large open source community.
[2]Kidane and Gloor (2007).

different departments in 2008, before smartphone usage became popular. Six departments took about three days on average to respond to mails, while one department was considerably slower. The employees in the slowly responding department reported much lower job satisfaction. In the meantime, in the age of smartphones, this behavior has become more prominent, with average response times of well-working groups in the two-hour range for employees getting hundreds of e-mails per day.

On the personal level, responsiveness is also an outstanding metric. How quickly you respond to others, and how quickly they will respond to you is an excellent indicator of the health of the relationship. The faster you answer to everybody else, the more passionate you are. The faster on average others answer to you, the more they respect you. The passion of Tim Berners-Lee in the early days of the Web was perfectly matched by the speed with which he answered his e-mails. The respect he got from the community of early Web developers was reflected in the speed with which they answered his e-mails.

5.5. HONEST SENTIMENT

In my initial work, I expected that being positive would be an indicator of successful projects and people. What I found, however, is that being honest is far more important. Using sophisticated machine learning algorithms we have developed software to measure positivity, negativity, and emotionality of language. While our software is not looking at the specific content of messages, we analyze positive and negative sentiment and emotionality of messages. Our software tool Condor uses a machine learning algorithm which can be trained with any large body of classified text, for example, with billions of tweets. We found that if the language is too positive, this might be an indicator of dissatisfied customers. For example, in a project with a global outsourcing service provider, we found that the more positive language a salesperson used in communicating with the customer, the less happy the customer was. On the other hand, in innovation teams we found that using more emotional language, defined as using more positive and negative text at the same time, was a predictor of more creative teams. When looking at employee attrition, we found that the employees most likely to terminate their work were becoming less emotional in their language, and showing less rotating leadership behavior.

5.6. SHARED CONTEXT

The more people start developing their own lingo, the more innovative they are. High-functioning teams also define their own language. When the World Wide Web was started, new words and acronyms like "HTML," "HTTP," "RDF," and "FOAF" were coined, and existing words like "web," "semantic web," and "apache" took on a new meaning. Our own software measures new word usage in two ways. First, it measures complexity of text as the frequency of rare words in the entire text collection. Looking at contents of e-mail of creative teams of medical researchers, we found that the more focused they were on inventing their own vocabulary by using words in a specific way and coining new abbreviations to discuss their new ideas, the more creative and effective they were. On the other hand, we found that the more complex the language of salespeople was, the less satisfied their customers were. Secondly, we also track the diffusion of new words in a community. If somebody introduces a new word in a group, using it for the first time in a message sent to others, we measure how quickly others pick up the word. The more somebody succeeds in introducing new words, the more influential she or he is. When Tim Berners-Lee created the Web, he introduced new uses for the words "web" and "browser," and over time added a whole list of acronyms such as HTTP, HTML, RDF, OWL, and "semantic web" to our language, reflecting his influence on today's society.

In sum, these six "honest signals of collaboration" use the existing structure, timing, and content of messages as indicators of performance. While measuring creativity and performance can be elusive, the six honest signals for collaboration can easily and repeatedly be tracked over time.

5.7. MORE HONEST SIGNALS

Using body-worn sensors, the sociometric badges, we found additional fascinating results. We measured if people looked into each other's eyes, how close they were to each other, how excited they were in their body movements, and how many turns in speaking two communication partners took. Comparing the interaction behavior with the results of a survey, where people reported how much they trusted the other person, allowed us to come up with surprising results about trust. The more we look others into the eyes, the more we trust them: When measuring face-to-face interaction using sociometric badges in teams of software developers, we found that the more people were looked at, the more they were trusted. Measuring face-to-face interaction in teams using socio-metric badges, we found that the less people speak in meetings, the more they are trusted. It also turns out that extroverts are less liked than introverts: in an experiment with sociometric badges measuring frequency of face-to-face interaction, extroverts were the most peripheral.[3] The more we trust others, the more creative we will be: in an experiment in a graduate student seminar we found that their peers from the other teams rated the creative output of teams where team members trusted each other the most highly.

The more we mirror each other's body language, the more we get into flow, the positive mood of elatement where we do not feel stress anymore. In a project measuring interpersonal interaction of jazz musicians through sociometric badges,[4] we found that the more musicians started moving in synch by mirroring each other as measured with an accelerometer, the better was their creative output, measured by the intensity of the applause by the audience. In other words, the more the musicians swing in synch, the happier is their audience.

5.8. THE SIX HONEST SIGNALS APPLY THE FOUR PRINCIPLES OF SOCIAL QUANTUM PHYSICS

Not just measuring, but actively encouraging the six honest signals of collaboration leads to improved collaboration, resulting in more innovation. I call this process

---

[3]Gloor, Oster, Raz, Pentland, and Schoder (2010).
[4]Gloor, Oster, and Fischbach (2013).

"virtual mirroring," showing individuals their own communication behavior, and telling them what behavior encourages collaboration and innovation, causing them to "reflect and reboot." Analyzing the six signals in combination and mirroring them back to the individual will encourage adherence to the five laws of collaboration described in Chapter 6. This application of the six honest signals of collaboration leads to improved communication resulting in more innovation. It is based on the four principles of social quantum physics. It starts with the particle/wave duality: we are perceiving individuals in the analysis of the six honest signals of collaboration as fixed bodies, but we measure their interaction as probabilities of conversing with each other in communication structures, dynamics, and shared context. Tracking central leadership and balanced contribution, the rotation in leadership, the speed of the response, the emotionality of messages exchanged, and the shared use of novel words delivers only an absolute value for a certain point in time, just like measuring physical particles does. Just like physical particles, humans are influenced most by their immediate surrounding. But like physical particles, individuals further away and the context they are in also exude a subtle influence on the individual. Our human sensory system analyzes all of these influences, leading to an emphatic response to the environment.

The six honest signals of collaboration allow us to measure the entanglement between two individuals. The individuals might take turns in rotating leadership, or they might work as perfectly synchronized teams. For instance, when we studied jazz musicians in concert, we found that the more their energy levels oscillate in parallel, the more the jazz band is in group flow, resulting in a more fired-up audience. In other words, the more the jazz band is entangled, the happier its customers are. We also found similar entanglement through measuring the six honest signals of collaboration through e-mail archives of teams, where for instance an entangled team shows a low variation in contribution index, or a highly homogeneous usage of novel words distinguishing it from other teams.

By mirroring the communication behavior of a team back to the team members causing their reflection, we are applying the Heisenberg uncertainty principle: if we measure the communication behavior of individuals and groups of people, and tell them what we are measuring, we will change their behavior. We were able to show this by improving satisfaction of the customers of an outsourcing provider through virtual mirroring of the outsourcing company employees working for the customer. We showed the outsourcing employees their six honest signals of collaboration, and told them which communication behavior produced happier customers. In turn, the employees changed their behavior — providing stronger, less rotating leadership, faster responsiveness, and less overly positive language — leading to happier customers.

We also find the future changing the interpretation of the past: for example the Croatian Wikipedians are "rewriting"[5] the history of the Ustasha, a right-wing fascist organization during the Second World War in

---

[5]https://meta.wikimedia.org/wiki/Requests_for_comment/2013_issues_on_Croatian_Wikipedia

Croatia, attempting to "clean" it of its Nazi past. The future also rewrites the past for individuals. Looking at an individual virtual mirror shows a view of the past that the individual did not have at the time the communication was happening. For an example of a virtual mirror see my own e-mail network of January 2016 shown in Section 8.1 in Figure 22. Looking at this network will show hidden relationships I was not aware of when the e-mail exchange was happening, thus altering my view of past events and rebooting my own behavior.

Collective consciousness in and by itself is an "agnostic" aggregated mind of groups of individuals that can arise in competitive and collaborative swarms. Just to give a negative example, ISIS has been extremely successful in creating collective awareness of its "cause" among disgruntled Muslim youth under the pretense of creating a new caliphate under the laws of the Koran. Its "queen bees" are using the Internet, YouTube, Twitter, and Instagram masterfully to reach their constituency. However, the goal of this book is to leverage collective consciousness to foster and nurture collaboration for increased creativity. To build a collaboratively cohesive swarm, individuals will grow their personal networks through CINs or COINs, which were introduced in Chapter 4. For them to function, they have to adhere to core ethical principles discussed in the next chapter.

MAIN LESSONS LEARNED

- The six honest signals of collaboration measure network structure, network dynamics, and network content.

- The two network structure-based signals are "strong leadership" and "balanced contribution."

- The two network dynamics-based signals are "rotating leadership" and "responsiveness."

- The two network contents-based signals are "honest sentiment" and "shared context."

- The sociometric badges measure additional signals based on face-to-face interaction.

6

THE ETHICAL LAYER: FIVE LAWS

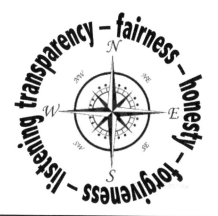

CHAPTER CONTENTS

- Transparency.

- Fairness.

- Honesty.

- Forgiveness.

- Listening.

In a public vote at the town hall meeting on May 4, 2015, the Swiss town of Duernten (population 7000) decided to return $250,000 to a worker, who had not filled out his tax declaration since 1995 due to dyslexia. In successively higher tax bills, the tax authorities had overcharged Ernst Suter by $280,000, forcing him to sell land to pay taxes on money he had never made. As a worker in a butcher's shop, Suter made about $60,000 a year, which, by Swiss standards, is a fairly low salary. Based on information from the town administration, the tax office of the canton of Zurich had second-guessed Suter's income at about $300,000 per year, and sent him tax bills accordingly, which Suter always paid, nearly forcing him into bankruptcy more than once. Only when Suter ran totally dry, did the branch of the town government that has the task to collect late payments, the office of payment enforcement, or "Betreibungsamt" in Swiss German, pass on the case to a custodian, who brought the whole tragedy to light.

This is where things took a positive turn for Ernst Suter. After the custodian sent a detailed list of the overpayments to all citizens in Duernten, the town hall meeting decided in December 2014 to return the money. When the mayor of the town and his tax administration dragged their feet and decided to cut the return into half — because in the Swiss system, half of the collected town tax of individuals is passed on to the canton — citizens of Duernten took the matter into their own hands. They again put the issue on the agenda of their town hall meeting in May, voting overwhelmingly in Suter's favour.

Fairness and ethical behavior are more important than strict adherence to the letter of the law. In this case, the swarm — the town hall meeting — also censored its leaders, asking the elected town officials to not only return the $250,000 they had taken from Suter, but even to make sure, in case the canton would want to tax the return payment as income, to allocate an additional $75,000 to pay for the income tax. They also asked the mayor to formally apologize to Suter. This shows that the swarm — the citizens of Duernten — knows better than the leaders what is fair, independent of what the tax code says.

6.1. RATINGS, NOT RANKINGS! — MERITOCRACY, NOT HIERARCHY!

When I started my research into swarm creativity in 2002, I assumed that collaborative groups would operate in an egalitarian way. I assumed that communities like Linux, open source developers, or Wikipedia editors would be made up of large crowds of people where everybody contributed evenly. However, what I found was the opposite. There are strong leaders at the top, Jimmy Wales, the cofounder of Wikipedia, and Linus Torvalds, the creator of Linux, still have a strong say. While top leadership is open to anybody, it is taken by the most competent. The rules and responsibilities of the leaders are clearly defined, and open for everybody to see. This leads to having the most passionate and intrinsically motivated leaders at the top, who care about the cause the most. Everybody can aspire to be a leader; however, their contributions are continuously being evaluated, and the members of the community democratically elect their own leaders. For example, for Wikipedia's leaders, their peer-given awards called "barnstars," number of edits, and number of resolved conflicts provide clear metrics to judge them. The objective is to measure and rate the contributions, not to declare winners and losers; in short, leaders are based on ratings, not rankings, on meritocracy, not hierarchy.

How does such a meritocratic rating system work? When looking at the evolution of individual value systems, we find a progression from egoism to loyalty to moral. At the most basic level, the individual organism, to survive, has to put its own basic needs first. When individuals are close to starvation, they will fend for themselves. In a society with more disposable resources, individuals will develop loyalty toward people close to them. They will still, however, put the needs of the group to which they feel loyal ahead of the needs of society at large. Only when all basic needs are covered, will members of a society start behaving in an ethically responsible and moral way.

We can observe a similar progression from competition and egoism to collaboration and altruism in different national cultures. Strong emphasis on the individual leads to unabashed capitalism, where the value of people is measured by the size of their bank account. This is what we find in the United States. According to US free market morals, it is okay for the company Turing Pharmaceutical to buy orphaned drugs against rare diseases, hiking the price for a single pill over night from $13.50 to $750, thus bringing the price for individual patients to a hundred thousand dollars per year. Pharmaceutical company Valeant pursues a similar business model, buying the rights to older, generic drugs, and raising prices by up to 500%. Valeant was a darling of "well-respected investors" like earlier mentioned Bill Ackmann, CEO of hedge fund Pershing Capital, who was hailed as a "good" capitalist and "philanthropist," investing billions into Valeant. While there is no law against such price-gouging behavior, it is definitively not ethical. Turing and Valeant are not really pharmaceutical companies, but financial reengineering firms. While pharmaceutical companies invest huge sums into developing new drugs, Turing and Valeant are capitalism at its worst, trying to wring out as much money as possible from old drugs, where they have a captive customer base, namely the patients of chronic diseases whose survival depends on their drugs. The research and development (R&D) costs of these drugs have been written off, and so the owners of Turing and Valeant are free to open the financial spigot as widely "as the market will bear," without any concerns for the suffering of their customers. Capitalism does not care about what is ethical, but about what is legal. And laws are made such that loopholes can be found. A US executive has the fiduciary duty to optimize earnings for the shareholders in a company. CEOs chasing tax loopholes and storing money abroad to create as much "value" as possible for their shareholders therefore do nothing but their duty by law. As my former business partner in a US company — right before we started suing each other — told me, "personally, Peter, I am your friend, but as the CEO of my company it is my fiduciary duty to squeeze you as much as possible to create as much value as possible for my shareholders." (He thought he was the largest shareholder.)

Figure 13: From Egoism to Altruism.

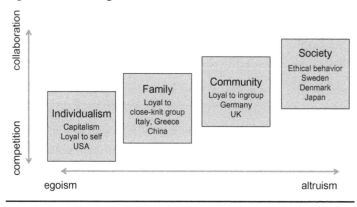

In cultures which emphasize loyalty to the family and longtime friends — Italy, Greece, and China come to mind — individuals will renounce brazen competition for collaboration among family members. In Italy, the family is seen as the bulwark to protect individuals from abuse and mistreatment by the state. The child owes loyalty to the parents, not society. As an Italian friend once told me, "If my mother would kill somebody, it would be my duty to stand by her and defend her against the state" (Figure 13).

Exclusive focus on the family and longtime friends as unit of cohesiveness and collaboration is against the benefit of society at large. In a society like Germany or the United Kingdom, people develop strong bonds within associations and communities. However, these groups bond together for mutual benefit against society. While I was teaching a course in Germany over the last 12 years, there was barely a year where I was not stranded at the airport or a train station either because of a strike of the Lufthansa pilots or a strike of the railway employees.

Notably both of these professional groups already have a lot of privileges in Germany, but are not shy in using their collective clout to extend these privileges. On a side note, there is an even darker side to this ingroup-centric behavior, as members of an ingroup will stick together to keep outsiders out. This has been shown most strikingly in Germany's darkest hour, where the Nazis were most popular in towns where there were the most civic associations such as small animal breeding, singing, and gymnastics associations.[1]

In northern European countries such as Denmark, Norway, or Sweden, we find a more reciprocal attitude where people expect the state to take good care of them, but are also willing to give back to the state. I was told the story of a Danish woman, just moving into retirement, not rich but squarely middle class, who refused to take Social Security payments from the state because she figured she had enough for her needs and wanted to leave the Social Security money for others who needed it more. I observed a similar behavior in Switzerland, where people carefully read their healthcare bill after treatment by the doctor, and question it item by item, although they would not have to pay it, as their healthcare provider covers it.

Meritocratic rating systems are following the same mechanisms as ethical behavior in Nordic countries: do what is good for society — or Linux, or Wikipedia, or Stack Overflow — in the end, it will be good for you as a member of this community, too.

---

[1] Satyanath, Voigtländer, and Voth (2013).

There are five key coordination mechanisms at play when people work together in an ethical way: transparency, fairness, honesty, forgiveness, and listening.

6.2. TRANSPARENCY

In the Middle Ages most people spent their whole lives in the village where they were born. In such a small world, it was impossible to hide any secrets; neighbors knew all there was about each other, and gossip among neighbors was the lubricant of society. This transparency assured honest behavior, as shaming and losing face was a powerful deterrent against asocial behavior. When in the age of the industrial revolution, long-distance travel was made easier, it became simpler to run, hide, and start a new life elsewhere. This created a powerful incentive to hide information, and the current turned against transparency. The Internet and Google, however, have reinstituted the small world network of the Middle Ages on a global scale, as any past transgressions such as inebriated college parties and real criminal activities are there for anybody to see on Facebook, Twitter, or Instagram, from anywhere on the world. The only way to hide is to totally change one's identity, which, in the age of LinkedIn and Facebook carries considerable social penalties as it basically means to build a new person and background.

In the age of collective intelligence and collective consciousness it is therefore much easier to accept transparency. If somebody has nothing to hide, there is no incentive to hide. Transparency encourages honest behavior, which creates mutual trust. For instance, Chinese citizens have low trust in their local government because its inner workings are shrouded in secrecy, and its rules are byzantine and impossible to penetrate for the ordinary citizen.[2] The Chinese state would work much better if Chinese citizens could trust their state. The best way for the state to create trust would be to operate more transparently.

The interesting thing is that once trust is established, there is no need for transparency anymore. People will trust a person with a favorable reputation, without asking for transparency. Once transparency can be taken for granted and trust is set up, it becomes much easier to do business. If there is no transparency, transaction costs are very high. I experienced this for myself when in July 2007 I was bringing 15 used computers to Ghana to be donated to schools. The shipping costs for the computers were about $800. It took me two weeks, and the services of a freight-handling agent at total cost of $700 to get the computers through customs in Ghana, because nobody trusted anybody else, and the entire process was totally nontransparent. For this amount of money I could have bought the same used computers on Accra's Makola market. That high trust reduces the need for transparency is also demonstrated in wealthy countries like Finland or Switzerland, which have a high tax compliance rate, without having to persecute taxpayers aggressively. In Greece or Italy, the tax official is your enemy, and the taxpayer is assumed guilty until proven innocent; in Finland and Switzerland, it's the other way round. Easily available transparency reduces the need for transparency. Trust given builds trust into society. By not controlling Swiss taxpayers in minuscule details, the

---

[2]See for example comparison in http://info.worldbank.org/governance/wgi/index.aspx#reports

tax evasion rate is much smaller than, for instance, in Italy, where each transaction must be documented and is supervised by the tax police.

In a classroom experiment, researchers showed that people are willing to reward transparency by paying more for products.[3] A company like Patagonia that publicly discloses the high moral and ethical quality of their production process can charge a higher price for their product. In the lab environment, study subjects were willing to pay double the price for a product that was produced in total transparency compared to a product produced in total opacity.

Having an active Wikipedia community might not only be good for transparency, it might even be good for the economy: In an analysis done in 2012, we compared for eight European countries the percentage of active Wikipedia editors with the corruption rankings of the countries from Transparency International and their credit default swap rate, that is the rate the government has to pay for loans as insurance against nonpayment. Greece had the highest rate to pay as well as the highest corruption index; this was well before the Greek currency crisis in spring 2015. Greece also had the lowest percentage of active Wikipedia editors, illustrating that comparatively fewer people there are willing to work for the greater good.

The Greek economy and Chinese bureaucracy try to leverage the "theory of mind" for their own advantage, where people are trying to outcompete each other by reading each other's mind, playing the game of "I think

---

[3]Kraft, Valdes, and Zheng (2014).

that you think that I think that you might think …"
Another example of opacity leading to missing trust
comes from the world of sports, where the selection of
the hosts for world championships and the Olympics is
a highly nontransparent process with low trust of the
public into the fairness of the process.

A more transparent society such as Canada, Switzerland,
or Denmark is not trying to hide problems in the closet and
leave them open to interpretation and mind reading, but
resolve them in public, positively "manipulating" people
by sharing the inner workings of the system. The
Wikipedia policies and guidelines are a prime example of
this approach; all conflicts are shared and fought out in
public. The result is arguably fair treatment of even highly
controversial topics such as gay marriage, gun control,
or abortion, and a global encyclopedia vastly superior
and up-to-date to all expert-managed, commercially run
encyclopedias.

6.3. FAIRNESS

Collaboration only works when the collaborators are
dealing fairly with each other. While every trick is
allowed to win among competitors, collaborators expect
fair treatment. One of the currencies collaborators want
to be paid in is peer recognition. The basic principle is to
give credit to whom credit is due. Linus Torvalds is well-
known for giving praise to other Linux contributors;
Wikipedia barnstars fulfill the same purpose.

Already in classical Rome fairness was one of the key
reasons for its thousand years of existence. In his book *A
History of Knowledge: Past, Present, and Future* Charles

Van Doren makes the case that the main reason for the one thousand years long success of the Roman empire was its adherence to one single written law, applicable to all. The Roman law basically laid out the rules and at least in theory treated every citizen the same, from emperor to commoner, even slaves were included. Van Doren concludes that mistreated subjects of despotic kings might not have fought the Roman conquerors wholeheartedly, after token resistance they rather preferred to join the Roman state with its clear laws and promise of fair treatment.

While fairness is hard to precisely define, it has been extensively tested by behavioral scientists in the "ultimatum game," where one person is allowed to split an amount of money with a second person.[4] The second person can accept or reject the deal; however, only when the second person accepts the deal is the first person allowed to keep her share of the money. It seems most people consider amounts below 30% as unfair. Although it would be better for the second person to keep, let's say 20% instead of nothing, she will usually reject the deal, so that both people end up having nothing. A study of 37 papers on ultimatum games found marked differences on the willingness of people to accept or reject the proposed deals, ranging from a Peruvian study where people were willing to accept 26% offers to a study in Paraguay where the first person on average offered 51%. The authors were however unable to map these differences to national characteristics. The conclusion seems obvious: anywhere in the world people are only willing to collaborate if they are treated fairly.

---

[4]Marlowe et al. (2008).

How can we encourage and support fair behavior? The answer lies in increased transparency. A threat of exposing unethical and unfair behavior will discourage a potential cheater from tricking. Shaming is a strong deterrent; transparency will keep people honest.

6.4. HONESTY

When former Ford CEO Alan Mulally took the helm of Ford motor company in 2006, in the first management meeting, his direct reports presented him with status reports that were color-coded green for "running smoothly," yellow for "problems," and red for "crisis." Although Ford was in serious crisis at that time, the status reports were almost exclusively green. Only one manager, Mark Fields, the head of Ford USA at that time, stood up and acknowledged serious problems with the tailgate latch of one of his models. When his peers waited for an angry outburst of Mulally about the apparent failure of Fields, Mulally stood up and applauded Fields for being brave enough to openly acknowledge his difficulties. Over the next three meetings, Mulally observed the problems of Fields going from red over yellow to green until the tailgate latch problem was solved. In 2014, Fields succeeded Mulally as Ford's CEO.

While it is nice to be nice, kindness and honesty are more important. In one of our projects automatically analyzing corporate e-mail using machine learning, we could confirm Mulally's instinctive behavior. Using computer-supported natural language processing, we compared customer satisfaction with the use of positive language of salespeople. We found that the more positive language the salesperson was using, the less satisfied the customer was. A much better predictor of customer satisfaction was the use of honest language, which we defined as using both positive and negative words.

I discovered the same while teaching my seminar on Collaborative Innovation Networks (COINs) described in Section 8.5 over a 12-year period. When I started the seminar in 2005, I was very positive and supportive in my feedback to the students, as I was afraid I would discourage them if I were too frank in my criticisms. However, over time I discovered that students did not take my overly positive comments seriously; they knew for themselves if something was not good, even if I was giving them half-hearted praise. In the meantime, I have switched to giving honest feedback, saying clearly what students did well, and what they did not so well. What I realized is that my consistent feedback built up much more trust and credibility, as seminar participants know now much better how to improve their work.

This ties in with latest research in K1 to K12 education, where the goal switched from teaching self-esteem to teaching resilience in the case of difficulties. Until very recently, teaching in US schools was optimized toward building up self-esteem in students, as research had found a correlation between self-esteem and success. However, it seems this was a classic case of confusing correlation with causation, as teaching students self-esteem leads them to developing a sense of entitlement, which does not let them recover in case of failure. Current research has found a much stronger link between success and resilience in case of difficulties.[5]

---

[5]Dumont and Provost (1999).

Parents and teachers do a disservice to their children if they shower them with indiscriminate praise. It is much better to be honest, and tell them not only when they excel, but also when they underperform, which will teach them at a young age to cope with and recover from failure.

Honesty for the individual means consistent and open behavior: Do what you say, and say what you do!

6.5. FORGIVENESS — TIT FOR TAT

In a team, giving somebody the benefit of the doubt makes collaboration more efficient. While the New Testament teaches us unrestricted forgiveness, experiments in behavioral economics have shown that this will lead to the exploitation of unconditional cooperators. Researchers in behavioral economics have found that we have the strong urge to punish cheaters, even if the punishment comes at a cost to ourselves. It seems this threat of punishment is needed to keep people honest — humans need both the carrot and the stick to adhere to the rules. Humans also have a much higher propensity to cheat if nobody watches, that's why transparency builds trust: it makes it much harder to cheat.

In a series of classic lab experiments, behavioral scientist Robert Axelrod showed that being kind and reciprocal are the most successful collaboration strategies. In these lab tests, researchers give participants the opportunity to collaborate or to defect, with rewards and punishments for collaborating and defecting. In the most popular of these games, the "prisoner's dilemma," a participant gets the biggest rewards if she cheats while her opponent is honest; honest opponents in this case get a big punishment for their good deed. Both are rewarded more modestly if both are honest. Axelrod found that an extension of another classic cooperation strategy called "tit for tat" works best. "Tit for tat" means collaborating on the first move when two strangers start working together, and mirroring the behavior of the opponent in subsequent moves. In sum, Axelrod concluded that being kind, being reciprocal, being fair, and not being tricky was the most successful strategy.

In simulations, behavioral scientists Martin Nowak and Karl Sigmund found that an extension of the "tit for tat" behavior introduced above in the prisoner's dilemma game, which they call "Pavlov," works better than unrestricted forgiveness. The Pavlov algorithm asks people to initially collaborate with their partners, if they cheat them, punish them once, and then go back to collaborating. The reason Nowak and Sigmund call this "Pavlov" is that they liken it to Pavlov's reflex-controlled behavior: the reflex is to cooperate, if cheated, punish once, and then go back to cooperation.

Most people would agree that killing Osama bin Laden was justified. We would also kill a mosquito that is sucking our blood, instead of letting it suck the blood — and maybe transmit malaria in the process. However, if the mosquito flies away instead of sucking blood, let it fly away. To punish somebody takes energy. Punishment should be seen as a corrective action for future better collaboration, not to take "revenge," as this only consumes additional energy from the one taking revenge. A simpler principle is "three strokes and you are out." If somebody cheats me once, I assume he made an honest mistake, I even give her or him the benefit of the doubt a second time, but if I am shortchanged the third time, I let them go and don't look back.

6.6. LISTENING

The art of listening is a key ingredient of collaborators. Competitors talk first, to make sure they are heard — just look at Donald Trump, he wants both the first and the last word in every discussion. Collaborators talk last, to make sure they hear everybody — Barack Obama is known to speak last in meetings, to make sure that everybody's opinion is heard before he makes up his own mind.

Nelson Mandela called the style of leadership where everybody is being heard "leading from the back." Leading from the back means not to be the official leader, but influencing the direction of the team by asking the right questions, listening to the answers, and moving the project forward, not the leader. Other metaphors that suggest the same style of listening-based leadership are the impresario, not the conductor, or the balloon pilot instead of the racecar driver. While the conductor gives precise instructions to the members of the orchestra, it is the impresario who pulls the strings from behind the scene and makes the entire concert possible. And while the racecar driver exerts full control over the car through steering wheel, accelerator pedal, and brakes, the balloon pilot needs to let the balloon go. The only way for the balloon pilot to influence the balloon is to decide about the time the balloon takes off, and on what altitude to fly. If a storm is coming, the pilot can either increase height, but if he increases it too much, there will be no air for breathing. If the pilot reduces height too much, the balloon will crash into the ground.

Now that we know what the key laws of *homo collaborensis* are — transparency, fairness, honesty, forgiveness, and listening — we are ready to investigate how adherences to these laws cannot just be measured by tracking communication patterns, but even be increased and thus collaboration quality improved by mirroring back an individual's behavior to the individual, thus triggering reflection and behavioral change.

6.7. THE SIX HONEST SIGNALS TRACK ADHERENCE TO THE FIVE LAWS OF COLLABORATION

The six honest signals of collaboration introduced in the previous chapter and the five laws of collaboration are tightly interlinked. By measuring the six honest signals of collaboration, we can track and even foster adherence to the five laws of collaboration. Figure 14 shows the mapping of the laws to the honest signals.

A leader can only show *strong leadership* over extended periods of time, if she is able to create a trust-based relationship with the members of her swarm. Generosity and *forgiveness*, where the leader holds back revenge if she feels slighted, and gives her communication partners the benefit of the doubt helps building trust, which helps building strong leadership. Pope Francis has demonstrated this with

Figure 14: The Six Honest Signals of Collaboration Track Adherence to the Five Laws of Ethical Collaboration.

Structure	Dynamics	Content
Strong Leadership	**Rotating Leadership**	**Honest Sentiment**
Forgiveness/Trust	Fairness/Transparency	Honesty
Balanced Contribution	**Responsiveness**	**Shared Context**
Fairness/Transparency	Respect & Passion	Listening

his leadership style of forgiveness, showing him as a strong and popular leader, who has the trust of his swarm.

A *balanced communication* style, where everybody contributes her fair share is an indicator of *fairness*. A transparent environment will lead to more fair behavior, and thus to more trust. Once trust is established, we do not need continuous transparency, as others will trust that we will treat them fairly without needing the capability to continuously check in on us. The Swiss government is an exemplar of balanced contribution, as it does not have one head of state, but seven ministers called "federal councilors" with equal power, who in combination are the Swiss head of state. This system has worked extremely well since 1848. When occasionally one councilor contributes too much or too little, he is not reelected by parliament, as has happened four times in the history of Switzerland, the last time to right-wing politician Christoph Blocher in 2007.

A leader can only practice *rotating leadership* if she can let go and delegate decision-making power to others. This has been demonstrated by open source leaders Linus Torvalds and Jimmy Wales, who put themselves under the same rules as any other Linux or Wikipedia contributor and delegate tasks to other leaders. The Wikipedia stewards are a group of elected leaders and final arbiters for each different language version of Wikipedia, who take turns as leaders and make final decisions about critical content such as the description of the Nazi past, or the pages about Angela Merkel or Donald Trump. A similar role is taken in Linux by the committers, who have the power to accept changes to the source code, and who are elected to their roles by popular vote.

By being *responsive* and on time we show respect to everybody. French king Louis XVIII reportedly said, "punctuality is the politeness of kings." As we have seen at the example of Tim Berners-Lee, the overall speed of response of a person is a proxy for individual passion and respect. Tim showed high passion by answering e-mail very quickly. Others showed him high respect by answering to his e-mails quickly as well.

By not being indiscriminately positive, but rather *honestly* telling what is good and also what is bad, leaders build better working relationships and thus ultimately more trust. Steve Jobs had a reputation for not suffering fools gladly. Rather, he was quite outspoken in his criticism, but he could also be quite charming if necessary. For example, his successor as Apple's CEO, Tim Cook, said, " no more than five minutes into my initial interview with Steve, I wanted to throw caution and logic to the wind and join Apple. My intuition already knew that joining Apple was a once in a lifetime opportunity to work for the creative genius, and to be on the executive team that could resurrect a great American company."[6]

Creating *shared context* by introducing a shared vocabulary will create not just a discussion, where one tries to convince others of their viewpoint, but — listening first — a true dialog, where we try to understand each other's viewpoint to achieve consensus. For instance, Barack Obama is known to speak last in any group meeting, thus creating a shared context by letting everybody contribute their honest opinion and to not intimidate other participants.

---

[6]https://en.wikipedia.org/wiki/Tim_Cook (retrieved March 26, 2016).

The next chapter describes how these networking structures and dynamics and ethical laws may be combined by individuals and groups to either compete or collaborate.

MAIN LESSONS LEARNED

- Transparency builds trust.

- Fairness means giving equal rights and obligations to all members of the swarm.

- Honesty is better than being uncritically positive.

- Punishing once and then going back to being forgiving works best.

- Leaders should talk last, and listen first.

7

THE COLLABORATION LAYER: FROM *HOMO COMPETITIVUS* TO *HOMO COLLABORENSIS*

CHAPTER CONTENTS

- Competitive Collaboration is competing internally to collaborate at the outside.

- Collaborative Competition is collaborating internally to compete at the outside.

- Stack Overflow is competitive collaboration; TopCoder is collaborative competition.

- Why humans have been getting less violent over the last 2000 years.

- Why altruism will beat egoism.

- Why "free markets" are everything but free.

- Why "cool" products are better than "hot" products.

When Chrysler and GM went bankrupt during the 2008 financial crisis, Ford CEO Alan Mulally should have jumped at the opportunity to get rid of his two biggest competitors. And yet, in a hearing in front of the US Senate, Mulally spoke for his two fallen rivals. Why on earth did he support the bailout of his two bankrupt competitors? At that time, Ford had mortgaged all its assets for a $23.6 billion loan to get through the crisis on its own and was in a much better financial shape than its rivals, offering Mulally a unique opportunity to dump his two largest competitors. And still, at a hearing in the Senate in Washington at the end of 2008, Mulally was supporting the government bailout of his competitors, against all principles of capitalism and free market economy, which should have led him to do everything to dispose of his competitors. The answer I heard him give to a student at a talk at MIT in 2015 showed him as a prime example of a competitive collaborator. As Mulally explained, bankruptcy of his two biggest competitors would not just have meant bankruptcy for them, but also bankruptcy for a large part of the American car parts manufacturers and car dealers, and thus of a large part of the US economy, up to 20% by some estimates. Also, if GM and Chrysler went bankrupt, their suppliers would have gone bankrupt, which Ford depended on, too. Ford needed the supply base to remain in business and supply parts to Ford as well. Mulally put the good of society, and collaboration with his competitors before winning the competition by destroying his opponents.

When I was working in 2000 as a consultant for the ill-fated merger between Daimler and Chrysler, I observed an opposite example in the car industry. Competition was inserted at the expense of collaboration, leading to total failure. At that time I was working as a partner at Deloitte, which was recruited to assist the DaimlerChrysler team to build Covisint, a car parts procurement marketplace. The goal of Covisint was to greatly lower car parts costs for its consortium members, which, besides DaimlerChrysler, were Ford and GM plus their alliance partners. Car parts suppliers such as Bosch or Visteon would have to bid against each other in online auctions to supply car models with brakes, transmissions, mufflers, and the like. I described this case in detail in my earlier book *Swarm Creativity*, although the consequences described here were then not as clear as they are now. Covisint turned out to be more than a double-edged sword for DaimlerChrysler. While DaimlerChrysler initially had great cost-savings through Covisint, the quality of the car parts they procured through competitive bidding were of lower quality, because competitive bidding destroyed the long-term relationships DaimlerChrysler had with its suppliers. This became obvious only much later when their premium Mercedes cars started having serious quality issues. Covisint was a prime example where collaboration to compete among car vendors destroyed the internal collaboration between the car manufacturers and their suppliers.

In the rest of this chapter, we will dig deeper to understand when and how it pays to compete, and when it is much better to collaborate.

7.1. ALTRUISM BEATS EGOISM

In his 2011 book *The Better Angels of Our Nature,* Steven Pinker presents a wealth of statistics to prove that humanity has become successively less violent. Tribal warfare was nine times as deadly, and the murder rate in medieval Europe 30 times higher than today. This decrease in violence is still ongoing, with today's wars killing a fraction of the people killed by wars in the past. In a 2015 update to his book, Pinker shows that this trend is continuing, with homicide rates further dropping, as are rape and violence against children. Pinker thus gives a convincing argument that altruism might be rising at the expense of egoism.

Using Google's analysis tools to read the collective mind of the Internet confirms the same trend. Google Ngrams has indexed millions of books published between 1800 and 2012 tracking the popularity of words over time. Looking at the word usage of "egoism" and comparing it with "altruism" in Google Ngrams shows that until 1920 altruism and egoism were running in parallel, with egoism slightly ahead. From 1920 to approximately 1975 was the age of egoism, with altruism rapidly declining until 1960. Since then altruism has been rebounding, overtaking egoism after 1975 (**Figure 15**).

Figure 15: Altruism Beats Egoism in Google Ngrams after 1980.

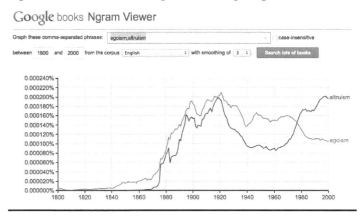

The *Oxford English Dictionary* shows a similar pattern, with the word "egoism" entering the English vocabulary in 1785, and the word "altruism" only entering English language in 1852. Zooming into the more recent past using Google trends gives a quasi-instantaneous window into the collective mind. Google trends show the popularity of Google searches broken down by search terms and geography. The importance of altruism still seems to be growing. There are roughly three times as many searches for "altruism" as there are for "egoism," with the frequency of searches for "altruism" going up, while searches for "egoism" are in slow decline (**Figure 16**).

Combining the statistical analysis of violence of Steven Pinker with the collective intelligence provided by Google shows a clear trend: we are getting more altruistic, more willing to restrict our selfish urges to the advantage of the community. As primatologists have shown, the benefits of living in a collaborative community extend beyond groups of humans.

Figure 16: In Google Search Trends, from 2005 to 2015, Interest in "Altruism" Is Going up, While Interest in "Egoism" Is Falling.

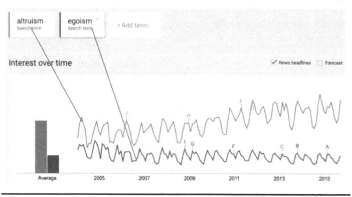

7.2. COLLABORATION GROWS PROPORTIONAL WITH POPULATION NUMBERS

When Dutch primatologist Carel van Schaik studied orang utans in Sumatra, he was puzzled to find that the orang utans in the region of Kluet were using tools to open otherwise inaccessible fruit, while the orang utans in the region of Batu-Batu were not able to figure out how to open the tasty Neesia tree fruits with their razor-sharp needles. What he found is that in Kluet, orang utans were living in groups, where the young learned to use sticks as tools from their teammates, while the solitary orang utans in Batu-Batu had no chance to collaborate and share the insights of a particularly innovative colleague. As long as they find enough food, orang utans living in close company, thus having the opportunity to learn from each other, can lead a better life. The solitary orang utans have no chance to share knowledge teaching each other how to access food difficult to reach.

The big question is when it is better to collaborate, and when it pays to compete. For the orang utans, it seems that population numbers have to do with competition or collaboration. When there is enough food, collaborate for a better life. When there is little food, it's everybody on their own, chasing away competitors fighting for scarce resources. Going back thousands of years in our own species' past, historians and anthropologists observe the same effect. Twenty thousand years ago, hunters and gatherers were competing for the same prey, while peasants in the Middle East about 10,000 years ago started living together in villages to more efficiently tend to their fields and share the fertile mud of the rivers. The more densely people started living together, the more rules they needed, to make living together less stressful. In principle, the strongest farmer could just claim the lion's share of the mud and water for his own field; however, this means that he would have to constantly watch his back, otherwise his neighbor might hit him over the head with his hoe to get the water for himself and his family. Then as now, competition leads to short-term gains, while collaboration enables a happier, long-term coexistence.

Human population has been growing exponentially in the last few years. While this enormous increase in numbers of humans brings a huge ecological burden for our planet, it also means that there are now many more human brains to communicate, collaborate, and innovate.

It seems that the closer humans are living together, the less competitive and the more collaborative they become. Violence has been going down since prehistoric times, and has never been as low as today. Steven Pinker has shown that in spite of terroristic attacks, society has become less and less violent. He argues that thanks to the progress of civilization, all kinds of violence, such as in wars, against women and homosexuals, and robbery and murder, have been in decline over centuries. For example, in 14th-century London there was more than one murder per 1000 inhabitants, compared to less than one per 100,000 inhabitants in today's London. Pinker proposes four reasons for the stunning reduction in violence: empathy, self-control, a moral sense, and reason. In Chapters 3–6, we have indeed seen that these are essential ingredients for successful collaboration (**Figure 17**).

The increase in human population, which led to a decrease in violence and an increase in speed of innovation, raises the question which organizational unit size of society works best. If an increase in population density leads to a decrease in violence, more collaboration and less competition, is having one large state with a

Figure 17: Human Population Growth Chart.

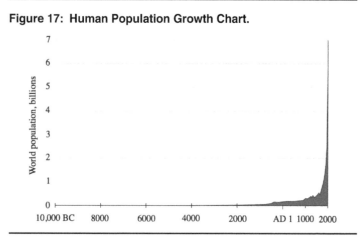

centralized government like France, Italy, or China better, or is a model like Northern Europe with many smaller states that have autonomous decision-making authority better? Looking at world history, it seems "delegating power to the edge," and placing as much responsibility as possible into the hands of the individual citizen is good for innovation. Times of decentralized "creative chaos" seem to be good for innovation. Renaissance Italy, with its fragmented city-states, and 19th-century Germany before German unification under the leadership of Bismarck in Prussia are well-researched hotbeds of innovation and creativity in arts and science.

Whether this decentralized structure reduces violence is a second question. The answer is that smaller organizational structures also help maintain civil order, as shaming and losing face are a major incentive to behave well. In medieval small-town structures, recognition and shunning by neighbors was a key means to keep local order. Francis Fukuyama has identified similar forces of modern society,[1] comparing Northern Europe with China or Italy. In China and Italy, the main unit of trust is the family, while trust in society at large is low. It seems that in these countries the smaller structures, such as sports, singing, or small animal breeding associations, which are prevalent in Germany and Northern Europe, are missing with the family filling in. It appears that a multidimensional social structure, where the social fabric through civic associations is strong, will lead to a more robust society with less violence.

---

[1]Fukuyama (1995).

7.3. EIGHTY PERCENT OF HUMANS ABHOR VIOLENCE

In related research, sociologist Randall Collins has shown[2] that most humans have a natural aversion against being violent. In the most provocative findings, US war historian S.L.A Marshall, interviewing countless soldiers during and after the Second World War, found that even in the most intensive fighting situations, only 15% of all soldiers fired their guns. This means, even if they were under heavy attack, where up to 80% of the soldiers would have had the opportunity to shoot back, only 15% pulled the trigger. While Marshall's numbers have been disputed by some high-ranking generals, according to Collins this is typical of senior managers, who get a distorted picture from reality, the further away they are from the frontline. On the other hand, sociologists found them to be correct. Ordinary soldiers also shy away from the most deadly elite killers in the army, the snipers in modern warfare. Snipers are a small minority, less than 1%; frequently they are disliked even by their own troops, because they are different, as "...they were emotionally distant, generally less sociable, more reserved than other troops" (Collins 2009, p. 384).

However, in spite of the majority of humankind abhorring violence, it seems today's society is still more driven by competition than by collaboration. At least, that's what we get when asking the Internet's crystal ball through Google Ngrams and Google Trends. The same trend is confirmed

---

[2]Collins (2009).

by the *Oxford English Dictionary*, which lists 1860 as the year in which the word "collaboration" has been used for the first time. In comparison, "competition" is much older; it was used for the first time in 1605 (**Figure 18**).

Collaboration does not even show up for the first 100 years of Google Ngram data collection. It grows slowly with a small spike during the Second World War, and only around 2000 is it growing again. Collaboration pales, however, in comparison with competition, which is growing rapidly from 1880 to the Second World War, perhaps triggered by the blunt capitalism prevalent in the first half of the 20th century. Only after 2000 does it seem to drop somewhat, but still eclipsing collaboration. Google trends from 2005 to 2015 shows a more differentiated picture. While collaboration seems to stagnate on a level about one-eighth of competition for this period, competition seems to have peaked in 2000, based on the prior Ngram analysis, and is slowly dropping in popularity since then, but still far more prominent than collaboration.

Figure 18: "Competition" Is Still Far More Popular until 2000 than "Collaboration" in Google Ngram.

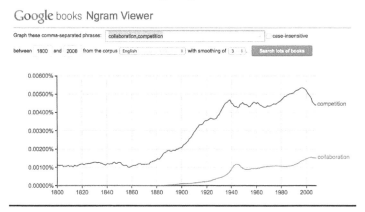

Figure 19: Google Search Trends Still Show Much More Interest for "Competition" than for "Collaboration."

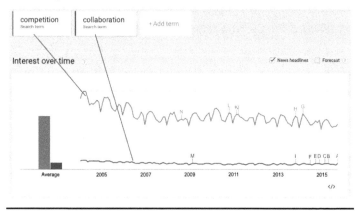

As the Google Search trend chart in **Figure 19** illustrates, our world still seems to be more driven by competition than by collaboration.

7.4. COLLABORATIVE COMPETITORS ARE EGOISTS, COMPETITIVE COLLABORATORS ARE ALTRUISTS

In this book, I make the case that all of us will be much better off if we invest into collaboration. The more we invest into collaboration and the less we invest into competition, the better. Our goal should be to channel our competitive energies into better collaboration. I make a fundamental distinction between "collaborative *competitors*" and "competitive *collaborators.*" Collaborative competitors are egoists, and they collaborate for their own benefit; competitive collaborators are altruists, and they compete to collaborate for the benefit of their group. Collaborative *competitors* collaborate to win; competitive *collaborators* compete to collaborate toward a shared goal. Two soccer teams playing against each other will engage in "collaborative competition," as the two teams will collaborate internally to compete against each other. Inside the team, there will be "competitive collaboration," as the members of the team compete for ownership of the ball, and for the fame of shooting a goal, but the team with the best internal collaboration will win the competition.

Legend has it that in the late Middle Ages and Renaissance, the Swiss peasant mercenaries became the most feared fighters of Europe, beating much larger and better-equipped armies of armored knights on horseback thanks to their motto "One for all, all for one." According to legend, the battle of the Swiss at Sempach in 1386 against the much stronger army of Habsburg Duke Leopold III of Austria was only won thanks to the self-sacrifice of Arnold of Winkelried, who, crying "take care of my wife and children" flung his body into the impenetrable phalanx of Habsburg spears opposing the Swiss. Catching the spears with his body, his self-sacrifice opened the way for the attack of the Swiss, leading to their total victory over the much larger and better-equipped Habsburg army. Winkelried was still collaborating to compete as the ultimate collaborator in the highly competitive business of waging war. However, he also was an altruist, as he gave is life for the shared goal of his Swiss swarm. This is a big exception, as collaborative competitors normally are driven by egoism.

The motivation of contributors to deeply collaborative endeavors such as Wikipedia is quite different. Collaboration trumps competition. While the Internet enables myriad examples of competitive collaboration, also further back in history people such as the merchants in the Dutch Republic, or the scientists of the Royal Society, competed to collaborate. The merchants of the VOC, the Vereenigde Oost-Indische Compagnie, or Dutch East India Company all shared the same goal. While the shareholders in Amsterdam each had the competitive goal of wanting to own the biggest house in town, their collaborative goal was the success of their company. Competition for collaboration was even more pronounced for the learned members of the British Royal Society. While Newton and Leibniz competed for the fame of having invented calculus, their collaborative goal was to further science by understanding gravity; they even developed some parts of the theory together.

E.O. Wilson in his book *The Social Conquest of Earth* describes the evolutionary progress of super-cooperative species such as bees, ants, and humans. Wilson calls them eusocial, "eu" meaning "true." To be eusocial, species must live together in multigenerational communities, practice a division of labor, and sacrifice at least part of their personal interest to the benefit of the group. Super-cooperators set aside their selfish desires, to join forces and self-sacrifice for the benefit of the hive or the tribe, in a transformation from competition to collaboration and altruism. This has led to ants, bees, and humans being spectacularly successful, living on all continents, and having the upper hand against other species. Wilson finds that altruistic collaboration is not just good for the group adhering to its principles, but even for the individual applying the behavior. While his altruistic behavior certainly did not personally help Swiss hero Winkelried, modern psychology has found that humans feel good if they help others. Even more, helping others also increases physical health of the altruistic individual. For example, researchers found that in a group of 2000 elderly members of the Presbyterian Church in the United States, the more members were helping others, the better was their mental health. Not only does it increase mental health, but more altruistic individuals also tend to be healthier and to live longer. In study after study, people volunteering their time doing good were getting older, and leading higher quality lives with less health impairments than more selfish people.

7.5. THE "DARK SIDE" OF COLLABORATION: COLLABORATIVE COMPETITION

Right after midnight of June 16, 1940, Marshal Pétain of France made his first broadcast to the French population, announcing sweeping collaboration with the German invaders of France. He went on to form the infamous Vichy puppet government, which collaborated with Nazi Germany all through the Second World War, until the Allied invasion in the Normandy led to the liberation of France. During the Vichy government the French republican motto "Liberté, égalité, fraternité" was replaced with "Work, family, fatherland" (Travail, famille, patrie). This switch in core values from egalitarian principles to ingroup-focused values, which stress "us against them," is typical for the dark side of collaboration. Within the group, there is collaboration, but the goal is to beat "them," "them" being the outside world.

Sometimes, even the most aggressive competitors collaborate — or conspire, to exploit their communities and customers. For instance, in 2013 currency traders at different banks conspired[3] to fix the exchange rate to increase their own profits. They had set up a cozy club in an Internet chat room where they were countertrading on large orders to buy foreign currency in the 60 seconds window before the trades were confirmed. This behavior is similar to a group of wolves that work far more efficiently when hunting in a pack. But similar to a wolfpack, collaborative competitors are in for the kill. Or in other words, they collaborate to compete more efficiently.

The same happens in its most extreme form in countries like North Korea, where the elites conspire to suppress their compatriots. In a pyramid of terror, the layer above suppresses the layer below for their own profit, playing to the human tendency of stratification and the desire to belong to a special, select group. In the case of North Korean dictator Kim Jong-un, as an absolutist despotic ruler, through a mix of terror and entitlements, he puts the group of generals right below him into a position of power toward the next lower layer. Reigning supremely, he punishes and kills as quickly as he rewards. If the defense minister falls asleep at an event presided over by Kim Jong-un, he is swiftly executed by a battery of anti-aircraft guns. By establishing a delicate balance of collaborative competition, Kim Jong-un succeeds in clinging to power. He is still on the same level as Qin Shi Huang, the first emperor of China, who unified China in 221 BC

---

[3]https://en.wikipedia.org/wiki/Forex_scandal

applying similar tactics. Qin Shi Huang not only had a terracotta army produced to serve him in afterlife, but also had the books of scholars who disagreed with him burned and them buried alive. Similar to Kim Jong-un, he had the habit of killing everybody objecting to his wishes including their family to the third degree.

The history of Europe up to the Second World War is a history of collaborative competition. In ever-changing alliances, the French, Spanish, Bavarian, Prussian, Habsburg, British, Scottish, Flemish, and many other major and minor kings, dukes, and princes realigned and collaborated to compete for supremacy in Europe. The countries of Europe in the 19th century can be seen as collaborative competitors, with competing nation states collaborating if it suited their needs. While the British, the French, and the Germans in the 19th century competed in conquering and exploiting the rest of the developing world, they occasionally banded together to share the plunder, for instance, in the Boxer war in China, where competitors Germany, the United Kingdom, and France collaborated to defeat the Chinese uprising.

Darwin identified this universal need for competition and survival of the fittest. Species will improve by competing for scarce resources, with the fittest winning the spoils. The same competitive spirit also imbued the free market economy, where Adam Smith's invisible hand is supposed to guarantee that through competition among vendors the customer will get the lowest price possible. It turns out, however, that this is not true, as competing producers will band together to the disadvantage of the consumer, to extract the highest possible price, providing a prime example of collaborative competition.

7.6. A PRIME EXAMPLE OF COLLABORATIVE COMPETITION: "FREE MARKETS" ARE EVERYTHING BUT "FREE"

It was assumed that Adam Smith's invisible hand would work to the advantage of the consumer, as vendors would offer a good at the lowest possible price to the consumer thanks to the wonders of "free" competition. Unfortunately, "free" markets are under the control of a select few collaborative competitors — for example, the Wall Street banks dominating the stock market, with no chance for the small investor to level the playing ground. This means that most of the time free markets have worked to the benefit of the producer, not the consumer. There are three key problems with the "free market economy," all driven by collaborative competition: information sharing, cartels, and unique resource access.

First, the consumer has an information disadvantage, as the producers know much more about their products than the consumer. For example, the small investor never has the same access to financial information as professional hedge fund managers. While legal persecution of insider trading has intensified, uncovering, for example, the foreign exchange rate rigging of the large banks mentioned in the previous section, it has by no means stopped. As long as a few key players control access to key resources, this behavior will continue.

Second, conspiring producers keep prices artificially high. While cartels occasionally get caught and punished, this is again a game where regulators never can catch up.

For example, when fuel prices spiked a few years ago, airlines all added the fuel surcharge. In the meantime, oil prices have sunk to historic lows, but no airline has reduced the price by removing the "fuel surcharge." It might not show up under this term anymore, but tickets have not gotten cheaper by the corresponding amount; if anything, they only got more expensive. Another great example of producers conspiring to the disadvantage of consumers is the widespread cheating of car manufacturers regarding exhaust emissions and fuel usage. The Volkswagen scandal, where Volkswagen installed cheating software on millions of diesel cars to pass stringent emissions requirements, is just the tip of the iceberg. Other car vendors such as GM and Mitsubishi got caught grossly inflating the gas mileage of their cars. These are exemplars of collaborative competition, where thousands of employees of the car manufacturer collaborate to cheat the consumer.

Third, critical resources are controlled by one or very few key players. For example, when Great Britain under Margret Thatcher's leadership privatized the British Rail system, rail quality plummeted and prices spiked, as the tracks were owned by one company, which had a monopoly on the tracks with no incentive to invest in improving them, and a lot of incentives to optimize income for its shareholders. Or the vast resources needed for introducing a new drug, which can only be financed by huge pharmaceutical companies. Having a virtual monopoly, they are able to charge immense drug prices for their captive audience. For example, patients in need of a novel revolutionary hepatitis C drug have no choice but to pay $95,000 for a three month treatment with this lifesaving drug.

"Free" markets are prime examples of collaborative competition. By having unrestricted freedom, "free" markets lead to economies like the 17th- and 18th-century plantations in the south of the United States, the West Indies, and Brazil, being driven by black slaves. While plantation owners did not exploit the slaves because of personal malignancy, the plantation owners' unrestricted freedom to make as much profit as possible led to huge suffering and abuse of the slaves. A recent example is the company Valeant, a US pharmaceutical company that buys well-established existing drugs, and then triples or quadruples their price, forcing healthcare providers and patients to be dependent on one-of-a-kind medication and pay vastly inflated prices. Valeant is not alone, for the AIDS drug Daraprim, infamous drug company Turing Pharmaceutical raised the price of a pill from $13.50 to $750 after it bought it from another pharmaceutical company. These are just a few egregious examples among myriad others of free markets extracting outrageous rents through collaborative competition.

7.7. THE "LIGHT SIDE" OF COLLABORATION: COMPETITIVE COLLABORATION

I am much more in favor of the new model of competitive collaboration. Exemplars of this new model to produce goods and services are the groups of writers, researchers, and software developers creating "free" knowledge. People working together in open content projects such as Wikipedia or open source software projects such as Linux are natural collaborators. Wikipedians and Linux developers primarily work together to reach their shared goal, and not for external recognition. Their main motivations are to learn new things, and to be recognized by their peers. This means that their main driver is collaboration, not competition.

The goal of competitive collaboration is to channel human's innate competitiveness into more efficient and effective collaboration. For instance, when software programmers share programming tricks and tips on the Internet forum Stack Overflow, they apply these principles of competitive collaboration. Stack Overflow is one of the top 100 websites on the Internet. Stack Overflow has collaboration written in its DNA, as expert software developers answer questions posed by less experienced programmers. This is very different from the Topcoder website, where programmers compete for a prize that will be paid out to one developer who comes up with the best solution for a particular problem. However, collaboration is far more popular than competition, as Topcoder only has Alexa rank 19,000. Admittedly, there are some fundamental differences between Stack Overflow and Topcoder. The main one is that the real work on Stack Overflow, building a specific solution to a problem, is done by the information seeker, with the community on Stack Overflow providing support, while on Topcoder, the company seeking a solution pays somebody else to come up with the solution. This means that in Topcoder the winner, the one with the best solution, gets money, whereas in Stack Overflow, there are no direct financial incentives. However, it seems being paid is much less popular than helping others (**Table 1**).

Table 1: Competitive Collaboration of Stack Overflow Compared against Collaborative Competition of Topcoder.

	Stack Overflow	Topcoder
Coordination Mechanism	**Collaboration**	**Competition**
Goal	Answer questions from software developers	Solve software development problems
Mode of operation	Developer asks question	Customer poses task
Motivation to participate	Help others (and build reputation)	Make money (and build reputation)
Solution is for....	The one asking the question **PLUS everybody else**	Only for the one asking the question
Community structure	Is homogeneous, the one answering can also ask a question	Is split into two: customers and coders
Alexa rank (Sept 10, 2016)	49	19,617

When somebody asked on Stack Overflow, "Is There Any Benefit to Participating on Sites Like TopCoder,"[4] one user gave the following reasons:

1. *They are useful to let you satisfy your thirst for knowledge.*

2. *TopCoder usually hosts competitions from various organizations, which pay you for solving real life problems.*

---

[4]http://programmers.stackexchange.com/questions/160986/is-there-any-benefit-to-participating-on-sites-like-topcoder-and-or-googlecode

3. *Usually the problems on Topcoder, GoogleCode, SPOJ, etc., are a subset of a real world problem, so solving them prepares for any extension of such problems in future.*

4. *Most importantly, actively participating in them or any such competition (even at the workplace) keeps your brain running and active.*

A 2013 study[5] found that Stack Overflow had 13 million registered users, out of which 443,000 had answered at least one question. Questions were answered on average within 11 minutes, with the 8% of questions that did not get any answer being deleted automatically by the system after a preset amount of time. This is quite different from Topcoder, which had just 794,000 users in 2015. Moreover, a study found that only 15% of these have ever participated in an algorithm competition, and less than 1% in a development competition.

The main use of Stack Overflow is for its readers, who are not registered users, but — similar to Wikipedia — only search its vast trove of answers for answers to problems of their own. This way, Stack Overflow is also far more useful and popular for the developer community than Topcoder, leading to an Alexa ranking of 49, and making Stack Overflow one of the most actively used developer websites. This entire aspect of providing usefulness to others barely exists in Topcoder, reflected in its much lower Alexa rank.

While it is pretty clear what gets people to participate on Topcoder — the hope of winning a competition and

----

[5]Wang, Lo, and Jiang (2013).

claiming its monetary award — the bigger question is what gets people to donate their time to answer questions on Stack Overflow. Why are Wikipedians working together? One answer is the "competition" part of "competitive collaboration," the warm and fuzzy feeling of being recognized and being voted for by their peers. Wikipedians are giving each other "Barnstars"; they are also voting each day for a "featured article," which gets a special star on its page and is featured on the Wikipedia home page for one day. Different from competitive people, who are striving for recognition from the world, collaborative people are mostly interested in peer recognition. It is enough for Wikipedia editors that other Wikipedia editors recognize their contributions. The same is true for the software developers on Stack Overflow, who are rewarded with reputation points and gold badges for the quality of their answers. While there is competition at the top of the list — it brings great honor to be on the top 1000 contributor list in Wikipedia, and to be in the top 0.01% percentile of Stack Overflow answer givers — this is competitive collaboration, and not collaborative competition.

Unquestionably, both competition and collaboration have been drivers of progress. The innovations sponsored by the X Prize foundation and the DARPA self-driving vehicle are just a few of the competitions that have triggered breakthrough innovation and research. Such high-profile competitions intend to motivate the smartest and the best to compete in developing innovations to further humanity. The underlying premise is that the "best solution" of a winning competitor will be the best possible solution. However, furthering humanity by declaring a winner has the large drawback that it leaves a lot of losers littered along the roadside.

Table 2 resumes the key differences between collaborative *competition* and competitive *collaboration*. While collaborative competition produces winners and losers, as happens, for example, in any sports competition, competitive collaboration only produces winners, as when musicians and their audience get together to enjoy a concert. As has been shown in many behavioral economics experiments, the most collaborative group wins over groups of egoists. This is also true if two groups of people with different opinions get together to talk through their different viewpoints. In a *discussion* each group tries to convince the other group of the advantages of their own viewpoint, while in a *dialog*, as shown succinctly in the booklet "on dialog" by physicist David Boehm, each group tries to

Table 2: Collaborative Competition Compared against Competitive Collaboration.

Collaborative Competition	Competitive Collaboration
TopCoder	Stackoverflow
Homo competitivus	Homo collaborensis
Sports	Music
Discussion	Dialog (David Boehm)
One winner, many losers	Everybody wins
You give, I take	We give, we take
Survival of the fittest?	Survival of the nicest?
←→	

first understand the viewpoint of the other group to together develop a mutually acceptable viewpoint. In competitive collaboration, everybody contributes, but everybody also gets back. In the end it's not the strongest fighter, but the people showing mutual respect and humility, who are thriving in an environment of competitive collaboration. I call this "being nice" in **Table 2**, although it could also be called "being kind." What matters is to not only show superficial politeness, but true respect, and empathy for the needs of others.

7.8. COMPETITION CREATES "HOT," COLLABORATION CREATES "COOL" PRODUCTS

Paris Hilton is "hot"; the iPhone and Tesla are "cool." In marketing, "hot" products are associated with sex and beautiful models. "Cool" products are attractive in their own right, through innovative features and superior usability. Whenever a company brings a new product to the market, it tries to make it the "hot" new thing through smart advertising, usually by adding scantily clad models to the product in the advertisements. Very few companies succeed in making their product also "cool." Steve Jobs was the master of "cool," creating with the Macintosh, iTunes, iPod, iPad, and iPhone one cool blockbuster product after the other. Elon Musk also seems to have the magic touch of "cool" with his Tesla cars.

Hot products are the product of competition; cool products are the product of collaboration. For instance, software company Atlassian, developer of a suite of software tools for software developers, is frequently associated with "cool." Its products, most prominently the project management tool JIRA, are sold without any marketing, directly from the Atlassian website. In 14 years, Atlassian grew from the two founders to 1400 employees and $320 million revenue in summer 2015. As Atlassian does not invest into making its products hot, it has no choice but to make them cool. On the other hand, if a company is selling an also-ran product, it has little chance other than trying to make its product "hot" to beat the competition, by running an advertising campaign that shows its product in the best possible light.

Obviously, it's much better to develop cool products than hot products. Once products are cool, the "hot" component can always be added. If "cool" is missing, it's impossible to add it back in. The best way to build cool products is to engage the "swarm," the group of core users that are passionate about the product, such as the software developers using the software tools sold by Atlassian. The swarm-building process is based on the framework of Collaborative Innovation Networks (COINs) introduced in Chapter 4. In the next chapter, we discuss how you as an individual can leverage collaboration and COINs to create small groups of intrinsically motivated people working together as competitive collaborators to create something radically new and cool.

MAIN LESSONS LEARNED

- A symphony orchestra or musical band engages in competitive collaboration.

- Two teams of soccer players engage in collaborative competition.

- Free markets are examples of collaborative competition.

- *Homo competitivus* is an egoist, while *homo collaborensis* is an altruist.

- "Cool" products win through superior quality, while "hot" products win through superior marketing.

8

BECOMING A COLLABORATIVE INDIVIDUAL

CHAPTER CONTENTS

- Individual recipe to become a swarm leader.

- Building happiness through social network engineering.

- Building your swarm on the Web.

- How to create your COIN.

- Blueprint for a COIN creation workshop.

- Tracking polluted water in Flint through a COIN.

- Creating "Renaissance Humans."

What do the insights about communication mean for the individual? How should each of us communicate to collaborate to innovate? What can we do to become competitive collaborators and not collaborative competitors?

Social network building skills are key, a process I call "socially engineering your network for success and happiness." To put it into the language of social networks: build "embeddedness" for personal happiness and "weak ties" for professional success. The more embedded we are in close-knit groups of good friends, and the more network closure we have — my friends knowing each other — the happier we are. The more time we spend with our friends, the more satisfied we are. It has been shown, however, that too much embeddedness is bad for business success[1] because in bad times we feel obliged to help our close friends in need, which might sink our own business, too. Also, if all our networking time is taken up communicating and connecting with close friends, we will miss out on new ideas and opportunities from the outside. The antidote for too much embeddedness is to also build bridges over structural holes in your personal network for business success. This was shown 40 years ago by Mark Granovetter, who wrote a seminal paper[2] pointing out that weak ties are essential for business success. Normally, it's not our close friends and family members who help us find a new job or new customers, but casual acquaintances or "weak ties" such as our hairdresser, somebody we talk to on the bus, an officemate, or somebody we meet at a conference. These are the people who bridge the "structural holes" in our networks.

---

[1]Uzzi (1997).
[2]Granovetter (1973).

While we are genetically wired to build embeddedness, we should strive to combine cultivating a small group of close friends to rely on in times of need with building a wide network of loose acquaintances for information gathering.

8.1. THE QUEST FOR HAPPINESS

When Swiss researcher Bruno Frey tried to identify reliable characteristics of happiness, a few things stood out. We are most unhappy when stuck in a commute; the shorter the daily trek, the happier we are. A second point which stood out even more was that the more time we have to spend in business meetings, the less happy we are. The more time we are able to spend with our friends, the happier we are. We want to be in control of our own destiny, and to be able to decide with whom to spend our time. In business meetings, and interacting with our boss, we have very little to say. With whom we spend time in our leisure, however, is something we can decide ourselves.

Therefore, for humans as members of a super-social species, being happy means being embedded in a group of good friends. Research has shown that the happiest Americans socialize for six to seven hours per day.[3] As has been demonstrated, having good friends is important both for happiness and health. It is also important with whom one spends time. If your best friends are

_____
[3]https://www.clintonfoundation.org/blog/2016/01/26/5-things-know-about-living-longer?utm_source=20160129HealthMatters&utm_medium=email&utm_content=20160129&utm_campaign=HealthMatters2016#sthash.QGHV7aJl.dpuf

overweight, there is a 40% chance you will also become overweight. If your friends are drug addicts, you are more likely to do drugs, too. If your friends pursue a sedentary lifestyle, you are more likely to pursue the same lifestyle. We therefore need to choose our friends well. In sociology, this tendency is called "homophily," or "birds of a feather flock together." This is not just true for members of the Western world, but has also been found for modern time stone-age hunter-gatherers in Tanzania, who choose their friends based on age, build, gender, body-fat proportion, strength of hand shake, and generosity.[4] The big question is whether we choose our friends based on similarity to us, or whether our friends become more and more similar to us. What researchers have found is that this transformation process cuts both ways, with people influencing each other and thus becoming increasingly similar to their friends,[5] and friends choosing their friends based on similar attributes.[6] The bottom line is: your friends are similar to you.

To reach the highest levels of happiness, we would like to be at the center of this group of friends, to be the "cool" girl or guy who is admired by everybody. The big question is, "what can I do to be cool?" Just buying everybody a drink is probably not the best way, although being nice and generous helps. The best way of being cool is being true to oneself, which in and of itself is hard to achieve, and is not an easy foundation for a cookbook recipe for coolness. There are general ways toward being at the center

---

[4]Apicella, Marlowe, Fowler, and Christakis (2012).
[5]Christakis and Fowler (2011).
[6]Aral, Muchnik, and Sundararajan (2009).

of a group as a good collaborator, as we have seen earlier, respecting the five laws of collaboration: be transparent, be fair, be honest, be forgiving, and be willing to listen. However, these are general rules that do not answer the final questions: "Who do I want to be? What do I want to do with my life? What gives meaning to my life?"

The way toward happiness seems to be a three-step process: Step one — find what motivates you. Step two — find others that share your goals. Step three — become a "cool" member of that group.

Being cool means to personify the values of the chosen peer group and being a loved participant of the self-selected swarm. Whether it is a congregation at church, a fraternity at a university, a sports club, or a choir or orchestra of hobby musicians, it is a self-selected "elite" group of special people where participants are proud to belong to. The group can be permanent; it can also just be assembled for the moment. Being a spectator at a football game, or going to a concert, makes us a temporary member of an ad hoc community. Participating at such an event puts us into fleeting companionship with other like-minded souls; we feel a spiritual brother- and sisterhood, and get into an elated mood of belonging.

The best way to become cool is to choose the "right" swarm, the group into whose goals you as a person wholeheartedly buy into. This is a chicken and egg situation, as only by trying out different groups, activities, associations, professions, and hobbies will people discover their community. On the other hand, when somebody is in a supportive community which will make them feel at home, they are much more likely to choose it as their swarm. Social network scientists Christakis and Fowler have found that homophily works both ways. On the one hand, people choose friends similar to them. On the other hand, people also become more and more similar to their friends. This two-way selection greatly assists in the formation of new swarms, because the longer a group stays together, the more similar its members will become, and the more they will start liking each other. The first step toward happiness is thus to find what we are passionate about. As a start, I suggest the simple three-step process listed in **Figure 20**, which is a simplified generalization of the coolfarming process shown in Figure 11.

The first step is identifying the topics one is passionate about. This sounds easy, but is anything but! As we usually choose friends who are similar to us, it helps to look at what our friends think is cool. Learning from them will help us identify our own passion. However, friendship is not necessarily a two-way street. You think you know who your friends are, but perhaps they do not know that you count them among your friends.

Figure 20: Three Steps for Building a Swarm.

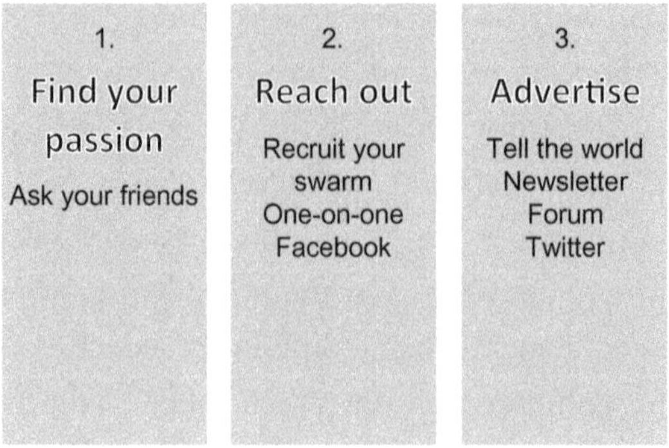

1.	2.	3.
Find your passion	Reach out	Advertise
Ask your friends	Recruit your swarm One-on-one Facebook	Tell the world Newsletter Forum Twitter

It has been repeatedly shown that there can be a large mismatch between reciprocal relationships. At school, everybody claims to be friends with the cool kids; the cool kids on the other hand are quite selective whom they count among their friends. As a remedy we propose a virtual mirroring process that tells you what the people with whom you communicate really think about you, applying the six honest signals of collaboration described in Chapter 4.

We have built a simple tool called galaxyscope that allows individuals to check to whom they are linked to on the Web. **Figure 21** shows a galaxyscope screen showing my own online social network. It gives a firsthand overview of my community, including some of my Twitter followers, some people I follow on Twitter, links

Figure 21: Galaxyscope (scope.galaxyadvisors.com) Tells the Users How Their Online Social Network Looks.

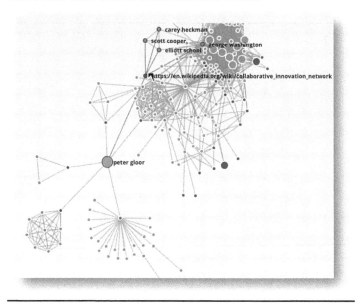

from and to the Wikipedia page where I am mentioned, as well as links from and to my blog, my MIT home page, and our software company galaxyadvisors.

As people are defining themselves through their friendship network, this virtual mirror will also tell them about their interests and passions through linking them to the interests of their friends. A more in-depth virtual mirror could be created by looking at the Facebook network, or depending on the age and sociodemographic background of the person, their personal e-mail, WhatsApp, Facebook Messenger, or Snapchat network. In professional life e-mail is still a major means of communication. Figure 22 shows my personal e-mail network automatically generated

Figure 22: E-Mail Social Network in January 2016, Automatically Created from My Mailbox.[a]

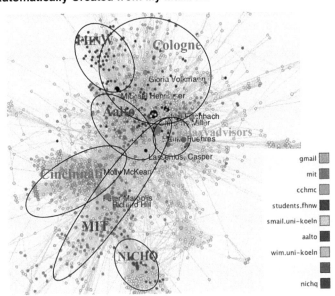

[a]For color pictures see online version of images, available at http://www.ickn.org/sociometrics/

by the software tool Condor from my mailbox in January 2016. Out team developed Condor over the last 14 years to create social network maps and calculate the six honest signals from online social media such as e-mail, Twitter, and the Web. Condor is explained in numerous examples in the companion book *Sociometrics and Human Relationships*.

Figure 22 shows the different communities I am a member of. I have already removed myself from the network, to focus on the communication among my friends and collaborators. Removing my own person to understand the relationships among my friends is good psychological practice. As **Figure 22** illustrates, there are seven major clusters of activity in my life. In the middle there is the galaxyadvisors cluster, representing our small software company, with my colleague Hauke Fuehres at the center. Next is the MIT Center for Collective Intelligence group, with our administrator Richard Hill being in the most prominent position. Then there are two healthcare related clusters: The Cincinnati Children's hospital Collaborative Chronic Care Networks (C3N) cluster shows Peter Margolis and Molly McKean as its most central participants (see Section 9.11). With the National Institute for Children Healthcare Quality (NICHQ) group I work in an infant mortality reduction Collaborative Improvement and Innovation Network (CoIIN) across all US states (see Section 9.12). The remaining three clusters mirror my teaching-related activities. The COIN seminar taking place in Germany at the University of Cologne and University of Bamberg shows my colleagues Kai Fischbach and Gloria Volkmann as most central participants (see Section 8.5). The COIN seminar at Aalto University Helsinki shows my colleagues

Casper Lassenius and Maria Paasivaara in the center. The third COIN seminar cluster is University of Applied Sciences Northwestern Switzerland Brugg (FHNW) with my colleague and co-lecturer Michael Henninger in the core. As this example illustrates, my mailbox perfectly mirrors the four legs of my professional life, working on growing our software company galaxyadvisors, teaching the COINs course at different universities, doing basic research at MIT, and putting my research insights to practical use in health-care. Through finding my friends I have found my passion.

The second step consists of recruiting others, to build the swarm. This might be done on Facebook, but is best done in a combination of direct face-to-face, phone, e-mail interaction, and social media networking. Once the core team is up and running, there comes the third step: tell the rest of the world about the greatness of your idea, to grow the swarm and increase acceptance of your idea. This can be done most efficiently using Twitter, blogs, newsletters, and online forums.

8.2. BUILDING YOUR SWARM ON THE WEB

Advertise what you are doing, and people will come find you!

This is the best way to recruit new team members for the COIN; however, this is also quite a slow way that takes a lot of patience. Online social media can help us both to advertise our ideas, and to identify and reach out to others who might be interested in what we are trying to create.

As Marshall McLuhan famously said, "the media is the message." When he coined this sentence in the fifties and sixties, he mostly alluded to movies. The Internet takes this idea much further, as it has changed society by empowering the individual to consume and disseminate information much faster and more targeted than movies ever could. McLuhan describes the image of the lightbulb, which creates a space at night that would otherwise be inaccessible in darkness. He compares TV and radio with the lightbulb that sheds light on everybody by broadcasting it. The Internet permits to narrow the lightbulb to a laser, focusing on an audience of one if need be.

Over the last 25 years using and studying social networks and collaborating on the Internet I noticed that the characteristics of usage changed drastically. What I write toady about how to use the different types of online social media might already be wrong by the time this book goes to press.

In the early years, before the Web became popular, e-mail was the main Internet application for communication. Until just a few years ago, when it was not possible to meet face-to-face, the phone was the preferred means of instantaneous communication. The phone has its place, even today, but communication nowadays is happening much more with text, WhatsApp, Facebook Messenger, Instagram, and Snapchat. SMS-texting teenagers send hundreds of text messages per week, if not per day. Project teams send hundreds of e-mail per day. Computer gamers communicate by chat for days nonstop.

The phone used to be the backbone of remote synchronous communication until 1990; it is now just one of many options to work together and stay in virtual face-to-face contact with loved ones. Skype, Google Hangout, and Web conferencing and online chat have become major means for closely collaborating teams to directly work together over long distance. In a research project — described in the next chapter — we found that the intensity and centrality of people in the videoconferencing network was the key predictor for the success of these teams. Sending and receiving e-mails is still key for companies as the main means of asynchronous long-distance communication. With the growing popularity of free Gmail, Hotmail, and Yahoo mail personal accounts, e-mail is also used a lot for private communication, and by being read on smartphones, it is being used as an instantaneous communication channel just like SMS. However, for close cooperation over long distance, instantaneous text in chat, for example, among software developers, or collaborating groups of computer gamers, has become most prevalent.

The virtual word is becoming a mirror of the real world: Katy Perry, Barack Obama, Lady Gaga, and Justin Bieber have the most followers on Twitter because they are real-world superstars. However, the opposite effect happens even more: anybody can become an Internet sensation overnight. However, this is fleeting coolness; the more such an Internet celebrity with hundreds of thousands of followers on YouTube or Twitter is trying to commercialize their fame and convert it into real cash, the less impact they will have.

Table 3 resumes the different ways social media can be used to build coolness. The usage patterns of Facebook and LinkedIn have already changed over the comparatively short lifetime of these two social networks. In the early days of Facebook and LinkedIn, it used to be that having more friends on LinkedIn or Facebook really set

Table 3: Usage of Different Social Media Platforms.

Social Media Reduced to Tag Lines:

- *Facebook* is for telling my friends how beautiful and happy I am.
- *Twitter* is for telling the world what I am thinking right now.
- *LinkedIn* is for managing my business contacts and finding a new job.
- *Blogs* are for sharing complex ideas with the world.
- *E-mail* and text chat are for doing productive work with others.
- *Web conferencing* and Skype are for overcoming obstacles, for teambuilding, and for doing productive work.

somebody apart as a great networker — today it just means that this person has nothing better to do than accumulating a lot of online contacts with little indication of the real-world popularity of the person. Not surprisingly, though, extroverts tend to have more Facebook or LinkedIn friends than introverts.[7]

This is even more prominent for Twitter, where marketing professionals spend a disproportionate amount of time building up a large group of followers. Most of the time, these followers are just following each other, forming a large, and mostly closed, echo chamber. A better metric for real-world popularity is the Twitter follower-to-following ratio. The more followers somebody has, and the less people she is following herself, the more popular somebody is in the real world. This is illustrated by Justin Bieber, Taylor Swift, Lady Gaga, Barack Obama, the Pope, and the Dalai Lama. A second metric of popularity is how quickly their tweets are retweeted.

LinkedIn is used for business contacts. Until two to three years ago, most people had 100–300 friends.

---

[7]Tong, Van Der Heide, Langwell, and Walther (2008).

However, because friends in LinkedIn and Facebook are not deleted — not even when they die — longtime LinkedIn users easily have more than 500 friends. The main application of LinkedIn is to advertise oneself for professional advancement, and for recruiters and HR professionals to identify new talent.

Facebook is used by two groups of people: self-promoting individual consultants use it as a means of distributing theirs or somebody else's ideas, and to approach and recruit potential customers. In these cases, they usually have over a 1000 friends. The majority though uses it to stay in touch with far-flung family and friends; they usually have 100–300 friends. The number of Facebook friends is also dependent on the nationality of the Facebook page owner. US college students easily can have 500–1000 friends, as they tend to friend a lot of people from their school. Chinese and Japanese, on the other hand, tend to be far more selective; they frequently have around 100 friends, but unlike US college students, these Facebook friends tend to be real-world friends, too.

Twitter has found a special niche in countries like the Philippines and Malaysia, where it is used like e-mail, for example, to announce the breakup of a romantic relationship. In highly privacy aware countries like Germany or Austria, Twitter is mostly used by politicians for self-promotion, by journalists to promote their writing, and marketers to promote their product, while the average citizen rarely tweets.

How can this all be applied to building your swarm? Advertising new ideas is done best on blog posts and with YouTube videos, where aspiring creators get the space to explain and present their new world-changing ideas. These ideas subsequently can be advertised on Twitter, Facebook, and LinkedIn, hopefully leading to expressions of interests of future potential members of the swarm. In the next step, community building can be done leveraging all types of social media. Members of the species Homo Collaborensis working on a project they are passionate about do not need orders for doing what needs to be done, but consensus. As the collaborative team shares a common goal, it is usually obvious what needs to be done. If decisions must to be taken, outcome is decided by what the Internet Engineering Task Force (IETF), an example of an early COIN, calls "rough consensus," where everybody has their say, until the direction emerges naturally.

The key insights about social networking, applicable both in professional and private life, are threefold. First, the quality of friends is far more important than the quantity. One trusted friend is worth hundreds of Twitter followers or LinkedIn friends. Second, there are some criteria that identify these trusted friends, for example, the speed of response. The faster the friend responds, and the more reliable and predictable the behavior, the higher the trust. Third, it's the quality of interactions that matters, and not the quantity. Whether it's tweets, e-mails, or blog posts, spamming the friendship network will drive the friends away. The goal is to make each Tweet, e-mail message, or blog post count. Say what you do, and do what you say!

Once you have found your swarm, the next question is how to build your own COIN. Or even better, join an already existing COIN, become a core member, and help it succeed.

8.3. HOW TO CREATE YOUR OWN COIN

COINs are never-ending engines of creativity. There are three simple steps that everybody can take to create their own COIN. The most important is to select the topic you are most passionate about, assuring that the motivation to join is not money, power, or glory, but the love about what you will be doing. Creating COINs is an infinite loop of finding like-minded people, getting together with them to brainstorm, developing new ideas, identifying leaders to take these ideas forward, and start innovating with them to convert the creative idea into a real product. This means repeating the following three steps ad infinitum:

1. Choose the topic you are totally passionate about, where you want to change the world.

2. Find others like you that share your passion about this topic.

3. Get together face-to-face in a half- or one-day work-shop to brainstorm what you want to focus on, and define a way forward, knowing that you will change this way forward many times. During this brainstorming phase, choose the topic you are most passionate about, and start again at step 1.

Figure 23 illustrates this never-ending loop of creativity.

The goal is to create a living collective mind, that constantly interacts asynchronously, and gets together virtually using Web conferencing, or face-to-face at one location synchronously at least once per month to build collective consciousness.

Figure 23: Never-Ending COINs Creation Process.

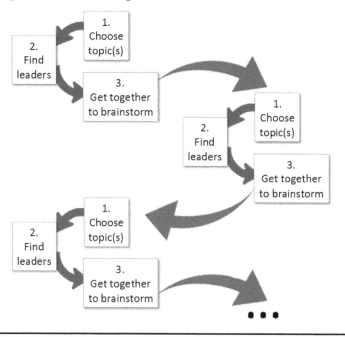

When we created our first two COINs on COINs, initially when I was a partner at Deloitte in 2000, and the second time as a visiting scholar at MIT in 2004, we found each other over the Internet, and started working together using Web videoconferencing and e-mail for over a year before we got a chance to meet face-to-face. By the time we had our first meeting in New York at Deloitte's headquarters, our COIN team had already worked together on defining what the focus of our consulting product offering would be — knowledge management — and iterated through a series of follow-up brainstorms, coming up with dozens of ideas of how we could develop different ideas such as knowledge management portals and diagnostic surveys. The key for the success of our COIN was the biweekly virtual brownbag, where we met using arcane Web conferencing technology. This allowed us to meet face-to-face virtually on a shoestring, using Webcams. As there were participants from central Europe, the United Kingdom, from all over the United States, and even from Australia, some participants always had to get up at odd hours in the middle of the night to join the Web meetings.

For most of the COINs I have been involved with since then, the instigators of the COIN brought other like-minded people together for a half-day to two-day co-located workshop where people were meeting face-to-face. This is a much faster way to build mutual trust and establish working relationships.

Let's look at how a poster COIN was born: The creation process of the Collaborative Chronic Care Networks C3N COIN provides an excellent example (see Section 9.11). Table 4 below shows the key milestones in the creation process of C3N. C3N is the brainchild of three academics, Peter Margolis and Michael Seid, medicine professors at Cincinnati Children's Hospital Medical Center, and Dick Colletti, a medicine professor at the University of Vermont. C3N was built on the foundations of an earlier initiative, ImproveCareNow, which is focused on transforming the healthcare and costs of Inflammatory Bowel Disease (IBD) by organizing a learning community among researchers, doctors, patients, and family members. Table 4 nicely illustrates the interplay between the leaders of C3N, initially Peter Margolis, Dick Colletti, and Michael Seid, later joined by George Dellal, choosing as their topic IBD, recruiting other early adopters to join their COIN. The three design meetings illustrate how the never-ending loop of creativity shown

Table 4: High-Level Timeline of C3N Project.

September 1, 2009	C3N grant officially started
January 25–26, 2010	First design meeting
April 9–11, 2010	ImproveCareNow (community of IBD/Crohn's doctors) learning session
May 25–27, 2010	Co-principal investigators meet with MIT Media Lab and Harvard researchers in Boston
July 15–16, 2010	Second design meeting
September 1, 2010	Start of second grant year
October 1, 2010	Start of Enhanced Registries grant to build an electronic patient registry
September 24–26, 2010	ImproveCareNow learning session
September 29–30, 2010	Third design meeting
March 18–20, 2011	ImproveCareNow learning session
May 19–20, 2011	"Inventing Breakthroughs Day" (IBDday) inviting patients and doctors to learn about C3N and fourth design session of core C3N team
September 1, 2011	Start of third grant year
September 16–18, 2011	ImproveCareNow learning session

in **Figure 23** led to the creation of 23 topic-specific COINs, addressing various needs of the IBD patients.

The results from a C3N brainstorming session at one of the first design meetings depicted in **Figure 24** illustrate the importance of meeting face-to-face to think the unthinkable. Bringing together like-minded people allowed the group of 20–40 participants to split into smaller subgroups, and come up with radically new ideas to better the lives of IBD patients. Involving people from all walks of life, IBD researchers, doctors, nurses, patients, and family members, unified in their passion to improve the daily lives of the patients, created a wide variety of creative ideas leading to breakthrough products. Spending the day together

Figure 24: Results from Group Brainstorming during a C3N Design Meeting.

in the same room was an incredibly energizing experience for all participants, fueling their enthusiasm to devote long hours back home to their cause, working in their respective COINs remotely, until meeting — in changing compositions — in the next design meeting.

Figure 25 illustrates the evolution of the C3N COINs from the beginning of 2011 to end of July 2014. The project officially started in 2009, and ended in July 2014. I had done some informal e-mail analysis with Condor right from the beginning based on the project leaders' mailboxes. From 2011 to 2014, we regularly collected the e-mail of up to 16 project members to analyze their communication patterns, and develop insights and interventions for better collaboration. Some of the key research results described in this book originated from this e-mail analysis.

Figure 25: Key COINs in the C3N from 2011 to 2014, COINs Each Year Automatically Calculated through the Community Detection Algorithm of Condor.[a]

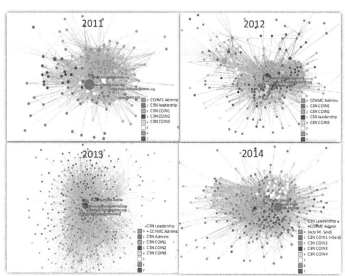

[a]For color pictures see online version of images, available at http://www.ickn.org/sociometrics/

Using the automatic community detection capability of Condor allowed us to identify the COINs' each network. In 2011, we found that the hospital administrators (in yellow) made up the largest cluster, followed by the project's leadership, which forms its own cluster (in green). The next three clusters correspond to three COINs, in turquoise, blue, and purple. In 2012, the hospital administration still made up the largest cluster (in yellow), but the two project leaders Michael Seid and Peter Margolis now joined a COIN working on a particular solution (blue).

In 2013, the two project leaders joined the administration cluster (yellow), which probably reflected their efforts to embed the results of their project into the permanent Cincinnati Children's Hospital administrative structure. In 2014, the two project leaders for the first time were not in the same community anymore, with Peter Margolis still in the administrative cluster (yellow), while Michael Seid joined one particular COIN (green).

Figure 26 illustrates the role of the C3N project on my life, and my participation in other COINs. This is done by looking at my own mailbox in one aggregated network picture, combining all e-mails from 2009 to 2015. The top part of Figure 26 shows the network including myself acting as the star attracting my own galaxy. The large yellow cluster includes our "COINonCOINs," the group of collaborators working together on developing the COINs concept further. It also includes most of the students participating in my COINs seminar from 2009 to 2015 (see Section 8.5). The second most important COIN is already the C3N project (green), followed by the Infant Mortality CoIIN (see Section 9.12) (turquoise), and then a cluster of various research projects with the research sponsors of MIT CCI (blue). The purple cluster shows a particularly active and cohesive COIN seminar group with students from MIT, Cologne, and Aalto University Helsinki from winter 2011.

The bottom part of Figure 26 shows the same data; only this time the central person in the network (myself) has been removed, and Condor's community detection algorithm rerun. With the main connector in the center gone, the core cluster (in yellow) becomes much smaller, and consists primarily of the members of the COINonCOINs, as well as the students of some COIN seminars where core members of the COINonCOINs were particularly involved. The C3N project team (green)

Figure 26: Peter's Mailbox from 2009 to 2015, COINs Identified through Condor's Automatic Community Detection Algorithm. Top Picture with Mailbox Owner (Peter) Included, Bottom Picture with Peter Removed.[a]

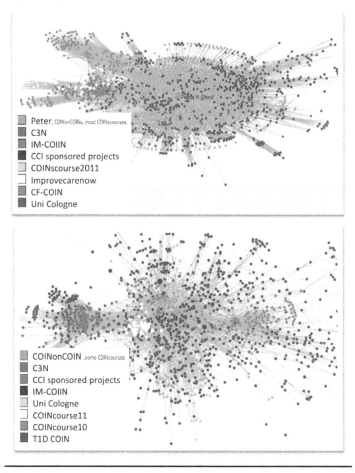

[a]For color pictures see online version of images, available at http://www.ickn.org/sociometrics/

is still the second most prominent cluster, followed by the MIT CCI-sponsored research projects (turquoise). The Infant Mortality CoIIN (blue) follows next, having switched the position with the MIT CCI-sponsored projects. Next are my collaborators over the years from University of Cologne (purple) and the COIN seminars from 2011 and 2010.

Figure 27 zooms into the yellow cluster from the bottom of Figure 26. It illustrates the collaboration among the core members of the COINonCOINs from 2009 to 2015, colored by the domain names of their e-mail addresses, indicating the nationality of the participants.

The peripheral nodes in Figure 27 are mostly students from FHNW Switzerland (yellow), Aalto University Helsinki (turquoise), University of Cologne (dark blue), and Universidad Cattolica di Santiago de Chile (light blue), connected to the core COIN by instructors from the same country who are core members of the

Figure 27: Largest cluster in Peter's Mailbox 2009–2015 ("Yellow Cluster" from Figure 26 Bottom), the Core COINonCOINs Community, People Colored by Domains from Their E-Mail Addresses.[a]

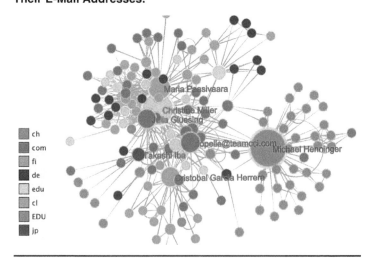

[a]For color pictures see online version of images, available at http://www.ickn.org/sociometrics/

COINonCOINs. Some of the students in the COINs seminar, particularly from Germany, MIT, and FHWN (dark blue, purple, and yellow dots in the periphery), also worked with COINs from the C3N project.

Figure 28 illustrates the same analysis for the C3N community from Figure 26, the green cluster in the network in Figure 26. Figure 28 mirrors my view of the C3N project, automatically extracted from my mailbox through automatic cluster analysis. The leaders of the project, Peter Margolis, Michael Seid, Dick Colletti, and George Dellal, all have central roles in the network also in my mailbox. Note that Figure 28 is fundamentally different from Figure 25, because the latter shows the *social* view combining all e-mail boxes of the main project participants, while the former shows *my* view (through my mailbox) of the C3N project.

Figure 28: C3N Cluster in Peter's Mailbox, 2009–2015 ("Green Cluster" from Bottom Picture in Figure 26), People Are Colored by Domains from Their E-Mail Addresses.[a]

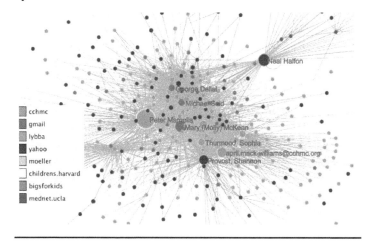

[a]For color pictures see online version of images, available at http://www.ickn.org/sociometrics/

But this network also shows the crucial role of informal leaders in my involvement with C3N, first of all Molly McKean, a junior project analyst fresh out of college, who became a key member of the C3N team, and was essential for our e-mail analysis project. Other key members, Sophia Thurmond, the C3N project manager of a COIN where I was part of, and Shannon Provost, a graduate student from University of Texas Austin who did her PhD thesis on the e-mail analysis project, also have central positions in the network. April Mack-Williams, the project administrator, also assumes a central position. Neil Halfon, a professor at USC, acts as a connector and bridge to another healthcare project outside the C3N project.

This drill-down analysis into the evolution of this poster COIN offers a unique view not possible through other means. By looking at the communication network of its participants, outside observers can deeply understand the team dynamics explaining the long-lasting impact of this project. This example illustrates both the outside group perspective obtained through the combined network analysis shown in **Figure 25**, as well as my personalized inside view through my own mailbox in **Figure 28**.

One of the key aspects of creating successful COINs is the initial COINs creation workshop, step 3 in the never-ending loop of creativity from **Figure 23**.

8.4. RUNNING YOUR OWN COIN CREATION WORKSHOP

When I get the opportunity to moderate an interactive hands-on COIN creation workshop, I usually employ a simple four-step process:

1. Stretch the imagination by short presentations from unrelated but topically similar innovators.

2. Conduct a plenary brainstorming, identifying topics and future thought leaders from among the participants.

3. Invite these thought leaders to lead small group discussions about their topics.

4. Define a roadmap for the COINs in small teams.

Usually people have been brought together because they are passionate about their topic, which means that participants will be highly motivated. In a typical COIN creation workshop, the first step consists of stretching the imagination of participants by inviting outside speakers that have tackled similar problems and have come up with creative solutions. For example, for a workshop about reducing infant mortality in the United States, I invited a sociology researcher studying networks among single mothers and welfare recipients in Northern Germany, or for a workshop developing new tourism ideas for Switzerland, the first presenter spoke about how he organized a theater festival in Berlin.

In the second step, participants are encouraged to think the unthinkable — no idea is too crazy. In the beginning, I formed small groups for this step, but I found that it works better to do this brainstorming in the plenary, as this helps the moderator to identify discussion leaders for step 3. When I moderate this phase, I try to get participants to develop their ideas and describe them in detail; all ideas are collected by a scribe and posted on the walls of the room.

In the third step, the ideas are whittled down, for example, by assigning votes from the participants to the ideas. The moderator also recruits discussion leaders for the next phase, by encouraging proposers of an idea to lead the discussion in the next step, or by prodding another participant to step in.

In the fourth step, participants split into small teams (the proto-COINs) and self-organize choosing the topic that interests them most. Each team is led by a discussion leader, frequently the one who proposed the idea in step 2. The goal of the team is to develop a vision statement and a roadmap laying out how the idea can be taken forward and turned into a prototype.

Over the last 12 years, I have tried to convert the general principles described in this chapter into a university course, to help students become better collaborators and creative members of virtual distributed teams.

8.5. THE COINS COURSE

To become successful Internet-enabled Renaissance Humans, we need a new type of curriculum, one that does not teach what percentage of GDP the United States spends on healthcare, or how the current political system works, but one that gets students to work together on developing new solutions for addressing burning issues of society. Most importantly, this curriculum also needs to teach how to innovate and collaborate with others over the Internet, crossing barriers of language, geography, and culture.

This is where the framework of the COINs course comes in, which takes first steps toward implementing such a curriculum. The COINs course has been taught for the last 12 years to students forming virtual teams participating from universities in Boston, Savannah, Helsinki, Cologne, Rome, Chile, and Switzerland, with majors in business, education, design, computer science, or sociology. In this course, students use and analyze social media to answer complex questions impacting society. It teaches students how to leverage virtual collaborative creativity in the Internet age. In particular, this course helps students understand and apply the dynamics of online communication using e-mail, social media, and the Web. This is done by online social network analysis using the software tool Condor developed by our team. Our course is unique in that it teaches a self-directed style of learning though competitive collaboration. While there is competition between teams and among team members for the best grades and ideas, the key objective is to collaborate. We strive to reward the individuals and teams who contribute most to the success of the entire class. Every team member is expected to step up and assume responsibility for the results of their teamwork.

The COINs course applies the four basic principles of social quantum physics: (1) entanglement and rotating leadership, (2) the wave–particle duality increasing empathy, (3) virtual mirroring triggering reflection, and (4) the future changing the past by pushing students to grow in new areas and continuously reinvent themselves.

Over the last 12 years, students in diverse teams hit many roadblocks of intercultural (mis)communication. For instance, it happened repeatedly that MIT students with Middle Eastern and North African roots and Finnish students in the same team had huge difficulties communicating. Finns are extremely punctual — meetings start and end on time by the minute. At the same time, Finns are very outspoken — if they don't agree with their team members' viewpoint, they will say so right away. Students with a Middle Eastern background, even tempered through some years at MIT, are on "polychromatic time," which means that meeting times are just taken as an approximation. Also, in Middle Eastern culture, not losing face is paramount, which means that if their counterparts bluntly tell them that they disagree, they take this as a personal insult. We learned that by making students aware of these issues upfront, we could increase understanding and empathy for team members from other cultures.

Over time, this led to "entanglement" among team members, as they started to develop a team identity over geographical and cultural boundaries. By telling them about the advantages of the six honest signals of collaboration — strong leadership, balanced contribution, rotating leadership, responsiveness, honest sentiment, and shared context — teams engaged in self-reflection, occasionally "rebooting" their way of working together, thus increasing their performance. Using virtual mirroring — applying the Heisenberg uncertainty principle — led to team members learning how well they were following the six honest signals, and changing their behavior toward applying them more consistently, which in turn led to better teamwork. They were shown network pictures like the ones in **Figure 29**: The big red dot in the middle and right picture is the instructor (myself), in the beginning the students communicated among themselves, in the middle

Figure 29: Social Network of COINs Course Student Teams at the Beginning, in the Middle, and at the End of the Course.[a]

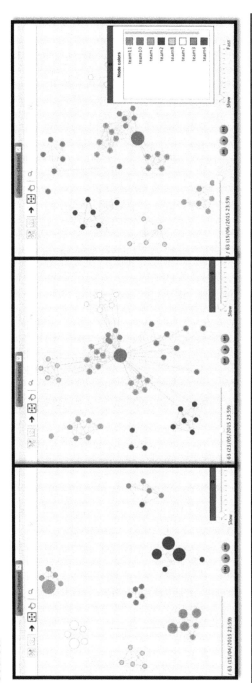

[a]For color pictures see online version of images, available at http://www.ickn.org/sociometrics/

of the project I had a central role, toward the end of the course, the students became much more self-organizing, with me only communicating with a few of the teams, while the others were working independently.

Using this visualization of the social network provides a system that is transparent enough to show the contributions of each individual to give them peer recognition. The picture shown in **Figure 30** visualizes the creativity of two different teams in a single picture.

The picture at left in **Figure 30** shows a creative and highly active team. It visualizes the rotating leadership; the more the picture looks like a "stormy sea," the more creative it is and the more different leaders are taking turns. The picture at right in **Figure 30** shows a low-performing team as a "calm sea," with no changes in leadership. In fact, only toward the end of the course did the team show some activity, with one leader becoming central. Looking at these pictures is like operating a time machine. The three snapshots in **Figure 29** can be watched in the Condor software tool as a movie, illustrating the team dynamics of the entire course. Through these movies, teams can gain a much better understanding of their past team actions, leading to the "future redefining the past" resulting in a reboot of their way of working together. The COINs course thus offers a showcase for applying the principles of social quantum physics to build collective awareness for increased collaboration. In sum, the COINs course is offering a blueprint for educating *homo collaborensis*, instead of training "homo competitivus."

Students in the COINs course have worked in many real-world projects. They have done some of

Figure 30: Temporal Social Surface of Two Teams, Calculated by Our Software Condor. *Notes:* **It illustrates how many times leaders in a team are changing over time. At left is a team with many leadership changes; at right, there are just two leaders visible, at the beginning and the end of the analysis period.**[a]

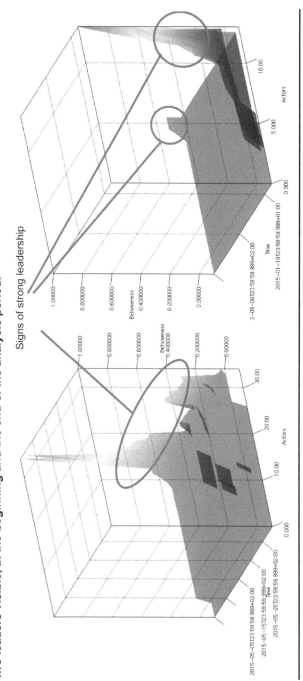

the e-mail-based social network analysis with companies described in Chapter 9. They have worked with the C3N team at Cincinnati's Children's Hospital described in Section 9.11 and the infant mortality CoIIN described in Section 9.12 led by the Health Resources Administration to build new medical COINs.

Another great example of a COIN of students (which has nothing to do with the COINs course described in this section) is how the scandal with polluted drinking water in Flint, Michigan, was exposed by a team of student volunteers from Virginia Tech.

8.6. TRACKING POLLUTED WATER IN FLINT, MICHIGAN

As a consequence of the huge problems of the US car industry in the early 21st century, the city of Flint in Michigan went bankrupt and was put under state receivership between 2011 and 2015. To save money, the town administration hatched an ill-fated scheme switching the water supply to directly pump water out of the Flint River. Unfortunately, the water from this source was highly contaminated with a chloride by-product, which led to corroding the water pipes to the homes, resulting in up to a thousand times the lead content in water considered safe.

The amazing part is that the detective work to expose the lead contamination was done by a professor and student COIN from Virginia Tech.[8] Marc Edwards, a

_____
[8]http://www.nytimes.com/2016/02/07/us/as-flint-fought-to-be-heard-virginia-tech-team-sounded-alarm.html

professor in civil and environmental engineering, collected a group of students and drove to Flint to test the water at the request of a citizen of Flint, LeeAnne Walters. Concerns of the citizens of Flint had earlier been ridiculed by the local authorities, and they had been assured that their drinking water was safe. What the student/professor group found was the opposite. In persistent work on and off site, and through forging friendships with locals, the Virginia Tech students found levels of lead in the drinking water vastly exceeding federal safety standards. Only after they repeatedly measured tap water and publicized their findings on a website they set up for this purpose, http://flintwaterstudy.org, did the Flint authorities finally act. Marc Edwards also started worrying about an outbreak of Legionnaire's disease in Flint, a type of pneumonia caused by Legionella bacteria. While state authorities had been aware of the outbreak, the public was only told after the Virginia Tech intervention.

For the students in the team from Virginia Tech, who came from different countries and disciplines, this was a unique opportunity to gain meaningful firsthand experience, and learn in the field. Hailing from places like Arizona, Virginia, India, and Singapore, they mostly studied environmental engineering. Doing this hands-on research gave them a motivational boost to do work which had a real impact, and acquire unique knowledge and skills. They are role models for this new way of COIN-based education, where student teams self-organize, supported by the teacher to learn and innovate in open-ended projects with the goals evolving along the way.

8.7. EDUCATING "RENAISSANCE HUMANS" — FROM HOMO COMPETITIVUS TO HOMO COLLABORENSIS

I have no special talent, I am only passionately curious.
— Albert Einstein

Humans make progress by learning from each other. The moment one stops learning new things, one gets old, or in the words of John Rooney, "The quickest way to become an old dog is to stop learning new tricks." However, just trying to be as good as the best is not enough. By learning from the best in the field and establishing so-called best practices will lead one to perfect the status quo, and inhibit radical change and improvement. Only by going where nobody else has been before, and by applying insights from other fields to the problems, and constantly questioning the state of the art, true progress is made. Learning and innovation grow together. Learning minds find out new things, understanding the patterns of nature and combining them in new ways, to make the world a better place, to increase happiness and satisfaction. At least for me, happiness and satisfaction come from understanding and applying new insights, creating a never-ending positive feedback loop of collaborative innovation and learning.

Today's education system teaches children to compete from an early age. They learn not just to compete in sports, but also in science and the arts, for instance to be the valedictorian in class. While it is a highly rewarding experience to be the valedictorian, this still leaves hundreds of children at the same school who are not the valedictorian, who are not considered winners, and who are thus consistently frustrated. Wouldn't it be much better to have an education system that places greater emphasis on collaboration and creativity than on competition?

Our schools teach collaborative competition, not competitive collaboration. Nonstop testing and scoring kill creativity of students at a young age, putting too much emphasis on winning the competition and being the best in class instead of learning how to work together. This is a pity, as the Internet would finally enable us to become true Renaissance humans. The scholastic ideal in Renaissance was to educate man — women at that time were rarely educated — to become a master of all disciplines. Leonardo da Vinci was the quintessential Renaissance man, excelling in all fields of science and arts, intellectually, artistically, socially, and physically. In the end, however, even Leonardo failed, as he just produced a few paintings, while his engineering feats mostly stayed in his sketchbooks — because he was missing similarly visionary and far-sighted collaborators. Today, for the first time, thanks to Google, Wikipedia, Massive Open Online Education (MOOCs), and additional online resources such as stackoverflow and the Khan Academy, we get a unique opportunity to become true Renaissance Humans — finding both the information we are looking for and the similarly minded collaborators, anywhere on the world.

As has been shown by Betsy Sparrow in a scientific experiment,[9] we include all this information available at our fingertips into our transactive memory. Already, Albert Einstein said, "never memorize something that you can look up in books." In the age of the Web, Google has

---

[9]Sparrow, Liu, and Wegner (2011).

replaced "books." In fact, this is what Betsy Sparrow found, naming it the "Google Effect," which means that we are not storing facts anymore in our brain, but applying the best search strategies for finding these facts on the Web using Google and other online search tools. Thanks to these resources, it's not just geniuses like Leonardo, but all of us who get the chance to be plugged into the knowledge of humanity, to become experts in anything we want, leveraging YouTube videos, TED talks, and countless online support and self-help forums. What is needed is an education system that trains students to make better use of their connected future.

While the success of firms such as Apple, Google, Facebook, or Tesla is testament to the skills of strong leaders such as Steve Jobs, Larry Page, Mark Zuckerberg, or Elon Musk, these leaders are also collaborators. As we have shown in this book, while there is a role for the strong leader, successful leaders are rotating leaders, delegating responsibility to whoever is best equipped to do a particular task. We therefore need to educate a new type of multidisciplinary leader, who is scientist and artist, and also teacher, entrepreneur, and manager. Elon Musk is not just the CEO of Tesla, but also an engineer and scientist who came up with the idea for the Hyperloop, a train where capsules ride on pressurized air driven by a linear induction motor, offering the potential to radically change mid-range transportation in urban areas. Besides two stints as the CEO of Google, Larry Page is also the inventor of Page Rank, the main search result-ranking algorithm behind the Google search engine and the instigator for many scientific pursuits of Google's parent company Alphabet. We should therefore strive to provide an education system that encourages this novel type of creative leadership, where the one with the best ideas takes the helm to lead a team by personal example and conviction.

In the next chapter, we look at how these insights can be extended from individuals to groups of people and organizations, and how they can self-organize and work together in competitive collaboration.

MAIN LESSONS LEARNED

- To become a happy individual, engineer your social networks by combining embeddedness into a group of good friends with weak ties to a large group of outside acquaintances.

- Using online social media, Twitter, Facebook, blogs, and e-mail allows everyone to create a personal swarm on the Web, joining people anywhere on the world, sharing the same goals and causes.

- New COINs can be created virtually; however, conducting physical face-to-face COIN-creation workshops still works best.

- The COINs course offers a blueprint to train physically distributed students to become virtual collaborators from different countries and cultures.

- "Renaissance humans" create new ideas collaboratively, leveraging the Web as a global knowledge source.

9

BECOMING A COLLABORATIVE ORGANIZATION

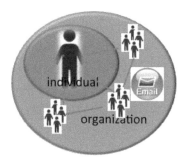

CHAPTER CONTENTS

- Swarm leaders take turns and are kind.

- Measuring customer satisfaction through the six honest signals of collaboration.

- Increasing organizational performance through virtual mirroring.

- Predicting employee attrition through the six honest signals of collaboration.

- Predicting sales success through the six honest signals of collaboration.

- Finding the most creative employees and successful start-ups through rotating leadership.

- Collaborative healthcare: C3N and IM-CoIIN.

How can the six honest signals and the principles of social quantum physics introduced in the preceding chapters be applied to increase organizational creativity? The key insight is that increasing organizational consciousness by building a culture of collaboration pays off. Based on the principles of social quantum physics, the goal for an organization is to create entanglement by nurturing empathy. The most important principle by far for group entanglement is rotating leadership. What happens when rotating leadership is replaced by one strong leader is vividly illustrated by King Gustavus II Adolphus in the following story.

9.1. STRONG LEADERSHIP ALONE SINKS THE STRONGEST SHIP

On a sunny day in August 1628, the newly built warship *Vasa*, the pride of the Swedish navy, set sail at the Stockholm shipyard for her maiden voyage. After 1300 meters, right in the Stockholm harbor, when the first light breeze hit her from the side, she capsized and rapidly sank — thanks to unfettered strong leadership.

In the Thirty Years' War in 17th century Europe, Protestant king Gustavus II Adolphus of Sweden single-handedly changed the power balance of war by leading his numerically inferior but better trained military force to victory in one battle after the other against the Catholic Holy Roman Emperor. At the same time, King Gustavus II Adolphus was also waging war against Poland, for which he desperately needed to upgrade his fleet of warships. He therefore ordered his shipbuilders to build a new ship that would beat all others, the *Vasa*, and make it the strongest warship in the Baltic. In a steady stream of letters, he personally ordered to add new features like a second cannon deck, and to increase its deck height so as to have a better platform when shooting down on the enemy. When his admirals told him that changing the construction plans would decrease seaworthiness and stability of the ship, he would not accept any contradiction, telling that "...whoever will not follow my orders will incur my personal wrath." When Swedish Admiral of the Fleet Klas Fleming had 30 men run back and forth on the newly built ship to test its seaworthiness, he had to stop the test after three runs because the ship started rolling left and right dangerously. However, nobody dared to tell the king. And thus on a sunny afternoon in 1628 the fully flagged *Vasa* left the shipyard. When, after one and a half miles out at sea, the first breeze softly hit *Vasa*, she capsized and sank like a stone, taking down 30 men. Fortunately, all other crewmembers were saved, as the ship was still in the harbor. A subsequent investigation into the catastrophe did not identify any culprits. His Majesty the king as well as everybody else involved concluded that it must have been an Act of God, as the ship had been built precisely according to the royal specification. And kings don't make mistakes. As we have seen earlier, being a strong leader in the vanguard of his troops helped King Gustavus II Adolphus win many battles. But it didn't help him to successfully complete an innovation project, such as building a novel warship. For such projects, rotating leadership, where collaborating leaders take turns, works much better.

9.2. HOW TO WIN THE NOBEL PRIZE? ANSWER: BE KIND!

While the *Vasa* illustrates how one autocratic leader can easily take down the whole ship, another Swede 200 years later started a new tradition of fostering collaborative innovation.

Alfred Nobel was by all accounts a highly creative entrepreneur and a prolific inventor with over 300 patents, who was writing poetry on the side. An avid traveller, he spoke six languages, and created a business empire with factories on all continents. While he made a major part of his riches by selling tools of war — he is most famous for having invented dynamite — at the end of his live he put his money into the service of peace and progress. On his deathbed, he willed the lion's share of his wealth to a foundation that was to use the interest of his fortune to give out five annual prizes in fields close to his own interests, for chemistry, physics, medicine, literature, and peace.

The rules for winning the Nobel Prize are such that they reward competitive collaborators over collaborative competitors. One cannot compete for the Nobel Prize, but has to be nominated by her or his peers. The final votes are given by a committee of academics. This means that scientists will be reluctant to nominate people who have been rude or arrogant against their peers. This leads to Nobel Prize winners not just being smart and creative, but also being nice. I stumbled on this by chance when I was speaking with a professor at a college in Florida. He told me that he had been fortunate enough to personally meet a few Nobel Prize winners in economics, a sixth Nobel Memorial Prize later added by the Swedish National Bank. What had struck him then was how kind and generous the Nobel Prize winners were compared to what he called the second tier of famous scientists. While the Nobel Prize winners were approachable and humble people, generous in giving praise and credit to others, the tier right below, such as editors-in-chief of the most prestigious journals, deans, chaired professors, and holders of other positions of authority, were arrogant, abrasive, claiming all good ideas for themselves, and visibly enjoying their power. This difference in personalities does seem to start to take effect much earlier, well before a Nobel Prize winner was getting nominated.[1] Comparing 68 Nobel laureates in medicine with 68 similarly scientifically productive and ranked scientists, researchers found that the Nobel laureates formed a clear network of dense collaboration, well before they got the Nobel Prize.

---

[1]Wagner, Horlings, Whetsell, Mattsson, and Nordqvist (2015).

This is an application of the "Homophily" or "Birds-of-a-feather-flock-together" principle, where like-minded people are searching each other out as collaborators. I have no proof for now, but I strongly suspect that it was the "kind and smart" property that brought the future Nobel laureates together in their younger years. This is quite different from the McKinsey inspired "we are the smartest guys in the room" culture of Enron, where a group of entirely extrinsically motivated people found each other to game the Californian energy system and play a host of other barely legal but clearly unethical games to enrich themselves at the public's expense.

9.3. FEEDBACK ON COMMUNICATION BUILDS COLLABORATIVE ORGANIZATIONS

What we can learn from King Gustavus II Adolphus and the Nobel Prize winners is that the six honest signals of collaboration are not just a scorecard of collaborativeness. Rather, by applying the four principles of social quantum physics — empathy, entanglement, reflection, and reboot — and encouraging people to behave according to the six honest signals will lead to more collaborative leaders and organizations. By hiring collaborators instead of competitors, and structuring the incentive system in a way that rewards collaboration, not competition, organizations will develop self-awareness through entanglement. This means, for instance, if a self-aware multinational organization encounters a serious problem in Singapore, its head office in London will learn about it minutes later, just like if somebody steps on your toes, your brain will register it instantaneously and you will step back. Such organizations will create a culture of working toward shared goals motivated not by winning individual competitions, but by collaboratively achieving common goals. Organizational alignment along shared goals means optimizing collaboration by improving communication.

In further applications of the principles of social quantum physics, virtually mirroring communication back to the individual and the organization can help increase collaboration. Showing individuals how they are doing in adhering to the six honest signals helps reduce uncertainty, and increases organizational collaboration leading to higher performance. The swarm building principles described above have been applied in our hundreds of research projects in numerous organizations over the last 14 years to increase collaboration in a variety of business settings. Our team has analyzed social networks in many different ways, originally by surveys, but very soon using e-mails exchanged between two people as a proxy for the social relationship between the two individuals, later extended by Twitter and blog links. Measuring the six honest signals through e-mail is like a probe into the organizational consciousness of a company. We used this approach to measure customer satisfaction, to predict employee attrition, to predict sales success of the sales force, and to identify the most creative staff members in research and development departments.

9.4. MEASURING CUSTOMER SATISFACTION

Happy people answer e-mail faster. They also use different language than unhappy people. Combining all the six honest signals allows to quite accurately predict their satisfaction. In one project, we analyzed the e-mail networks of employees of a global services provider, which provides accounting, HR, and other business process outsourcing services to hundreds of Fortune 500 and other large companies. Over a period of three years, we collected the e-mail of the outsourcing provider's employees for more than 20 of its customers. We then compared the six honest signals of collaboration — strong leadership, balanced contribution, rotating leadership, responsiveness, honest sentiment, and shared word usage — with customer satisfaction. To measure customer satisfaction, the outsourcing provider used "Net Promoter Score," a metric introduced by Fred Reichheld in a 2003 *Harvard Business Review* article. For measuring the Net Promoter Score, the service provider asks its customers the simple question "how likely are you to recommend me to your peers" on a score of one to 10, with 10 being the most likely to recommend, and with one to not recommend the provider at all.

We found that not only could we predict Net Promoter Score based on the e-mail behavior of the account managers of the service provider working for the particular customer, but we even were able to come up with recommendations for more efficient communication. While all six honest signals of collaboration were reliable indicators of customer satisfaction, we found that in particular if the account managers showed *strong leadership,* customer satisfaction increased. If network leaders became increasingly clearly visible, creating a more recognizable and stable set of client contact points and a disciplined, predictable flow of communication made the customer more satisfied. Account managers got to see their own communication network in social network pictures such as the one in **Figure 31** so they could reflect on their own behavior. In **Figure 31** each dot is a person, and each connecting line is at least one e-mail exchanged between two people. The size of the dot shows the importance of the person in the network (measured by a metric called "betweenness centrality").

The picture on the left in **Figure 31** shows a network where two people are clear leaders (the large dark dots in the center). The network on the right, taken from another organization, shows a network with many leaders (there are about a dozen large grey dots). A second metric that helped us to distinguish communication with happy customers from communication with unhappy customers was *balanced contribution*. Positive contributors send more than they receive; negative contributors are mostly information consumers. In the context of the outsourcing firm, we found that if a few people from the outsourcing provider were contributing massively more than the rest, this made customers happier. If, on the other hand,

Figure 31: Social Network Showing Strong Leadership (at Left) and Distributed Leadership (at Right).

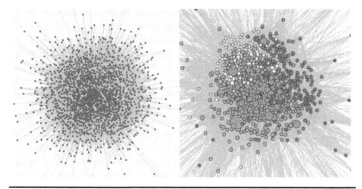

customers were flooded with information from many different sources, it made them unhappier. A third criterion was *responsiveness* of both service providers and customers. Service providers responding quickly to customers did not increase customer satisfaction per se; however, how quickly a customer responded to a message from a service provider staff member was a reliable indicator of customer satisfaction. Happy customers answer e-mails faster.

The fourth metric, which in my view is the most important one, is *rotating leadership* — or in this case "steady leadership." It seems that for a well-established outsourcing relationship, a "King Gustavus II Adolphus" type of strong leadership is better than many changes in this role. While for creative teams, rotating leadership is best with a few strong leaders taking turns, for the outsourcing provider steady leadership produced more satisfied customers. This means that the same two or three people were always in charge of the relationship, they were steady contributors of information flowing to the customers, and were reliable points of contact for information coming back from the customer. While in a project phase, creativity might be at a premium, once the relationship is established, reliability of communication with the provider is more important for the customer.

It pays to use honest language. Analyzing the content of the communication provided additional valuable cues to track customer satisfaction. We measured *honest sentiment* of the e-mail subject lines exchanged between service providers and customers. Because of privacy reasons we did not look at the content of the messages. While we were expecting that more positive sentiment in the communication would be indicative of happy customers, we found the opposite. The more positive the service providers were talking to the customers, the less happy the customers actually were. An even better predictor of customer satisfaction was the "honesty" of the language, that is both the positivity and negativity of the words used in the subject line. This means that if the language exchanged between customers and service providers was more emotional, the customer was happier. We defined emotional, or "honest" language as including both highly positive as well as highly negative words.

Finally, we also found that if the service providers were using simple language, the customer was happier. The sixth "honest signal" is based on *shared language*. We measured it between service providers and customers through new word usage and message complexity, again restricted to just analyzing the subject line. In innovation communities, we had found that if groups started using a novel vocabulary, making up their own acronyms and abbreviations, it was indicative of creative influence. For the relationships between outsourcing customers and providers, the opposite was true: the simpler the language used between the two parties, and the more adhering to standard English, the happier the customer was.

Through measuring the six honest signals of collaboration, the outsourcing provider was able to track collective consciousness between its customers and its employees working for the customer. This allowed the outsourcing provider not only to anticipate customer dissatisfaction flashpoints before they became a major issue, but even to increase collective consciousness through virtual mirroring.

9.5. INCREASING CUSTOMER SATISFACTION THROUGH VIRTUAL MIRRORING

Mirror mirror on the wall, who is the fairest of them all?

– Evil Queen, the stepmother of Snow White, asking if she is the most beautiful woman alive

The Heisenberg uncertainty principle suggests that if individuals become aware of their own communication behavior, this will change it for the better. Self-reflection through the eyes of others can be an eye-opening experience. In our work with the global service provider, we used the system above to calculate numeric scores for the six metrics: "strong leadership," "balanced contribution," "responsiveness," "rotating leadership," "honest sentiment," and "shared context." These scores, together with network pictures such as the one in **Figure 31**, were shown to people periodically in a process we call "virtual mirroring." Just like Snow White's stepmother, the Evil Queen, who had a mirror that always told her the truth, our virtual mirror will tell people the truth about how they communicate with others, and how they are seen by others. Our hypothesis is that through the Heisenberg uncertainty principle these "honest signals of collaboration" will induce the people looking into the virtual mirror to change their behavior through self-reflection.

We tested this hypothesis with the account managers of the service provider described in the previous section. Account managers of 24 large customers of the service provider were shown their virtual mirror every month for the duration of seven months. The virtual mirror was calculated not just for them, but also for all the members on their team, ranging in size from 10 people up to a few hundred. Additionally the account managers were also given recommendations how they and the staff members on their account might change their communication behavior to make the customers happier. After seven months the results were quite clear: compared to the 200 accounts whose managers did not get the virtual mirroring, the accounts of the 24 mirrored managers improved customer satisfaction by 5%. Customer satisfaction of the other 200 accounts without virtual mirroring, on the other hand, went down by 12%. Note that the only selection criterion for the 24 accounts to be included in our study was that they were using the e-mail system of the outsourcing service provider. The other 200 accounts were using the e-mail system of their customer, a criterion that had nothing to do with the overall performance of the teams. In all other aspects the two groups were alike.

We have applied the virtual mirroring process in different environments, mostly based on collecting e-mail archives. It was initially developed and tested with the COINs (Collaborative Innovation Networks) seminar described in detail in Section 8.5, where showing teams of students how they communicated greatly increased collaborative performance. It has also been applied in the context of collaborative healthcare, described later in Section 9.11, where teams of healthcare practitioners and researchers were shown their communication networks calculated from the e-mails they exchanged, to increase their collaboration efficiency and effectiveness.

9.6. MEASURING EMPLOYEE DISSATISFACTION

In the same global outsourcing company where we measured customer satisfaction, we also looked at employee satisfaction. As the ultimate criteria of satisfaction we took the attrition of employees, literally letting employees vote with their feet about how much they like their employer. More specifically, we collected the e-mail of the 3000 most senior employees of the 60,000-employee company over 18 months. We then looked if we could see any difference in the six honest signals of collaboration between people who had left the company over these 18 months and people still with the company. What we found is that there are really two categories of mid-level managers, let's call them the *nomads* and the *settlers*. Settlers stay with the company for extended periods of time; nomads switch company every few years. When looking at the communication network among peers at the outsourcing company, we found that nomads communicate much less with their peers, and more with outside parties. On the other hand, they are more passionate and responsive, they need less "pings" until they respond back, while others also show them more respect, needing less reminders until they answer back to nomads. Additionally, nomads are more "matter of fact" and less emotional in the e-mail subject lines. They are also less "close" to their peers in terms of social network distance. Overall, there emerges a picture of the nomads as being more emotionally balanced, of being well respected, being highly passionate about their work, and being more subject matter focused, and less status focused.

However, once nomads get frustrated at their workplace, turning from "happy nomads" to "unhappy nomads," they show a markedly different behavior. When they start looking for greener pastures, ready to leave their current employer, their communication patterns change. They start showing more closeness to their peers at the company, making efforts to contact strategically placed colleagues, while at the same time becoming more passive in their contribution patterns. However, others at the company need more nudges to answer to their e-mails, thus showing them less respect. Unhappy nomads start using more complex language in their e-mail subject headings, and they also change their networking position more frequently from being central to being peripheral, and back. Overall, the picture that emerges from the communication behavior of unhappy nomads is one of rejected love, of frustration, and of trying to reach out to better connected colleagues within their peer group trying to find opportunities within the company. However, this is usually to no avail, and therefore unhappy nomads will move on, to new opportunities at another company.

In our analysis at the outsourcing company, we were able to quite accurately distinguish "nomads" from "settlers," and also identify "happy" and "unhappy" nomads, leading to valuable suggestions for the organization of how to keep high-potential nomads happy by giving them more internal recognition and embedding them in peer-support nomad groups. Put in other words, as long as nomads are happy, they define collective consciousness as demonstrated through their rotating leadership behavior, and their passion and respect revealed through theirs and others' responsiveness. Once they are frustrated, they step outside the collective as shown through radically different communication patterns.

Besides predicting employee attrition, the same approach also works to predict sales success.

9.7. PREDICTING SALES SUCCESS

Analyzing just a small slice of communication data will predict how well the entire sales force of a huge enterprise is doing. In this project, we analyzed one week of the full e-mail archive of a high-tech company with over 90,000 employees, as well as one month of the company's Web conferencing data. We did not look at any content, neither in message body nor the subject line of the e-mail, only tracking structure and dynamics of the communication. We then compared the annual sales performance of the global sales force of the company with the communication behavior of the same people.

In general, we found that the fewer e-mails the sales force members sent, the more successful they were. The more passive they were in their mailing behavior, that is the less they sent compared to the number of e-mails they received, the more they sold. This means that just bombarding customers with e-mail is a poor sales strategy. On the other hand, we also found that if they were responsive to e-mails, meaning that it took them fewer nudges or "pings" from their customers until they responded, they were more successful.

We also noticed some national differences, confirming cultural stereotypes. In the Western world, and in the United States, Canada, and Germany, the global company trend of being more successful when sending less was confirmed (not that surprising, as this is a Western company). The less e-mail salespeople in the United States, Canada, and Germany sent and the faster they responded, the more they sold. In India, however, the leadership pattern was a better indicator of a successful salesperson: the more steady their communication behavior, and the less rotating leadership behavior they demonstrated, the more successful as salespeople they were. For Japan, the best predictor of a high-performing salesperson was focus: the fewer different communication partners they had, meaning that the more the salespeople focused on a few selected communication partners, the more successful they were.

We also noticed hierarchical differences between sales managers, and sales specialists across all geographical regions. For sales managers, the more steady leadership they showed, the more they sold. For sales specialists, it was their and their customers' speed of response: the faster they replied to each other, the more they sold. Finally, we also found that selling different types of products mandates different types of communication behavior. For sales specialists selling products in mature fields of technology, it's steady leadership that helps selling, while for sales specialists selling novel technology products, rotating leadership — associated with creativity — is the best predictor of high sales.

Besides analyzing the e-mail communication behavior, we also looked at the social networking behavior gathered through Web conferencing, particularly with the Webcam turned on. We found that Web conferencing was an even better predictor of sales success than e-mail. While the overall amount of Web conferencing interaction was lower than for e-mail, it was highly indicative of high sales. The more a pattern of rotating leadership emerged for a salesperson, switching between participating in and organizing Web conference sessions, the more successful the salesperson was. We also found that the more different communication partners a salesperson had, and the more proactive in setting up Web conferences a salesperson was, the higher was the sales success. These Web conferencing communication patterns were independent of geography, hierarchy level, and product line. The bottom line is that face-to-face interaction trumps e-mail communication, even in the virtual world: the more Web conferencing, particularly with the video camera turned on, and the less e-mails salespeople send, the more successful they are. A successful sales relationship is based on trust, and trust is much better built in face-to-face interaction than in e-mail. The more the sales force succeeded in creating shared collective consciousness with its customers, the more the customers were willing to buy its products.

9.8. IDENTIFYING THE MOST INNOVATIVE EMPLOYEES

Looking at communication tells a lot about individual and group creativity. Starting with the e-mail archive of the World Wide Web Consortium, we have studied the communication patterns of many particularly creative teams. The way how the Web's founder, Tim Berners-Lee, communicated provided the blueprint for many later projects analyzing communication patterns of particularly creative people.

For instance, in a global energy company we analyzed the corporate e-mail network to find the most innovative employees among the thousands of employees of the research and development department. We collected the complete e-mail traffic among a few thousand employees over 13 months. We also looked at how the R&D staff members communicated with outside researchers from universities. To test and verify our assumptions, we looked at which staff members filed for patents or published scientific papers. In addition, the company conferred annual awards for the best publication, and for the most innovative employees.

When measuring the six honest signals of collaboration, there were marked differences in communication behavior between innovators and their peers in the R&D department. The innovators were more respected, as their peers within the department answered them on average in 20 hours instead of the 22 hours it took for others to get a response. Innovators were also more passionate, as they answered e-mails with less nudging; on average it took others less than two e-mails to elicit a response from innovators, and their peers took more than two nudges until they responded. Innovators also showed more rotating leadership; over the entire observation period of 13 months, they changed their network position 170 times from being leaders to being listeners, compared to their peers who showed the rotating leadership behavior on average for 166 times. The most striking difference however was the intrinsic motivation they showed within their peer group, which we measured by calculating the centrality of their social network position. We used a metric called "betweenness" which measures information flow in the network, as access to information is access to power. It turned out that innovators are over three times less central — and thus attention seeking — than their peers. They are also more passive senders of e-mail in terms of their contribution of new messages. When restricting the communication to the local lab of the innovators, however, their pattern flipped, and they became more central within their local lab network than their peers. This means that innovators are much more focused in their communication.

The picture also changes when we switch our lens from analyzing the communication within the R&D department to analyzing the communication with external universities. The innovators get more mails from senders with university e-mail addresses, and they are more proactive in sending e-mail to university researchers compared to their peers within the R&D department. Their rotating leadership behavior becomes even more pronounced in communication with universities; they change their position from being the leader to the listeners 65 times in the 13 months observation period, compared to 41 rotational changes in leadership for their peers within the company. Innovators also talk with more different people at the university over these 13 months, initiating an e-mail dialog with 56 outside people instead of 37.

We also found that output-oriented innovators — the ones producing papers and patents — communicate quite differently from outcome oriented innovators — the ones garnering awards for being most innovative and for writing the best paper. Paper and patent writing innovators show more introvert behavior than their peers, while award winning innovators show more extrovert behavior: while on average innovators send less e-mail than their peers, award-winning innovators were the most active senders and receivers of e-mail in the entire R&D department. However, it seems that paper- and patent-writing innovators are more respected than award-winning innovators, as they were responded faster than award-winning innovators. Paper- and patent-writing innovators are less central — more introvert — than award-winning innovators, who must be highly visible in order to be nominated for their awards. Award-winning innovators also show more rotating leadership, switching between leading and listening, than the more introvert paper- and patent-writing innovators.

Finally, we also looked at whether there is a difference between repeat innovators — who have been included at least twice on the list of most innovative researchers — and one-shot innovators. We found that repeat innovators send twice as much e-mail to their peers, and also receive much more e-mail than one-shot innovators. Repeat innovators show higher rotating leadership, changing from leading to listening 30% more than one-shot innovators. They also have slightly higher respect — they are responded a bit faster, and are somewhat more central in the network.

In sum, we find that intrinsically motivated innovators can be found by looking at the "honest signals of collaboration," with signs of respect shown as rapid response by others, and the innovators showing high passion by answering their e-mails faster than their peers. A second key insight is that innovators are less "political" in their e-mailing behavior by sending much less e-mail within their organization. They are the "queen bees" of building collective consciousness within the R&D organization by rather using their communication bandwidth to reach out to outside parties to develop new innovative ideas instead of sending "political" e-mails to colleagues within the company.

9.9. FINDING THE MOST INNOVATIVE BIOTECH START-UPS IN BOSTON

Similar patterns of creativity were confirmed studying social networks of members of the R&D departments of biotech start-ups in the greater Boston area. This project was motivated by an earlier project with 100 software start-ups in Israel,[2] where we had looked at communication between the CEOs of these start-ups in 1998; information about the communication was collected in personal interviews with the CEOs. We then checked six years later, in 2004, which of the software start-ups were still around, having survived the dotcom crash and the burst of the e-Business bubble. At that time, we had found that the start-up CEOs who had been willing to participate in the interview three years before the dotcom crash had a much higher chance of surviving the dotcom crash, demonstrating that thinking outside the box, and collaborating with academics was a good long-term predictor of success. We also found that the more connected a CEO was to her peers at the helm of the other start-ups, the higher the chances of survival for her start-up.

In the follow-on project in the greater Boston area, we were trying to further untangle the connection between communication and location of start-up entrepreneurs. For the duration of a year, from 2005 to 2006, Ornit Raz, a

---

[2]Raz and Gloor (2007).

post-doc at MIT, collected the communication network of 10% of all members of the R&D departments of 200 biotech start-ups through an online survey. At a random day per week, for the duration of one year, selected members of the research staff got an e-mail with a link to an online survey, where they reported with whom they had spoken on that day face-to-face, on the phone, or exchanged an e-mail. They reported on communication with other start-ups, with large pharmaceutical companies, with research hospitals, and with university researchers.

We used the data from this project to investigate two related questions: "does location matter for communication," and "does location help for start-up performance?" We measured creative performance of the start-ups as the number of patent applications they filed in the three subsequent years after the communication data was collected, as direct financial data for the start-ups was not available. The results were quite clear. We found that location greatly boosted communication. Companies located inside a circle with a radius of seven kilometers with the center between Harvard and MIT communicated exponentially more with each other than the companies outside this circle.[3] However, communication did not translate into creative performance.[4] Two other criteria were much better predictors of high patent application count, our proxy for high innovation capability. The first one was network position in the communication network, independent of location. Biotech companies, which were highly central in the R&D communication network and

[3]Allen, Raz, and Gloor (2009).
[4]Allen, Gloor, Raz, Woerner, and Fronzetti (2016).

also located inside the Boston biotech cluster, had on average 20 patent applications in the next two years. Companies located in the center of the Boston biotech cluster, but peripheral in the communication network, had only five patent applications. Companies not central in the communication network, and located outside of Boston on average had only three patent applications in 2006 and 2007. Companies central in the communication network, but located outside the Boston biotech cluster, however, had 23 patent applications. This means that the more central a company was in the communication network — and not the geographical network — the higher was its creative performance.

The second criterion of innovation was rotating leadership. The more the R&D leaders of a company changed their network position from being peripheral to being central and back, the more patent applications the company filed. In sum, this project confirmed the results we obtained from innovators inside the company outlined in the previous section: communicating intensively with a lot of outside peers, and passing the baton back and forth are the most important predictors of creativity.

Besides numerous applications in industry, competitive collaboration is also prevalent in many fields of healthcare.

9.10. COLLABORATIVE HEALTHCARE

Mens sana in corpore sano — a healthy mind in a healthy body (Latin)

My friend Arlette provides an eye-opening experience illustrating the positive power of collaboration on health.

Arlette has cystic fibrosis and celebrated her 60th birthday in 2015. Most other cystic fibrosis patients of Arlette's generation did not live over 20. Cystic fibrosis is a chronic disease, which children inherit from parents through their gene combination. It is characterized by an overproduction of mucus in the lungs, leading to breathing difficulties, reduced growth, and secondary diseases like diabetes. When Arlette was born, the life expectancy of a patient with cystic fibrosis was about 10 years. I met Arlette in 2000; at 45 she was already then unusually old for a patient with cystic fibroses. With an unquestioningly positive, accepting attitude toward life, and collaborating closely within a close-knit support network of relatives, friends, and other cystic fibrosis patients, Arlette succeeded to reach a biblical age for cystic fibrosis patients. A key factor for her longevity was the loving care of her parents during her youth, and then the warm relationships she created with about 50 close friends over her lifetime, demonstrating the positive effects of embeddedness in social networks. It also helps that Arlette was trained as a pharmacist's assistant, so she was able to medicate herself, and treat many of her ailments. You can listen to Arlette tell her life story on YouTube.[5]

The goal of collaborative healthcare is to empower patients like Arlette to take their life into their own hands, and collaboratively, with their health providers, doctors, nurses, and insurers, lead a healthy high-quality life. Collaborative healthcare needs collaborative leaders like Arlette, who are willing to not just care for themselves, but

---

[5]Arlette Maurer — 60 years with Cystic Fibrosis https://www.youtube.com/watch?v=1UnTkyEVVSs

share and help others to innovate and lead better lives. Frequently these leaders are patients themselves. I call them "empowered patients," as besides being afflicted with the disease they are working to cure, they also have training as nurses, doctors, or researchers. Frequently they also have family members and loved ones who suffer from this condition. By having a lot of "skin in the game," these patient-researchers will be highly motivated and passionate leaders of these collaboration teams.

9.11. COLLABORATIVE CHRONIC CARE NETWORKS

Collaborative Chronic Care Networks (C3N) are a key example of collaborative healthcare. C3Ns have been invented in 2009 by two professors at Cincinnati Children's Hospital, Peter Margolis and Michael Seid, and Richard Colletti, a professor at University of Vermont. C3Ns grew out of an earlier project of Peter and Richard, ImproveCareNow, which brought together patients of Crohn's disease and their family members with Crohn's doctors to one- to two-day learning sessions combined with sharing patient data of participating hospitals across the United States. Crohn's disease or inflammatory bowel disease (IBD) is a chronic disease of the intestines. Crohn's is incurable until now; the goal of treatment is to drive the disease into remission and allow patients to lead a normal life.

The C3Ns project was funded by the National Institute of Health with a multimillion-dollar grant in 2009. C3Ns combine concepts of process improvement, learning communities, lead user innovation, and COINs. The objective of C3Ns is to leverage the innovative ideas of the patients, by combining them in small teams with researchers and medical providers such as doctors and nurses. They collaborate to improve the lives of the patients, with the long-term vision of developing a cure for Crohn's. Patients meet at regular learning sessions; over the past years, a small core team of C3N researchers has built a self-organizing, vibrant research community of hundreds of patients, clinicians, and researchers working on improving the lives of patients. Twenty-seven creative ideas have been picked up by COINs, 23 have seen the light of day, and are rolled out to thousands of patients with Crohn's. Topics for the C3N COINs range from mentoring programs, patient guidelines, and self-help videos to online matchmaking tools, data collection smartphone apps, and games for better managing the disease. Most importantly, remission rates of the Crohn's patients participating in the C3Ns have been going up steeply. Since 2014 the concept of C3Ns has been extended from Crohn's to pediatric kidney transplant patients and cystic fibrosis. Using the same blueprint, groups of patients, caregivers, providers, and researchers have come together to develop innovations for kidney transplant and cystic fibrosis patients.

The process consists of three parallel streams. In the first work stream, patient innovators, family members, medical researchers, and doctors meet virtually and face-to-face, to develop new innovations to improve the lives of the patients. In "virtual brownbag" sessions, novel ideas are shared among the group. In addition, in a series of design meetings, the group, usually about 50 to 70 people strong, gets together for two days to brainstorm and innovate, and create dozens of new COINs around breakthrough ideas. For example, for the cystic fibrosis design meeting, teams developed over 50 innovative ideas, ranging from patient monitoring apps, community building, to onboarding guidelines for new patients and parents. These ideas were then taken up by the innovation teams, and turned into real prototypes and tested with patient groups.

The second work stream consists of larger gatherings of doctors and patients structured as learning sessions, applying the Breakthrough Series method developed by IHI, the Institute for Healthcare Improvement in Cambridge MA. IHI was created by a team of medical researchers around Don Berwick 20 years ago with a focus on building learning communities in healthcare. The learning sessions focus on process improvements by putting a measurement system in place and implementing best practices among participants from many different institutions.

The third work stream develops a patient data registry, to collect patient records on a case-by-case basis. Its goal is to build a database of patient records across participating institutions, not just with hospitals and physicians in the United States; links also have been fostered with similar patient registries in Northern European countries, the United Kingdom, Canada, and other countries in Europe, Australia, and elsewhere. These registries extend existing patient databases, for example, by the Cystic Fibrosis Foundation of the United States which through their patient registry has been able to develop breakthrough medication and treatment regimens, greatly extending the lifespan of cystic fibrosis patients. Similar registries are built through ImproveCareNow for Crohn's patients, and for the pediatric kidney transplant patient communities.

By fostering collaboration among health providers such as doctors and nurses, patients, patient family members, and researchers, C3Ns have the potential to increase the quality of life exponentially for patients of chronic diseases. The key is to put patient innovators into the center, with doctors and researchers learning from them, and not the other way around.

9.12. INFANT MORTALITY COIINS

Collaborative Improvement and Innovation Networks (CoIINs), created by the Maternal and Child Health Bureau of the US Health Resources and Services Administration since 2012, are another great example of collaborative healthcare. They have been started by Michael Lu, the associate administrator of the Maternal and Child Health Bureau (MCHB) of the US Department of Health. These CoIINs combine social workers and health administrators of all 50 US states to address the disparities in infant mortality between middle-class children and children from low-income backgrounds. CoIINs bring together leaders from the community, grassroots activists, and government officials to develop novel ideas to reduce infant mortality and provide children born in poverty with better prospects for their later lives. The main Infant Mortality CoIIN is focused on health administrators mostly on the US state level, trying to develop new policies and interventions by running learning sessions conducted according to the IHI Breakthrough Series model. Health administrators are trying to increase awareness of risky behavior for infants and mothers, such as smoking while pregnant, reducing preterm births, and unsafe sleep habits for babies. In a second Home Visiting CoIIN, social workers, the "home visitors," get together to increase the efficiency of the "Home Visiting Program." The social workers, the "home visitors," visit expecting and young low-income mothers at home in the first few years after the infant's birth to help disadvantaged mothers improve infant and maternal health, and prevent abuse and neglect.

The goal is not just to create learning communities, but, inspired through the C3Ns, to also create innovation teams — COINs — that develop radical innovations to drastically reduce infant mortality. For example, in one of these COINs, a group of state health administrators and researchers work together to bring ideas for trauma-informed care to fruition: It has been found that adverse childhood experiences in the first few years of an infant have the potential to wreak havoc on the entire remaining life of the future adult. Traumatic experiences such as childhood rape, violent treatment of the mother in front of the child, or incarceration of a parent will lead to health-averse adult behavior such as severe obesity, alcohol and drug abuse, and smoking, resulting in bad health through diseases such as depression, diabetes, and cancer. By raising awareness of the bad effects of traumatic experiences in early childhood, and by increasing resilience to traumatic experiences, the vicious circle can be broken.

After having been in operation for three years, a vibrant ecosystem of health CoIINs addressing all aspects of maternal and child health has developed. It operates on three levels. On the top level, administrators in

Washington and the 50 US states collaborate and innovate to develop better policies and programs to improve the quality of care and of life of mother and infant. On the middle level, social workers on the ground collaborate and innovate to directly work with mothers and their family members to improve the environment for the newborns in many ways. And most exciting, on the grassroots level, mothers, fathers, grandparents, and other family members self-organize, supported by home visitors and social workers, and by state policies, to provide a nurturing environment for the future lives of their children.

In our work supporting both the C3N and the Infant Mortality CoIINs, we have supported the COIN creation process through coolfarming innovative ideas for better care of Crohn's patients and mothers and infants. We have also measured the progress in creating collective consciousness within the COINs by analyzing its communication behavior through e-mail analysis, and by providing virtual mirroring to its leaders. This has helped the COIN leaders to recognize emergent junior leaders, nurturing a new generation of young guides and mentors to the community. At the same time, virtual mirroring has also helped weaving a more dense community network, as it has made visible otherwise hidden connections between different groups working on similar topics on Crohn's disease, cystic fibrosis, and infant mortality.

9.13. FROM COMPETITIVE TO COLLABORATIVE OPEN SOURCE HEALTHCARE

This aspect of patients collaborating with researchers to share their patient data records for further research allows them to actively contribute to new insights regarding their own disease. A new Open Science model, based on conducting research in public-private partnership, is pioneered by Sage Bionetworks, which collects, analyzes, and shares complex biological data, for instance, providing smartphone-based data collection apps to patients to contribute their own data on breast cancer and melanomas. Similar to Jonas Salk, who refused to patent the polio vaccine, saying, "There is no patent. Could you patent the sun?" the results for Sage Bionetworks research will be freely available.

As long as mainstream healthcare is still run through unfettered capitalism and competition, collaborative healthcare leads a niche existence. Pharmaceutical companies still try to outcompete each other in optimizing revenue for their shareholders. For instance, a breakthrough treatment against hepatitis C in the form of novel and highly effective drugs Harvoni and Sovaldi by Gilead, costs $1000 per pill, summing up to almost $100,000 per treatment. The only way to get Gilead to reduce the prices was through competition, as competitor AbbVie was bringing competing drugs to the market.[6] Or even worse, Turing Pharmaceuticals funded by former investment banker Martin Shkreli obtained licenses for out-of-patent drugs, and raised their prices by up to 5000%, for instance, increasing the price of the AIDs drug Daraprim from $13.50 to $750 per pill. As long as investors and authorities are willing to accept such highly competitive

---

[6]http://time.com/3643996/hepatitis-c-drugs/

and amoral behavior, collaborative competition will trump competitive collaboration — also in healthcare.

Valeant and Turing are shocking examples of competitive healthcare. However, there is hope, as such companies as Sage Bionetworks are combining collaborative healthcare with open source principles. Sage Bionetworks integrates patients into the research and development process while applying an open source computational modeling process inspired by open source software development. While it is still early days, if open source software development is any guide, the future for open source healthcare should be bright. Whether it is open source drug development, or open source software development, learning from each other — "stepping on the shoulders of giants," as Isaac Newton said — is one of the key advantages of the open source process.

The main findings from this chapter is that to increase organizational collaboration, one can measure and optimize rotating leadership, passion and respect, and honest sentiment, through virtual mirroring. Passion is measured as the time it takes an individual to respond to others. Respect is measured as the time it takes everybody else to answer to the individual. To measure and increase organizational innovativeness, measure and increase COIN creation and destruction. The more new COINs are created — which means that by definition some old ones will be destroyed — the more creative is the company or organization.

In the final chapter, we will look at what the future might bring to a society where money is complemented by social capital, and competitive collaboration has become widely accepted.

MAIN LESSONS LEARNED

- Swarm leaders are respectful, humble, kind, and take turns.

- Measuring the six honest signals of collaboration, and providing them as a virtual mirror to members of the organization will increase organizational performance, satisfaction, and creativity.

- The six honest signals of collaboration can predict and improve customer satisfaction, employee attrition and satisfaction, sales success, and employee creativity.

- COINs also help create breakthrough solutions for patients of chronic diseases, and to reduce infant mortality.

10

BUILDING A COLLABORATIVE SOCIETY

CHAPTER CONTENTS

- Transparency creates trust.

- From financial capital management to social capital management.

- Become a bonobo, not a chimpanzee.

- We will become collectively conscious.

In the final chapter, we will explore the environment that swarms live in. Similar to social insects, human swarms both influence and are influenced by society and the surrounding ecosystem. Today's generation of millennials, their basic needs met, is looking more for meaning than for money in their jobs — although they of course also expect to be compensated well. How do intrinsically motivated, self-organizing groups such as Wikipedians, Stack Overflow contributors, and teams like the Collaborative Chronic Care Networks (C3Ns), infant mortality COINs, or student COINs shape their environment? What can today's large companies do to tap into this energy among all their stakeholders? It starts with the workforce, going over suppliers and customers, ending with society and the entire ecosystem of our planet.

One of the first points to consider when creating a COIN is that they are about everything but coins. This means that if the first members join a COIN because they are paid to do so, the COIN will never get off the ground. People might be paid for joining a COIN, but they join because they are passionate about the goals of the COIN, not because they are paid. The key challenge for the initial COIN members is to create and maintain a culture of trust and give-and-take. As has been explained in Chapter 6, trust and transparency go together. Transparency creates trust; once trust is established, there is no need for extensive transparency anymore. While respecting individual privacy is important, being transparent is more important than respecting privacy at all costs — as has been shown when the mental depression of Germanwings pilot Andreas Lubitz was well known to his psychiatrist, who was not allowed to communicate this to Lubitz' employer, with deadly consequences for the 149 passengers and crew on the aircraft that Lubitz crashed into a mountain. Once trust through transparency is established, social capital will become the main engine that keeps the COIN going, which in the end will also — if so desired and planned — lead to financial capital.

The following story explains very nicely how transparency, trust, and social capital are all linked together, and when missing, will also destroy financial capital.

10.1. NO TRANSPARENCY, NO TRUST, NO BUSINESS

A few years ago I was part of a weird story that, depending on how you read it, got me to miss a multimillion-dollar investment into my company, or more likely, saved me from wasting 25,000 euros on expensive Rolex watches. It illustrates the essential role of trust for innovation and collaboration.

In January 2011, I got an e-mail out of the blue. It was from "Clive," an investment advisor working for an investment advisory firm in Hong Kong who was looking for investment opportunities. When I googled his company, its Web presence looked reasonable. Clive told me that he was working as an advisor for a wealthy investor in the United Arab Emirates who was interested in investing a substantial sum in our software start-up galaxyadvisors. After a few more e-mails, Clive told me the name of his distinguished customer, Mohamed Al Ketbi, a relative of the king of the United Arab Emirates and oil minister of the same country.[1]

---

[1] I changed the names of Clive and Mohamed, as they most likely were not the real Clive and Mohamed.

Clive gave me Al Ketbi's Yahoo e-mail address. A quick check in Google told me that this Al Ketbi indeed seemed to exist. When I sent Al Ketbi an e-mail, he responded the next day and proposed a skype call. After some scheduling problems on his side, we finally spoke a few words on skype, although the technical quality was quite bad, and I never got video skype to work, so we ended up using mostly skype chat. Al Ketbi expressed serious interest in investing 5 million dollars in galaxyadvisors. Al Ketbi asked me to fly to Dublin and meet his investment banker as well as a certain Phenton Craigg, his advisor in Dublin, who would do the due diligence and be the interface to the investment banker. Al Ketbi also gave me his mobile phone number with an area code from the United Arab Emirates.

We agreed that I would fly to Dublin in June and meet Phenton Craigg and the investment banker. Al Ketbi also offered to reimburse me for my travel expenses. He then suggested that as a compensation for Phenton Craigg's due diligence services I should buy two Rolex watches to give to Craigg during our meeting in Dublin at the airport. As I found this a bit strange to give a big gift to somebody who would evaluate my own business, I decided to bring along one of my books for Phenton Craigg instead. However, I was now really curious how the story would unfold and therefore decided to invest $600 in a cheap ticket to Dublin and meet Phenton and the investment banker in person.

When I arrived at the airport hotel in Dublin, Phenton met me in the lobby, and the investment banker was nowhere around. Phenton was a well-dressed black fellow, with a British accent, who told me that he was originally from the Bahamas, and had worked as a diplomat, which was how he had gotten to know Al Ketbi.

However, Phenton did not seem to be that interested in our business plan, and in the end he asked me if Al Ketbi had not asked me to give him a gift. I then told Phenton that I had a book for him as a gift, which did not really satisfy him that much. He finally left, telling me that the investment banker unfortunately was not available that day. As soon as Phenton had left, I got an upset phone call from Al Ketbi, asking me why I had not given the two Rolex watches to Phenton Craigg, whereas I told Al Ketbi that I did not think that paying somebody to evaluate my own product was appropriate (although on a side note, this is how rating companies such as Moody's, Fitch, and Standard & Poor's operate: countries and companies pay them to get their own rating).

Although I cannot prove it, I strongly suspect that Clive, Al Ketbi (probably not the real ones), and Craigg were all the same person; let's call him Phenton, because that's the name he gave to me. Phenton smartly crafted his investment story, bringing in other personalities along the way. As an intuitive psychologist he used the fact that we trust groups of people more than a single person, however great his story. Most likely Phenton engineered his fantasy tale to have two brand new Rolex watches hand-delivered to him in Dublin. But maybe I missed a tremendous opportunity to get a multimillion-dollar investment in our start-up.

10.2. SOCIAL CAPITAL TRUMPS FINANCIAL CAPITAL

In their book *The Second Machine Age*, Erik Brynjolfsson and Andrew McAfee argue that the computer will replace menial jobs, such as manufacturing cars, assembling computers, or stitching clothes. Newly emerging technologies such as 3-D printers might speed up this trend, permitting to 3-D print new clothes or even an entire house, while in vitro meat production might allow us to eat steaks created in the lab artificially from meat cells with no need for farmers to breed and slaughter cattle for meat production, garment worker to sew clothes, or construction workers to build houses.

Having large groups of people made jobless through advances of computer technology as projected in the *Second Machine Age* was the horror of society in the Victorian Age, where it was believed that "idleness is at the root of all evil." While "the second machine age" might lead to a doomsday scenario with billions of unemployed workers desperately rioting for work, I anticipate a much brighter future where people will not "work" anymore, but do the activities that give meaning to their lives. As humans draw energy from being with "people like themselves," they will be choosing their activities according to their wishes and likes, to collaborate with other like-minded people on whatever they are passionate about.

These developments indicate that society is improving the foundations for a humane existence.

Two concrete trends toward untangling money from bringing more meaning into life are the discussion about increasing the minimum wage in the United States to afford people subsisting on minimum salary a better existence, and the "unconditional basic income," called *bedingungsloses Grundeinkommen* in Germany and Switzerland where the idea is gaining a lot of traction. While increasing the salary of the working poor to allow them a decent life is unquestionably an improvement of the status quo, unconditional basic income is currently being discussed in different Northern European countries, which are taking baby steps toward such a future. The underlying idea of the unconditional basic income is precisely that, namely providing an income to everybody that is unconditional of his or her contribution to the economy and society. The Netherlands and Finland will be starting a pilot in local communities to collect experience on the consequences; Switzerland voted in 2016 about introducing the unconditional basic income in 2016, although rejecting the proposal. The unconditional basic income would pay everybody an unconditional salary, to free them for whatever they would like to do. However, unconditional basic income raises the question what people would do with their newly gained free time if they don't have to work anymore. Twenty thousand years ago, our hunter-gatherer ancestors had the unconditional basic income, as they contributed to and got from their family what they needed. As they had to carry their entire household on their back, it was just not possible for one individual to become much richer than the other tribe members, which means that everybody had access to a similar unconditional basic income. The key difference however was that the sharing of the basic income happened within the small band, while the Netherlands or Finland would offer it to everybody of their five to sixteen million citizens.

The two main questions of the unconditional basic income are, first, what people will be doing with all their spare time, and secondly, how fair it is toward all the "lazy" people who will not contribute toward society's needs, but are just consuming whatever they are given? Looking at today's stone age hunter-gatherers suggests that lazy people get less than hardworking hunters, but that, at least as long as there is enough, everybody gets a share of the catch. This would not be different for the unconditional basic income, as the size of this income is low compared to a professional income.

There have always been both hardworking and lazy people. This is true not just for people. Any swarm is made up of "hardworking bees" and "lazy bees." This even applies to the real bees, as bee researchers found that only a small fraction of bees are the busy honey collectors we admire so much. A much larger part of the swarm spends their lives more or less actively tending to the needs of the swarm staying at home, or even resting outside and enjoying the sun. Half of the swarm does not work at all: male bees, the drones, basically spend their entire (albeit short) lives just eating and sleeping and waiting for their chance to mate. This also suggests that human society will not fall apart because of all the "lazy bees" just being outside, consuming the unconditional basic income, and enjoying the sun. The "busy bees" will obtain their reward from getting meaning by contributing toward improving society, following the motivation pyramid introduced in Chapter 2, progressing from money, to power, to glory, to love, to wisdom. The motivation pyramid suggests that in order to find meaning in live, people living off the unconditional basic income will still work toward gaining money, power, glory, love, and wisdom, if only to maintain their self-esteem. The hope however is that everybody will discover what their passion is, and find more meaning in life than just consuming food and entertainment. Already the Romans discovered this, when they were buying social peace at home by providing *panem et circences*, "bread and games" to the common people in Rome for free. As the population lost civic engagement, Rome was not able to field a native army anymore; in the end Rome was overrun by the barbarians. The key therefore is to keep everybody intrinsically motivated and active.

Microfinance, making small loans available to the working poor without access to mainstream banking, has been promoted as a promising step toward self-help. It is a way for underprivileged people to get access to capital and work their own way out of their poverty. As poor people do not have collateral to pledge against a loan, they pledge their social capital instead. However, it would be better to lift everybody up to a level of wealth to get direct access to financial services provided by financial institutions to most citizens of the Western world. But even better would be to replace financial capital by social capital. While Mohammad Yunus and his Grameen Bank got a Nobel Prize for introducing micro-loans in Bangladesh, it has been shown by Yale researchers Dean Karlan and Jonathan Zinman[2] that microfinance by itself does very little to alleviate poverty. Only in combination with providing long-term coaching can the poor permanently improve their social standing. This provides another argument for rotating leadership between micro-entrepreneurs and their coaches to keep the social fabric intact, and provide social capital together with financial capital.

---

[2]Karlan and Zinman (2011).

10.3. BITCOIN: TRUST WITHOUT TRANSPARENCY

The virtual currency bitcoin demonstrates this trend toward hard coin being replaced by social capital. Bitcoin has no guarantor at all other than the anonymous swarm of people owning some of it, and the trust that if somebody wants to sell bitcoins, somebody else will be willing to buy them for a good price. Or to put it in other words, when I buy bitcoin, I buy into the social capital of the bitcoin swarm. However, while the economy of the United States backs the US dollar, the backers of bitcoin are totally anonymous. As the total amount of liquid bitcoin is comparatively small to major real-world currencies, the exchange rate of bitcoin fluctuates wildly. In this sense, investing into the social capital of the anonymous bitcoin swarm is a risky undertaking. As there is no government backing this currency, the owner of bitcoin has to trust the swarm that there will always be somebody willing to take it. In this sense, it operates like a pyramid scheme, driven by investors looking to get rich by attracting other to their swarm of bitcoin owners. Bitcoin therefore offers an explosive mix of financial capital and social capital, with the very real risk of burning gambling owners of bitcoin badly.

Simply owning money, even lots of it, is rewarded less and less, with banks in the most secure economies such as Sweden and Switzerland now offering negative interest rates to investors looking to safely park large amounts of money. Somebody depositing a substantial sum at a Swedish or Swiss bank will not get interest, but will have to pay the bank for this privilege. The capitalist is punished for accumulating money. The conclusion of these trends is that hoarding money becomes less desirable. What we really are accumulating is social capital, either in the form of trust into a state's economy that once my retirement comes, the state will be capable of paying my pension, or into the anonymous swarm of bitcoin owners. The final scenario would be a society where social capital replaces financial capital. Accumulating financial capital is a way to stockpile social capital. Social capital is like personalized financial capital: if I do a favor to you, you will reciprocate the favor in time of my need. If I have accumulated enough money, I can buy your help and don't need social capital. However, uncoupling financial and social capital leads to unethical hoarding of financial capital, at the expense of social capital. As long as it is acceptable for a hedge fund manager to become a billionaire by buying off-patent drugs, and boosting the price of a pill from $13.50 to $750, all social capital is destroyed. This trend leads to worrying disparities in the United States, with the top fifth of all earners controlling 90% of the US wealth, and the bottom 20% owning basically nothing, with disastrous consequences for their health and well-being. As long as our unconditional love affair with capitalism lasts, this will not be changing. As long as the value of an individual is measured by the size of her or his bank account, the smartest will strive to accumulate as much financial capital as possible. In a world ruled by financial capital, however, there is no place for friendship and altruism. Such a society resembles the medieval world, where the strongest and most cunning knights acquired the largest fiefdoms by sheer strength of their arms, only today brains have replaced brawn.

10.4. TRANSPARENCY TRUMPS PRIVACY!

In the Germanwings disaster, the numerous physicians and psychiatrists he had previously visited, knew that pilot Andreas Lubitz had suicidal thoughts and was unfit to pilot an aircraft. Germany's strict privacy rules restricted them from communicating this to his supervisors at Lufthansa, thus enabling Lubitz to take off March 24, 2015, subsequently crashing flight Germanwings 9525, killing himself and an airplane full of innocent passengers. In a more transparent society, the doctors would have shared Lubitz' mental health problems with his employer. This obsession with privacy in lieu of transparency allowed a single pilot gone astray to create a massacre.

For an example of why we need transparency, look at bitcoin. This currency has no real-world economy backing it like the US economy backing the dollar, or Europe's backing the euro. There are no paper bills, and no gold in the vaults of a central bank as collateral. The only reason bitcoin works — and it is far from clear that it will succeed in the long run — is because its algorithm is open source and can be verified by anybody. Everybody willing to invest the money to print their own bitcoin can fire up a "bitcoin printing press" consisting of a battery of computers that will crunch the digital numbers that make up a bitcoin. The only obstacles are figuring out how to run the software, and buying the supercomputers capable of running it. The single reason bitcoin can exist at all is because its creation process is totally transparent, and transparency builds trust into bitcoin. On a side note, the nontransparent nature of who owns the bitcoins might also be its main obstacle to mainstream acceptance, as bitcoins have become a preferred means of payment of criminals for illegal activities.

As discussed in the introduction of this book, it seems that collective intelligence as measured through Google search trends values altruism over egoism. However, society does not seem to be ready yet to embrace transparency. At least that's what doing a background check in Google ngrams and Google trends shows: privacy is more popular than transparency. According to the *Oxford English Dictionary* both of these words were used at the end of the 16th century for the first time: "privacy" in 1534, and "transparency" in 1591. As Google Ngrams shows in **Figure 32**, in the 19th century, privacy and transparency occupied similar levels of mindshare. This radically changed in the 1960s, with privacy becoming an increasingly important topic until 2000. The most recent development, documented in Google trends from 2005 to

Figure 32: Privacy beats transparency in Google Ngrams after 1900.

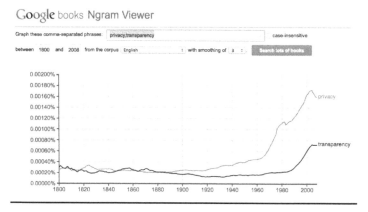

Figure 33: Privacy is searched more than transparency since 2005 as shown in Google search trends.

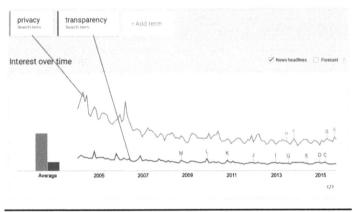

2015, shows a similar picture, with privacy trumping transparency (**Figure 33**).

I am convinced that we are heading toward a world where transparency will have priority over privacy. We are sharing formerly intimate secrets like who is in love with whom on Twitter and Facebook, which just a few years ago were thought of as being entirely private. While for instance Europe has strict privacy laws, the November 2015 terrorist attacks in Paris poked big holes in these laws. Transparency encourages ethical behavior, as nobody wants to be seen as a cheater in public. Ethical behavior is based on fairness, and on the golden rule: "don't do unto others what you don't want others do unto you!" Allowing others to see what I am doing unto them will keep me away from actually doing it. Shaming is a powerful enforcer of ethical behavior and fairness. While everybody has some secrets they would like nobody to know, keeping the major topics transparent keeps us honest.

10.5. CHIMPANZEE OR BONOBO?

When motivating the benefits of collaboration in Section 7.2 we studied insights of primate researcher Carel van Schaik about orang utans. Comparing the activities of chimpanzees and bonobos gives an even stronger argument for collaborative behavior. When two chimpanzees who do not know each other meet for the first time, they will carefully approach each other, ready to flee or attack at the first sign. Their stress hormones surge, they will do posturing to impress each other, while trying to decide whether to fight or to flee. The story is very different for the closest relatives of the chimpanzees, the bonobos. When two bonobos meet for the first time,[3] their pleasure and trust hormones surge[4] and they will get together in close body contact, sharing food, and maybe engage in sex. Chimpanzees are archetypical competitors; bonobos are collaborators.

Key competitors in the 2016 US presidential elections show similar behavior. Showman extraordinaire and billionaire Donald Trump is a clear chimpanzee, posturing to impress others, raising stress hormones, and trying to close the best deals to #MakeAmericaGreatAgain (that's the Twitter hashtag of his campaign). Donald Trump is the epitome of competition; he despises losers, and fires people at a whim. He does not want to pay taxes, and boasts about having others pay for the billion dollar bankruptcies of his gambling and real estate failures, amassing a billion dollar fortune for himself in the process. He is motivated by being admired and envied.

---

[3]http://www.primates.com/bonobos/bonobosexsoc.html
[4]Staes et al. (2014).

His onetime Democrat competitor, Vermont senator Bernie Sanders, fits much better into bonobo territory. He cares about sustainability, global warming, keeping the world a livable habitat, and providing healthcare for everybody. One of his key proposals is free public education for all. He invites his followers to #feelTheBern (the Twitter hashtag of his campaign). While Trump's campaign is led from the top, Bernie Sanders successfully tapped in the creative energies of the swarm. His website FeelTheBern.org has been developed autonomously by volunteers contributing their design and software development skills for free, without official leadership by his campaign office. His behavior is similar to bonobo culture, showing empathy, caring, and feelings.

While writing this paragraph, I am sitting in a Starbucks in Santiago de Chile's plush Providencia neighborhood. People bustling by are well dressed and busy. The streets are squeaky clean, with a lot of leafy trees and blooming flowers — it's spring in Santiago right now — adding to the nice picture. Contrast this with the neighborhood behind "Plaza de Armas," where streets are gritty and much less clean, and beggars fill the street. While Chile is the most affluent and well-organized of the Latin American countries, its population still seems to be split in two worlds. Providencia is the liberal, optimistic, forward-looking world of "green," where people care about sustainability, global warming, and social responsibility, and bike rentals are everywhere. The area behind "Plaza de Armas" is the seamy, gritty, poor against rich, noisy world of "black," where people stick to the values of the past, and their best hope of escaping poverty is winning the lottery. This pattern shows up all around the world. Whether it is Tokyo, Beijing, San Francisco, New York, London, or Helsinki, there is the contrast between "green" — open for new and "black" — conserving the tradition. Green is where the hip and young want to be; black is where guardians of tradition are. Green people are motivated intrinsically, they derive meaning from what they do, while black people's motivation is extrinsic, their ulterior motive is getting external recognition.

Most religion is black. Catholic priests are not just wearing black, but they are also excellent preservers of the past. More than 1500 years after the Roman Empire collapsed, Rome still is the center of the world — at least the Catholic world. The wealth and riches accumulated in the Vatican museum and Saint Peter's Basilica show of an elite ruling the Western world and extracting tithes from Manila to Santiago and Cape Town to Budapest, investing the money into building among the most splendid palaces of the world. And the Catholic Church is still running strong. Current Pope Francis is doing a masterful job combining black and green, demonstrating perfect swarm-based leadership. In a project where we measured the most influential thought leaders in the world each year for the last four years,[5] Pope Francis has come up as the most inspirational and admired thought leader globally for the last two years. Personally humble, he has given up on living in the pontifical palace, preferring to stay in a modest three-room apartment. He invites climate-change scientists to a summit in Rome, and even extends careful feelers to homosexuals.

------

[5]http://www.huffingtonpost.com/nathan-gardels/world-influential-voices-2015_b_8729486.html

Donald Trump, Bernie Sanders, and Pope Francis have all succeeded in growing a swarm of passionate bees. By showing strong leadership, even without providing any concrete answers, Donald Trump succeeded to lead the crowded camp of Republican US presidential contenders in 2016. Showing a much more nuanced approach, Bernie Sanders combined emotional intelligence and empathy with rotating leadership to get into a neck-to-neck race with Hillary Clinton for the democratic presidential election. But according to our thought leader, coolhunting, humble, honest, and approachable Pope Francis beats them both as a moral and spiritual authority.

10.6. COLLABORATION, HAPPINESS, AND ECONOMIC SUCCESS: SHARED PROSPERITY

Switzerland delivers a strong case in point. According to the 2015 World happiness report[6] it is the happiest country on Earth. While some of its citizens' happiness might come from eating the most chocolate — chocolate containing various chemicals such as theobromine, caffeine, and serotonin that all influence mood positively — there is a deeper link to collaboration and economic success. Switzerland is economically very successful, with a global wealth ranking by GDP among the top 10 wealthiest nations in all country rankings.[7]

It is also a fairly collaborative one, as I can attest. For a start, it does not have a commander-in-chief, it has seven of them. There is no Swiss president, the seven ministers are

---

[6]http://worldhappiness.report
[7]https://en.wikipedia.org/wiki/List_of_countries_by_GDP_(PPP)_per_capita

peers and together, they are the Swiss head of state. They take turns as formal head of state year-by-year, demonstrating rotating leadership at the very top. Compared to the number of inhabitants, Switzerland has a disproportionate share of large multinational companies, which, according to sociologist Francis Fukuyama, is a key indicator of spontaneous sociability.[8] The three largest European companies on the 2015 *Financial Times* Global 500 list of most valuable companies[9] hail from Switzerland. Novartis is number 10 on the list, Nestle number 14, and Roche number 16. The top five companies are all from the United States, with Apple and ExxonMobil leading the list, followed by Berkshire Hathaway, Google, and Microsoft. Fukuyama defines spontaneous sociability as cooperative behavior, and the subordination of personal goals to shared goals — key facets of collaboration. There is one key difference however between Switzerland and the United States, home to by far the most Global 500 most valuable companies: while the United States invests a disproportionate amount of its GDP in its army, Switzerland invests a recognizable share of its GDP in the International Committee of the Red Cross (ICRC). While the mighty US Army has no adversary capable of taking it on in conventional warfare, the ICRC assumes the far less glamorous task of taking care of the victims of war. To be fair, the United States was also the largest payer of ICRC expenses in 2013, the most recent year I was able to find any numbers,[10] with 260 million dollars,

[8]Fukuyama (1995).
[9]http://www.ft.com/intl/indepth/ft500
[10]https://www.icrc.org/eng/assets/files/annual-report/current/icrc-annual-report-financial-overview-2013-eng.pdf (retrieved March 18, 2016)

followed by the United Kingdom with 163 million, and
Switzerland with 120 million. To put this in relationship
with the national GDP, Switzerland invests compared to the
size of its GDP 10 times as much in the ICRC as the United
States. Also, other than the United States which has been
more or less continuously at war somewhere on the world
for the last 200 years, the last aggressive war of Switzerland
was the battle of Marignano in Northern Italy in 1515,
leading to the Swiss declaration of eternal neutrality; the
last time Switzerland was fighting within its own borders
was a civil war in 1847 claiming fewer than 100 lives. For
the last 150 years, collaboration has been trumping over
competition, leading to impressive economic success and
happiness.

Figure 34 illustrates how competition interferes with
the three related building blocks of a positive life: collaboration, economic success, and happiness. As Figure 34
illustrates, competition can interfere with any of the three
building blocks. Overly competitive behavior will negatively impact happiness, economic success, and of course

Figure 34: Relationship between collaboration, economic success, and happiness.

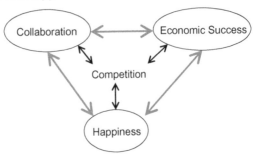

collaboration. A company emphasizing collaboration over competition will have happier employees and higher economic success if it succeeds in channeling the competitive urges of its employees toward collaboration, nurturing a collaborative culture instead. Not "up or out," but "one for all, all for one" should be the goal. The aim is to not let competition interfere, but leverage our competitive urges for better collaboration in competitive collaboration, as has been laid out in this book. Building collective consciousness through empathy and entanglement, and improving collaboration through reflect and reboot will lead to more happiness and economic success.

Emphasis on collaboration instead of competition is nothing new, rather ancient Chinese philosopher Laozi said it all in the 6th century BC, over 2500 years ago.

> *Truthful words are not pleasant,*
> *Pleasant words are not trustworthy;*
> *Those who are good do not dispute,*
> *Those who are disputatious are not good;*
> *Those who know are not learned,*
> *Those who are learned do not know.*
> *The Sage does not store up things,*
> *The more he does for people, the more he has;*
> *The more he gives, the more he gains.*
> *The Way of Heaven,*
> *Is benefitting, not harming.*
> *The Way of the Sage,*
> *Is acting, not contending.*

Chapter 81 of Tao Te Ching *by Laozi, (https://en. wikisource.org/wiki/Translation:Tao_Te_Ching)*

10.7. A COLLECTIVE COLLABORATIVE FUTURE

Congratulations for having read this book so far! By being interested in this new way of conducting business and private life, you already prequalify as a collaborator. You probably knew what you have been reading all along; it's just that the framework described in this book makes the benefits of proactive humble leadership, and shifting emphasis from competition to collaboration measurable and tangible.

While doing close to a hundred projects studying communication and collaboration with many companies, nonprofits, and other organizations over the last 14 years, I found that the managers and leaders who were interested in working with our team probably did not need us, as they were already instinctively doing all the things you have been reading about in this book. For instance, when analyzing start-up entrepreneurs, just the willingness to work with our team was one of the key predictors of their long-term success, as we found when looking at the communication network between software start-up CEOs in Israel, described in Section 9.9: The best predictor of their start-up's survival from 1998 to 2005 was their willingness to answer our survey questions in 1999. My friends Julia Gluesing and Ken Riopelle had a similar anecdotal experience, when in 2006 they proposed to study collaboration within the R&D departments at Ford, GM, and DaimlerChrysler. After initial interest, GM and DaimlerChrysler withdrew from the project, and two years later in 2009 GM and Chrysler went bankrupt. Ford stayed with Julia and Ken's project, studying collaboration in their global R&D department by analyzing its e-mail using the Condor tool mentioned in Section 8.1. Ford got through the 2008–2010 financial crisis on its own, without bankruptcy! While this example is of course anecdotal, it still gives evidence to the point that natural collaborators like Allan Mulally, the CEO of Ford in those critical years, are instinctively applying the principles described in the five-layer model of collaboration shown in Figure 1.

The four principles of social quantum physics introduced in Chapter 3 provide an excellent framework for where we will be heading. Just like quantum physics opened a new way of looking at the mechanics of how elementary particles interact, social quantum physics shows a new way of looking at human interaction and collaboration. The four principles "empathy," "entanglement," "reflect," and "reboot" lay out a roadmap of where a more collaborative future might take us.

In the future, we will have understood the "honest signals" for all these different channels of communication, and by applying entanglement and the Heisenberg uncertainty principle, come to a world of collective awareness through immediate transparent communication.

Science fiction writers have for a long time been predicting a future where artificial intelligence will become smarter than humanity. By now, illustrious pundits[11] such as Stephen Hawking or Elon Musk openly worry that this development might lead to an apocalypse. Such a superhumanly intelligent computer, which potentially has the capability to destroy humanity, could be hijacked by a super villain, or might simply decide there is no need

---

[11]http://time.com/3614349/artificial-intelligence-singularity-stephen-hawking-elon-musk/

for humans. The risk is that either a despot like Kim Jong-un or a terrorist organization like ISIS might program this super-intelligence for their own sinister purpose, to claim world leadership, or that this artificial super-intelligence simply will take over. Science fiction author Isaac Asimov has foreseen this in his Three Laws of Robotics first mentioned in a short story published in 1942, which state that: (1) A robot may not injure a human being or, through inaction, allow a human being to come to harm. (2) A robot must obey the orders given it by human beings except where such orders would conflict with the First Law. (3) A robot must protect its own existence as long as such protection does not conflict with the First or Second Law. As long as artificial super-intelligence obeys Asimov's Three Laws of Robotics, we have little to worry about. Or, as Marvin Minsky said, "Will robots inherit the earth? Yes, but they will be our children."

While it is imaginable that a malicious genius programmer can work around the Three Laws of Robotics, he or she would have to beat the combined intelligence of the rest of the world. The safeguard against malicious super-hackers is transparency. Open knowledge sharing on Stack Overflow, Reddit, Wikipedia, and the many specialized hacker forums allows the collaborative developers of the world to defeat secretive software developers working for Kim Jong-un or ISIS. Chances that ISIS-affiliated programmers succeed in creating an artificial super-intelligence are slim, as the skills of terrorists not really extend too far into software development. Also, the pool of innovative programmers working for Kim Jong-un is quite small compared to the legions of knowledge-sharing software developers in the Western world. To quote again Marvin Minsky, "it's very important to have friends who can solve problems you can't." The benefits of knowledge sharing through open source are leveraged both by individual developers and large corporations like Google, Microsoft, Apple, or IBM, which are open-sourcing a large part of their most advanced algorithms and software. For example, bitcoin would not have been successful if it were not available as open source software, its algorithms accessible to anybody willing to invest the brain time to understand the source code. As open source programmer Eric Raymond says, "given enough eye balls, all bugs are shallow." To take this one step further, the collective intelligence will build global consciousness through entanglement.

In his story "The Last Question" Isaac Asimov describes an increasingly collectively conscious future, where humanity loses innovation to the first superhuman intelligent computer around 2060 (which, on a side note, is slightly after 2045, the date Ray Kurzweil predicts for the singularity — when computers will be capable of improving themselves). According to Asimov's story, in 2060, Multivac, the first self-learning, self-programming, self-improving computer, is incapable of answering the question if the heat death of the universe can be avoided. Over billions of years, an increasingly immortal and genetically engineered humanity asks successions of increasingly more powerful and smarter generations of Multivacs the same question, with the computer always answering "insufficient data for meaningful answer." Trillions of years in the future, our successors, now bodiless and collectively intelligent inhabiting trillions of worlds in many galaxies and merged with the computer — earth and sun have become a white dwarf in the meantime — watches all the stars flicker out. With nobody to answer anymore, the computer finally states: "Let there be light!" And there was light.

MAIN LESSONS LEARNED

- Privacy matters; however, transparency is more important.

- Financial capital frequently gets in the way of social capital.

- It is better to be a bonobo than a chimpanzee.

- Focusing on collaboration instead of competition might not make us richer, but it definitively makes us happier.

BIOGRAPHY

 **Peter A. Gloor** is Research Scientist at the Center for Collective Intelligence at MIT's Sloan School of Management where he leads a project exploring Collaborative Innovation Networks. He is also Founder and Chief Creative Officer of software company galaxyadvisors, a Honorary Professor at University of Cologne, Distinguished Visiting Professor at P. Universidad Católica de Chile, and Honorary Professor at Jilin University, Changchun, China. Earlier, he was a partner with Deloitte and PwC, and a manager at UBS. He got his Ph.D. in computer science from the University of Zurich and was a Post-Doc at the MIT Lab for Computer Science. In his spare time, Peter likes to work on projects bridging the digital divide, enjoy nature, and play the piano.

REFERENCES

Allen, T. J., Gloor, P., Raz, O., Woerner, S., & Fronzetti, A. (2016). The power of knowledge sharing reciprocal relationships for startup success. *Journal of Small Business and Enterprise Development*, 23(3), 636–651.

Allen, T. J., Raz, O., & Gloor, P. (2009). *Does geographic clustering still benefit high tech new ventures? The case of the Cambridge/Boston Biotech cluster.* Working Paper MIT ESD-WP-2009-01.

Apicella, C. L., Marlowe, F. W., Fowler, J. H., & Christakis, N. A. (2012). Social networks and cooperation in hunter-gatherers. *Nature*, 481(7382), 497–501.

Aral, S., Muchnik, L., & Sundararajan, A. (2009). Distinguishing influence-based contagion from homophily-driven diffusion in dynamic networks. *Proceedings of the National Academy of Sciences*, 106(51), 21544–21549.

Arlette Maurer-60 years with Cystic Fibrosis. Retrieved from https://www.youtube.com/watch?v=1UnTkyEVVSs

Axelrod, R., & Hamilton, W. D. (1981). The evolution of cooperation. *Science*, 211(4489), 1390–1396.

Bohm, D. (2004). *On dialogue*. London: Routledge.

Brynjolfsson, E., & McAfee, A. (2014). *The second machine age: work, progress, and prosperity in a time of brilliant technologies*. New York, NY: WW Norton & Company.

Carter, J. R., & Irons, M. D. (1991). Are economists different, and if so, why? *The Journal of Economic Perspectives*, 5(2), 171–177.

Christakis, N. A., & Fowler, J. H. (2011). *Connected: The amazing power of social networks and how they shape our lives*. London: HarperPress.

Collins, R. (2009). *Violence: A micro-sociological theory*. Santa Barbara, CA: Greenwood Publishing Group.

Donnay, G. F., Rankin, S. K., Lopez-Gonzalez, M., Jiradejvong, P., & Limb, C. J. (2014). Neural substrates of interactive musical improvisation: An fMRI study of 'trading fours' in jazz. *PLoS ONE*, 9(2), e88665. doi:10.1371/journal.pone.0088665

Dumont, M., & Provost, M. A. (1999). Resilience in adolescents: Protective role of social support, coping strategies, self-esteem, and social activities on experience of stress and depression. *Journal of Youth and Adolescence*, 28(3), 343–363.

Dunbar, R. (1998). *Grooming, gossip, and the evolution of language*. Cambridge, MA: Harvard University Press.

Felitti, V. J., Anda, R. F., Nordenberg, D., Williamson, D. F., Spitz, A. M., Edwards, V., … Marks, J. S. (1998). Relationship of childhood abuse and household dysfunction to many of the leading causes of death in adults: The adverse childhood experiences (ACE) study.

American Journal of Preventive Medicine, 14(4), 245–258.

Frank, R. H., Gilovich, T., & Regan, D. T. (1993). Does studying economics inhibit cooperation?. *The Journal of Economic Perspectives*, 7(2), 159–171.

Frey, B. S., & Meier, S. (2003). Are political economists selfish and indoctrinated? Evidence from a natural experiment. *Economic Inquiry*, 41(3), 448–462.

Fukuyama, F. (1995). *Trust, the social virtues & the creation of prosperity*. New York, NY: The Free Press.

Gloor, P. A., Oster, D., Raz, O., Pentland, A., & Schoder, D. (2010). The virtual mirror: Reflecting on the social and psychological self to increase organizational creativity. *International Studies of Management & Organization*, 40(2), 74–94.

Gloor, P., Oster, D., & Fischbach, K. (2013). JazzFlow – Analyzing "Group Flow" among Jazz Musicians through "Honest Signals". KI – Artificial Intelligence, 27(1), 37–43.

Granovetter, M. S. (1973). The strength of weak ties. *American Journal of Sociology*, 78, 1360–1380.

New York Times. (2016). How Larry Page's obsessions became Google's business. *New York Times*, January 22. Retrieved from http://www.nytimes.com/2016/01/24/technology/larry-page-google-founder-is-still-innovator-in-chief.html?

http://info.worldbank.org/governance/wgi/index.aspx#reports

http://programmers.stackexchange.com/questions/
160986/is-there-any-benefit-to-participating-on-sites-like-
topcoder-and-or-googlecode

http://quantum-mind.co.uk

http://time.com/3614349/artificial-intelligence-singularity-
stephen-hawking-elon-musk/

http://time.com/3643996/hepatitis-c-drugs/

http://worldhappiness.report

http://www.ft.com/intl/indepth/ft500

http://www.huffingtonpost.com/nathan-gardels/world-
influential-voices-2015_b_8729486.html

http://www.nytimes.com/2015/05/03/magazine/want-a-
steady-income-theres-an-app-for-that.htm

http://www.nytimes.com/2015/11/10/business/dealbook/
ackmans-enigmatic-investment-philosophy.html?nl=
todaysheadlines&emc=edit_th_20151110

http://www.nytimes.com/2016/02/07/health/zika-virus-
brazil-how-it-spread-explained.html

http://www.nytimes.com/2016/02/07/us/as-flint-fought-
to-be-heard-virginia-tech-team-sounded-alarm.html

http://www.primates.com/bonobos/bonobosexsoc.html

https://en.wikipedia.org/wiki/Forex_scandal

https://en.wikipedia.org/wiki/List_of_countries_by_GDP_
(PPP)_per_capita

https://en.wikipedia.org/wiki/Tim_Cook. Accessed
onMarch 26, 2016.

https://en.wikipedia.org/wiki/Wikipedia:List_of_Wikipedians_by_number_of_edits

https://meta.wikimedia.org/wiki/Requests_for_comment/2013_issues_on_Croatian_Wikipedia

https://stats.wikimedia.org/EN/TablesWikipediansEditsGt5.htm

https://www.clintonfoundation.org/blog/2016/01/26/5-things-know-about-living-longer?utm_source=20160129HealthMatters&utm_medium=email&utm_content=20160129&utm_campaign=HealthMatters2016#sthash.QGHV7aJl.dpuf

https://www.icrc.org/eng/assets/files/annual-report/current/icrc-annual-report-financial-overview-2013-eng.pdf. Accessed on March 18, 2016.

https://www.ted.com/talks/charles_limb_your_brain_on_improv?language=en

Jemielniak, D. (2014). *Common knowledge?: An ethnography of Wikipedia*. Stanford, CA: Stanford University Press.

Karlan, D., & Zinman, J. (2011). Microcredit in theory and practice: Using randomized credit scoring for impact evaluation. *Science, 332*(6035), 1278–1284.

Kidane, Y., & Gloor, P. (2007). Correlating temporal communication patterns of the eclipse open source community with performance and creativity. *Computational & Mathematical Organization Theory, 13*(1), 17–27.

Kraft, T., Valdes, L., & Zheng, Y. (2014). Transparency and indirect reciprocity in social responsibility: An incentivized experiment. Available at SSRN 2518627.

Lammers, J., Stapel, D. A., & Galinsky, A. D. (2010). Power increases hypocrisy moralizing in reasoning, immorality in behavior. *Psychological Science*, *21*(5), 737–744.

Lammers, J., Stoker, J. I., Jordan, J., Pollmann, M., & Stapel, D. A. (2011). Power increases infidelity among men and women. *Psychological Science*, *22*(9), 1191–1197.

Leavitt, H. J. (1989). Educating our MBAs: On teaching what we haven't taught. *California Management Review*, *31*(3), 38–50.

Madore, K. P., & Schacter, D. L. (2015). Remembering the past and imagining the future: Selective effects of an episodic specificity induction on detail generation. *The Quarterly Journal of Experimental Psychology*.

Marlowe, F. W., Berbesque, J. C., Barr, A., Barrett, C., Bolyanatz, A., Cardenas, J. C., ... Henrich, N. (2008). More 'altruistic' punishment in larger societies. *Proceedings of the Royal Society of London B: Biological Sciences*, *275*(1634), 587–592.

Nemoto, K., & Gloor, P. (2010). Analyzing cultural differences in collaborative innovation networks by analyzing editing behavior in different-language Wikipedias. Procedia – Social and Behavioral Sciences (Vol. 26), 2011, Proceedings COINs 2010, *Collaborative innovations networks conference*, Savannah, GA, October 7–9.

Nemoto, K., Gloor, P., & Laubacher, R. (2011). Social capital increases efficiency of collaboration among Wikipedia editors, ACM Hypertext 2011. *22nd ACM conference on Hypertext and Hypermedia*, Eindhoven, NL, June 6–9.

Nishi, A., Shirado, H., Rand, D. G., & Christakis, N. A. (2015). Inequality and visibility of wealth in experimental social networks. *Nature, 526*(7573), 426–429.

Nowak, M., & Sigmund, K. (1993). A strategy of win-stay, lose-shift that outperforms tit-for-tat in the Prisoner's Dilemma game. *Nature, 364*(6432), 56–58.

Oosterbeek, H., Sloof, R., & Van De Kuilen, G. (2004). Cultural differences in ultimatum game experiments: Evidence from a meta-analysis. *Experimental Economics, 7*(2), 171–188.

Pentland, A. (2008). *Honest signals – How they shape our world*. Cambridge, MA: MIT Press.

Pentland, A. (2015). *Social physics: How social networks can make us smarter*. New York, NY: Penguin Books.

Piff, P. K., Stancato, D. M., Côté, S., Mendoza-Denton, R., & Keltner, D. (2012). Higher social class predicts increased unethical behavior. *Proceedings of the National Academy of Sciences, 109*(11), 4086–4091.

Pinker, S. (2011). *The better angels of our nature: The decline of violence in history and its causes*. London: Penguin.

Raz, O., & Gloor, P. A. (2007). Size really matters-new insights for start-ups' survival. *Management Science, 53*(2), 169–177.

Ridley, M. (1997). *The origins of virtue: Human instincts and the evolution of cooperation.* London: Penguin.

Satyanath, S., Voigtländer, N., & Voth, H. J. (2013). *Bowling for fascism: Social capital and the rise of the Nazi Party* (No. w19201). National Bureau of Economic Research.

Schwartz, C., Meisenhelder, J. B., Ma, Y., & Reed, G. (2003). *Psychosomatic Medicine, 65,* 778–785.

Seeley, T. D. (2010). *Honeybee democracy.* Princeton, NJ: Princeton University Press.

Shmotkin, D., Blumstein, T., & Modan, B. (2003). Beyond keeping active: Concomitants of being a volunteer in old-old age. *Psychology and Aging, 18*(3), 602.

Sorkin, A. S. (2015). Bill Ackman's enigmatic approach to Valeant pharmaceuticals. *New York Times,* November 9.

Sparrow, B., Liu, J., & Wegner, D. M. (2011). Google effects on memory: Cognitive consequences of having information at our fingertips. *Science, 333*(6043), 776–778.

Staes, N., Stevens, J. M. G., Helsen, P., Hillyer, M., Korody, M., & Eens, M. (2014). Oxytocin and vasopressin receptor gene variation as a proximate base for inter- and intraspecific behavioral differences in bonobos and chimpanzees. *PLoS ONE, 9*(11), e113364. doi:10.1371/journal.pone.0113364

Stossel, J., & Johnson, S. (2007). *Doing good and feeling better.* Retrieved from http://abcnews.go.com/2020/story?id=2685717&page=1

Tong, S. T., Van Der Heide, B., Langwell, L., & Walther, J. B. (2008). Too much of a good thing? The relationship between number of friends and interpersonal impressions on Facebook. *Journal of Computer-Mediated Communication*, *13*(3), 531−549.

Uzzi, B. (1997). Social structure and competition in inter-firm networks: The paradox of embeddedness. *Administrative Science Quarterly*, *42*, 35−67.

Van Doren, C. L. (1992). *A history of knowledge: Past, present, and future*. New York, NY: Random House Digital, Inc.

Wagner, C. S., Horlings, E., Whetsell, T. A., Mattsson, P., & Nordqvist, K. (2015). Do Nobel Laureates create prize-winning networks? An analysis of collaborative research in physiology or medicine. *PloS ONE*, *10*(7), e0134164.

Wang, S., Lo, D., & Jiang, L. (2013). An empirical study on developer interactions in stackoverflow. Singapore Management University, 18−22 March.

Wilson, E. O. (2012). *The social conquest of earth*. New York, NY: WW Norton & Company.

Yap, A. J., Wazlawek, A. S., Lucas, B. J., Cuddy, A. J., & Carney, D. R. (2013). The ergonomics of dishonesty the effect of incidental posture on stealing, cheating, and traffic violations. *Psychological Science*, *24*(11), 2281−2289.

Young, S. M., & Pinsky, D. (2006). Narcissism and celebrity. *Journal of Research in Personality*, *40*(5), 463−471.

INDEX

W   Take?

returned or ren~
ne r'   Approach
—   To
N   u Conservati n

What Will It Take?

A Deeper Approach To Nature Conservation

Iain Scott

HPT Books

First published in 1999
by HPT Books

HPT Books is part of
The Human Potential Trust
The Oasis
Highbrook Lane
West Hoathly
Sussex RH19 4PL
England

Proceeds from the sale of this book, including
the author's royalties, will be used for charitable work.

ISBN 1-899131-03-5

Cartoons by Jake Fern
Cover photograph by Iain Scott:
Mirror Lake, Yosemite National Park, California

Typeset by Jenny England, Woking, Surrey
Printed and bound by Biddles Ltd, Guildford, Surrey

Contents

This book is dedicated to Niel Briers-Louw
- a South African farmer and friend -
who knows how to be thoughtful, caring, and giving.

And also to James Bennett, aged 9;
dreams of the future can come true with lots of hard work.

Acknowledgements

Thank you to everyone who read and commented on the draft manuscript.

Special thanks to my colleagues Jake Fern for drawing the cartoons, Charlie Budd for his assistance with checking facts and figures, and Jonathan Brauner for always being willing to help whenever needed. Sarah, my wife and colleague, worked hard to get the manuscript ready - yet another expression of her love for nature.

Joni Mitchell kindly granted permission to quote the lyrics of her song *Big Yellow Taxi*.

Introduction

Most people are now generally aware of the damage being done to the environment. It is widely known that countless species are endangered. Rainforests are being cut down at an alarming rate. There is pollution of the air, water, and land. High above us, holes in the ozone layer are threatening health. Our climate might be changing. Environmental organisations such as Greenpeace, Friends of the Earth, and the Worldwide Fund for Nature (WWF) have become household names. We have been asked to help save the whales and urged to recycle our drink cans. We are "environmentally aware". Furthermore, today's children are learning about the environment at school and are often talked about as being the generation which will make a difference.

But will they? And does our "environmental awareness" really amount to much? How are the various organisations spending the funds donated to save our natural world? Can we always trust what they tell us? These are important questions which need to be asked and answered.

Giant pandas cannot survive without bamboo. Hippopotamuses need to spend the day submerged in rivers, lakes, pools, or mud hollows to keep cool. The seeds of certain plants have to pass through the digestive system of a bird or other animal before they can germinate. Elephants require a lot of space. Fish will die if the waters in which they live become grossly polluted. Migratory birds depend upon over-wintering destinations. Life is interconnected. Ecosystems are complex networks. If we destroy or alter an ecosystem, we threaten some or all of those species within it. Through upsetting the natural balance of our planet, we might also be risking human survival. So, in considering the environmental issue, we cannot afford to mess about. We must clearly identify and understand what is happening, then act accordingly.

The spirit or ethic of the conservation movement must be admired and applauded. It represents a growing awareness which has arisen from the perception that something is wrong and needs to be corrected. It also represents a hope that solutions can be found and it signifies the beginning of actual change. Many thousands of individuals all over the world are trying to make a stand – wanting to save our endangered wildlife, wild places, and overall environment. More and more of the general public are adding their voices and support to the call for environmental protection. Governments are starting to listen.

So far, however, we have merely made the first step or two towards restoring a safe and balanced environment for everyone and everything. The conservation movement is still in its infancy. Most organisations exaggerate their few successes and limited progress – conveniently ignoring their many failures. The mainstream conservation movement is seriously in danger of losing its way, seemingly unaware of (or perhaps unwilling to formally acknowledge) the fundamental factors which are causing our environmental crisis. We now need to gain a more mature awareness of what is required to prevent further problems and, where possible, to correct the damage already done. The present level of "environmental awareness" is an important beginning – a step or two in the right direction – but it is not yet anywhere near enough.

This book is a plea for a deeper approach to nature conservation. The current shallow approach cannot succeed in achieving its core objectives; a few battles may be won, but the overall war against environmental disaster will be lost. Therefore, a new attitude and a wider understanding is required. A thorough re-consideration is urgently needed.

The contents of *What Will It Take?* will appeal to a wide range of readers: To those members of the general public who are concerned about saving endangered species, stopping further habitat destruction, and achieving clean air, water, and land so that we can all thrive without unnecessary threats to our health. To those who are actively working for the environment – whether their involvement is at local, national, or international level. To anyone else who is campaigning for a better world – because the issue of nature conservation is intrinsically linked to the need for social change. To decision-makers in government and business – as the need for this deeper approach is undeniable and they will sooner or later have to adjust their policies accordingly. To parents who want their children to grow up being responsible, caring, and safe. To teachers and their students – who realise that today's future will quickly become tomorrow's present.

This is not a technical book which might only interest environmental specialists. It is simply written and hopefully easy to read. My words are intended to appeal to both your head and your heart – rather than being too intellectual or else playing the emotional game regardless of rational thinking. My aim is to help broaden perspective and focus minds on what it will take to save our planet's wildlife and natural environment.

I never try to be politically correct. Instead, my preference is always to rely on straightforwardness – to tell it the way I see it. As you will soon discover, my views are not conventionally "green". Nor are they typically anti-industry or anti-progress.

Some people differentiate between "conservationists" and "environmentalists". They do so to clarify a particular emphasis that one person or group may have as different from another's. I choose to use both terms as meaning the same. A few intellectual experts might frown on this, but the average reader will hopefully benefit from my simpler terminology.

At the heart of my reasoning is the need to challenge human selfishness and greed. A self-orientated psychology is common to *Homo sapiens*. This is the "me, me, me" or "I want more" mentality. Selfish behaviour is nowadays increasing, both in complexity and opportunity for expression. Few would disagree that selfishness is widespread and a root cause of many environmental problems. Nevertheless, the extent of selfishness is usually underestimated. It is also a factor frequently overlooked when forming strategies to combat what is going wrong in the world.

Although I am critical of a lot of what is presently happening, my criticism is constructive. I am neither an optimist nor a pessimist. Optimists too often rely on hope, with no actual basis for their optimism. And pessimists are usually little more than optimists with experience. In contrast, I am a realist. It is always best to face the facts, no matter how undesirable or uncomfortable they might be. At present, human beings have become intelligent – but not yet fully civilised. We need to evolve further.....to develop an alternative to our current dysfunctional situation. I have no doubt that a real, logical, and practical solution exists to our many problems. The chapters ahead will explain why a different attitude to nature conservation is needed – and make clear the substance of this deeper approach.

Iain Scott
Sussex, December 1998

SECTION ONE: BEGINNINGS

1

Something is wrong

The lyrics of this song, written in 1970, were true then and are still highly relevant now:

> *They paved paradise*
> *And put up a parking lot*
> *With a pink hotel, a boutique*
> *And a swinging hot spot*
> *Don't it always seem to go*
> *That you don't know what you've got*
> *Till it's gone*
> *They paved paradise*
> *And put up a parking lot*
>
> *They took all the trees*
> *And put them in a tree museum*
> *And they charged the people*
> *A dollar and a half just to see 'em*
> *Don't it always seem to go*
> *That you don't know what you've got*
> *Till it's gone*
> *They paved paradise*
> *And put up a parking lot*
>
> *Hey farmer farmer*
> *Put away that DDT now*
> *Give me spots on my apples*

15

> *But leave me the birds and the bees*
> *Please!*
> *Don't it always seem to go*
> *That you don't know what you've got*
> *Till it's gone*
> *They paved paradise*
> *And put up a parking lot*
>
> *Late last night*
> *I heard the screen door slam*
> *And a big yellow taxi*
> *Took away my old man*
> *Don't it always seem to go*
> *That you don't know what you've got*
> *Till it's gone*
> *They paved paradise*
> *And put up a parking lot*

Big Yellow Taxi by Joni Mitchell

i. Mercury poisoning

One of the first signs that something was wrong occurred during the late 1950s at Minamata Bay in the south of Japan. Local cats began behaving strangely; they staggered about, then died. Shortly afterwards, humans started having shaking fits and developed paralysis. Babies were born brain damaged and blind. By 1960, over 70 people were dead and thousands of others seriously ill.

A chemical company in Minamata Bay was suspected, as it pumped industrial waste including tonnes of mercury into the sea. Investigating scientists confirmed that the fish were absorbing mercury into their bodies – and cats and people who ate the fish were being poisoned. The company denied responsibility and did not seem to care; they continued to pump mercury into the sea for another 10 years. As a country, Japan was determined to catch up with the fast-growing wealthy economy of the United States of America.

In 1997, Minamata Bay was declared safe to fish in once again. Since the 1970s, the bay had had a giant net across it to stop fish entering; this has now finally been removed. Meanwhile, mercury pollution continues elsewhere in the world in countries as far apart as Turkey and Brazil.

ii. DDT

Dichlorodiphenyltrichloroethane (DDT) was extensively used in the 1950s and 1960s as a chemical insecticide. Evidence emerged that DDT became concentrated as it progressed up the food chain. Levels in rivers and estuaries might have been low, for example, but the small organisms such as plankton and shrimps contained higher levels; fish which ate them had even higher levels of the chemical and fish-eating birds accumulated still more. The egg-shells of affected birds became thinner as a result, causing reproductive failure.

Brown pelicans on an island off the California coast were amongst those failing to breed. Researchers were shocked to see that out of 12,000 nesting attempts, just two youngsters were produced. Almost all the eggs had been crushed by the weight of the incubating parent birds due to the thinness of the shells caused by DDT poisoning.

Following an earlier voluntary ban, Britain officially banned DDT in 1984 – yet, hypocritically, exports of this dangerous chemical rose from 1,840 kg to 125,503 kg. The USA ban on its use dates back to 1972, but exports of DDT continued totalling millions of kilograms per year.

iii. The seal hunt

Photographs and documentary film of the annual Canadian harp seal hunt first provoked worldwide public concern in 1964. Harrowing bloody images showed hunters bludgeoning newborn whitecoat seal pups to death. These baby seals were even being skinned alive in front of their mothers. Here was a clear case of humans brutalising hundreds of thousands of helpless animals, motivated by greed and self-interest.

The Canadian government supported the sealing industry. They tried to censor the world's media and intimidate animal welfare organisations who wanted to monitor or protest against the hunt. Throughout the 1960s and 1970s, this resulted in many confrontations between the police and sealers on one side and journalists, photographers, film crews, and activists on the other. Protesters tried to shield the bodies of seal pups with their own, only to be quickly arrested. Other activists sprayed harmless dye on the animals to make the pelts unmarketable. Meanwhile, over two million whitecoat seal pups were killed.

The actress Brigitte Bardot went out on the ice with the protesters. In the middle of her press conference, sealers responded to the French sex-symbol by throwing the bloody carcass of a freshly-skinned seal pup at her.

In the early 1980s, European Union countries banned imports of whitecoat furs – effectively ending the commercial hunt of these baby seals. But the slaughter did not stop. Hunters then concentrated on "beaters" (pups around 25 days old) and older seals.

In 1996, the Canadian government agreed to a killing quota of 250,000 harp seals; (by 1998, the annual quota had risen to 285,000). This political decision to increase the hunt was in response to a collapse of the North West Atlantic stocks of cod and other fish in 1992. Many fishermen blamed harp seals. Scientists from 15 countries insisted that overfishing by humans was to blame, adding that the Atlantic cod constitutes less than 2–3% of a harp seal's diet. On this occasion, the scientific view was conveniently ignored. One product of the hunt in particular has "excellent" economic value: seal penises, which are in great demand in Asia for use as aphrodisiacs. Sealers have reportedly been offered twice as much for a male carcass as a female one.

Whether seals are killed for their fur, meat, or penises is irrelevant. And the big question is not whether harp seals could withstand an increased hunt; they almost certainly could, as they are a common species. Rather, we need to examine the criteria by which the killing of wildlife is justified, and think about who decides what these are. We should specifically ask ourselves if the currently fashionable theory of "sustainable use of wildlife" is ethical.

The harp seal is not the first animal to be extensively hunted in Atlantic Canada. The Atlantic walrus was hunted to extinction from all areas south of Labrador by the mid-1800s. The sea mink was hunted to extinction by 1900. The grey seal was hunted so severely that this population was believed to be extinct in 1949, although it has since recovered. The great auk was hunted to extinction by the mid-1800s. The Labrador duck was hunted to extinction by 1875. Fewer than 1000 harlequin ducks remain in eastern North America; numbers continue to decline, probably as a result of hunting, despite the species being classified as endangered.

iv. Ashtrays

On New Year's Day, 1978, the dead body of a male gorilla was found in Rwanda's forest undergrowth. The young silver-back gorilla had been repeatedly stabbed with spears. His head and both hands had been hacked off and carried away.

This gruesome story made news headlines worldwide. This was a famous gorilla, called Digit, who had featured in many documentaries and articles about Dian Fossey's work in Rwanda with the endangered mountain gorillas. Digit had also been used by the Rwandan tourist bureau; the caption on a poster read "Come to meet him in Rwanda".

The poachers were soon caught. Why had they mutilated the gorilla's body? The hands were to be made into ashtrays and the skull into a trophy for sale to tourists. Seven months later, two more gorillas from Digit's family group were found similarly killed and mutilated.

Two decades later, according to the Dian Fossey Gorilla Fund, no fewer than eight mountain gorillas were deliberately killed by humans in 1995. Up to 10 more were shot by soldiers in May 1997.

Returning to 1995, one of the winning entries in the Wildlife Photographer of the Year competition was of a lowland gorilla head, cut off and lying in a bowl on a kitchen shelf next to a bunch of bananas. The Swiss photographer, Karl Ammann, was staying in a village in southern Cameroon when he learned that a local man had just shot a female gorilla. The animal had been killed for the police chief of the next village, who had supplied the rifle and ammunition. As payment, the hunter was allowed to keep the gorilla's head and one of her arms.

v. Eggs

In 1978, a regular visitor to the British Museum's ornithological department at Tring in Hertfordshire was searched by the security guards as he was about to leave. He had nearly two dozen rare birds' eggs hidden underneath his loose-fitting trousers.

The man had been visiting the museum for over two years, often several times each week. Investigations revealed that he had been steadily stealing from the national reference collection throughout this period. Museum staff were shocked at the scale of the theft. A total of 30,000 eggs had been taken!

Unfortunately, hardly any of the rare eggs were recovered. The thief was a major trader in the egg-collectors' black market and he had already sold most of his plunder. Many of the eggs came from birds now endangered or extinct and so were irreplaceable. Collectors and thieves will more usually rob birds' nests of "live" eggs in the wild.

Another part of the wildlife market trades in birds for falconry. High prices are known to be paid by rich Arabs for rare species. The thieves and smugglers seem not to care that a bird is endangered – other than the fact that this increases its value. The financial rewards of such crimes often outweigh the risk of fines or even possible imprisonment if caught.

vi. Oil spill

There have been a number of publicised cases of oil spillage accidents at sea during the past few decades. Most memorable is perhaps that of the Exxon *Valdez*. In March 1989, approximately 10 million gallons of crude oil spilt from the Exxon *Valdez* tanker into Prince William Sound, Alaska. Some of the huge oil slick travelled more than 400 miles. About 1,500 miles of coastline were affected.

By mid-1990, 35,000 dead sea birds of 89 species had actually been found. Estimates for the total number of sea birds killed – 600,000 – were based on this figure. Also found dead were 10,000 sea otters, 16 whales, and 147 bald eagles. Only 25% of migratory salmon returned to the area the next year to spawn; the spawning grounds of black cod and herring were also severely affected. I especially remember seeing on the TV news a devastated wildlife ranger collecting up the barely-recognisable corpses of sea otters; a year before, I had personally spent many hours watching and photographing these fascinating and playful creatures at Monterey in California.

Investigations later revealed that the tanker was being piloted illegally by the third mate at the time of the accident. The captain's blood tested positive for significant amounts of alcohol; he was sacked by Exxon and prosecuted by the authorities. It took 10 hours until the first oil containment booms and other equipment arrived; by then, much of the oil had dispersed over too large an area to be effectively controlled. Exxon eventually had to spend US$2 billion on a lengthy clean-up operation – and still more on legal damages awarded to local people.

2

A continuing – and possibly worsening – situation

i. Extinction

Extinction is forever. This is a sobering thought and a grim reality. Once a species is extinct, we cannot do anything to help it. It is gone. Numerous extinctions have occurred since life began. The dinosaurs are the best-known examples of this. But there is a difference between the natural process of extinction and human-caused extinction. Natural extinctions have always left space for new species to evolve and flourish – whereas the current human-dominated situation does not. The diversity of life is being reduced and therefore lost.

After four decades of modern conservation effort, our environmental crisis is continuing; indeed, it seems to be getting worse. Edward O. Wilson, the Harvard University conservation biologist, cautiously estimates that human-caused species extinction accelerated from approximately 1,000 species per year in the 1970s to more than 27,000 species per year by the early 1990s. Sandra Postel, an academic who contributed to the 1992 Worldwatch Institute report, estimated species extinction to be 140 per day – two times greater than Wilson's estimate.

Another scientific study, published in 1997 by Jennifer Hughes, Gretchen Daily, and Paul Ehrlich, looked at the same question of species extinction but also went further. Estimates of current extinction rates are largely based on species-area relationships and the rate of habitat loss due to deforestation. They accepted a very cautious estimated rate of tropical deforestation of 0.8% per year (whilst noting that a more accurate rate is probably 2%) and assumed that there are 14 million species globally with two-thirds of all species existing in tropical rainforests. (Other people think there could be as many as 30 million species in total.) Their calculations reveal that tropical forest biodiversity is declining by roughly 14,000 to 40,000 species per year – or two to five species per hour. They go on to estimate that there are about 200 genetically-distinct populations per species (a total of 1.1 to 6.6 billion wildlife populations globally). Of these, 16 million populations per year, or approximately 1,800 per hour, are being exterminated *in tropical forests alone.* This loss of population diversity is extremely worrying and suggests that future rates of species extinction might be three to eight times higher than current figures, as the overall abundance of biodiversity in nature is presently being severely reduced.

Sceptics have argued that we do not know exactly how many species are becoming extinct. We still cannot even be sure about the total number of species in existence. But does this really matter? We must, of course, be cautious whilst there is uncertainty – though surely a best-judgement means of assessing the situation is sufficient in this instance, as there can be no doubt that humans are actually destroying huge areas of habitat such as tropical rainforest. If a house was burning down, would you wait until you knew the exact list of contents before calling the fire brigade? Excessive caution can be misplaced and irresponsible.

One in four of our modern medicines owes its origin to the properties of plant species. The most commonly quoted example is Madagascar's rosy periwinkle. Two drugs have been derived from this wild plant and are used to great effect in the treatment of cancer. Whereas a child suffering from leukaemia in 1960 only had about one chance in five of remission, this has now increased to four chances in five – largely due to the medicine discovered from the rosy periwinkle. Commercial sales from this single discovery have been calculated as being US$200 million per year in the USA alone. A lesser known example is the contraceptive pill, which was derived from a West African forest plant.

Worldwide, the commercial value of all plant-based prescription drugs is approximately US$40 billion per year. We have yet to analyse the biochemical properties of most wild plant species.....yet we are recklessly destroying them.

ii. Pandas

The Worldwide Fund for Nature (WWF) was founded in 1961 (when it was then known as the World Wildlife Fund). WWF boasts that it "raises and spends more money on the conservation of wildlife than any other organisation in the world." As you most probably know, WWF's logo is a panda.

Most researchers think there are between 1,200 and 1,500 giant pandas in the wild. This is higher than the commonly quoted figure of 1,000 – but the difference is due to the inaccuracy of past censuses rather than any actual increase in the population. Unfortunately, the remaining pandas are fragmented in 24 small populations of between 10 to 80 individuals. So the loss of even one panda is critical.

Deforestation was so severe between 1975 and 1985 that some 50% of the pandas' habitat disappeared. Poaching now appears to be the biggest threat; £6,000 has been known to be paid for a single pelt in countries such as Taiwan, Hong Kong, and Japan. In 1988, one search of villages in the Sichuan Province of China uncovered 146 pelts. The Chinese government has recently given long jail sentences to poachers. But pandas are still dying due to poaching of other animals – many of which are highly prized as ingredients of traditional medicine. The traps which snare other mammals also kill pandas.

Chinese efforts have largely concentrated on captive-breeding, often using tiny concrete cages. Huge amounts of money have been spent on building breeding centres and monitoring stations, together with all the additional expenses of staff and equipment. This has resulted in there being more facilities for captive pandas than there are pandas in captivity.

In America and Europe, giant pandas are big business for zoos. No other animal is more popular with visitors. The exhibition of one panda by the Toledo Zoo in Ohio during 1988 was calculated to have brought the zoo an extra £2.2 million, for example, as well as £51 million profit for the city due to increased tourism. The Chinese authorities are well aware of this "panda power" appeal and seem happy to arrange panda loans for about a million US dollars per year. During 1995, a female called Yan Yan was rented to Berlin Zoo. The loan coincided with Yan Yan's narrow window of fertility – female pandas are only fertile for 48–72 hours each year – thereby losing any chance of her mating back in China. Yan Yan arrived at Berlin Zoo on April 14th 1995 and is to stay there until the spring of the year 2000, "unless a new agreement is worked out before that date."

There has been a relatively poor record of breeding giant pandas in captivity. And many of the babies produced have failed to survive for longer than a year. The fact is that pandas have died faster in zoos and so-called breeding centres than they have been able to reproduce. They have been taken from the wild and so far there has not been a single reintroduction. Indeed, the financial incentives mentioned above mean that wild young pandas have frequently been "rescued" because they are often discovered alone – even though research has shown that mothers will leave their babies for up to 52 hours whilst they forage. So, not surprisingly, the majority of pandas in captivity began their life in the wild.

WWF, in order to become the first foreign conservation organisation in China, agreed to fund the Wolong Breeding Centre at the cost of £1 million. Further money has been spent on a variety of other questionable construction projects. The giant panda continues to be endangered.

iii. Rhinos

The rhino has existed on Earth for more than 40 million years. There are five species: the black rhino and white rhino range throughout Africa; the Sumatran rhino, great Indian one-horned rhino, and Javan rhino inhabit Asia. Since the early 1960s, documentary film makers and conservation groups have been telling us that all rhino species are seriously endangered. As rhinos – like the giant panda – are amongst the "popular" animals whose plight has been publicised time after time after time, surely the situation has now improved? Unfortunately, it has not.

For every 100 rhinos living in the early 1970s, only three remain today – a terrible decline of 97%. This is despite an international trade ban in rhino products since 1977. In Zimbabwe, for example, black rhinos decreased in numbers from about 2000 in 1989 to just 263 in 1995.

Poaching has been the main cause of the problem. Rhino horn is used in powdered form for herbal medicines in Asia and carved into handles for ornamental daggers in Yemen. One kilogram in weight sells for approximately US$20,000 and up to US$60,000 on the street, making even a single rhino horn valuable and a quick source of making money. Taiwanese authorities claimed that horn was available in less than 1% of pharmacies during the early 1990s, yet investigators found rhino parts in 79% of the shops they visited.

In the early 1990s, a number of conservationists believed that the dehorning of rhinos would help deter poachers. The idea sounded simple and it generated a lot of publicity. WWF and others were keen to provide funding. Dehorning is expensive and it has to be repeated annually due to the horn regrowth. It is a risky process which might result in the death of an animal from stress associated with drug immobilisation. On the positive side, some argued that the removed rhino horn could be sold – subject to a change in the CITES agreement (Convention on International Trade in Endangered Species) – thereby generating additional funds for conservation. But it seems that dehorning has been a failure. In Zimbabwe's Hwange National Park, 83 out of 85 rhinos were killed by poachers within six months during 1993. The poachers merely cut out whatever horn was left.

Furthermore, research in 1994 suggested that dehorned rhinos were less able to protect themselves or their offspring.

South African private game reserves seem to have done the most to safeguard the white and black rhinos. They have created intensive protection zones using fencing and armed guards. Labour is cheap and the private reserve owners take a hard approach towards anyone suspected of poaching. However, many of the poor people are alienated by this tough business approach and resentment has been increasing.

The Asian species have the lowest numbers of all. The Javan rhino is precariously clinging onto existence, with about 50 surviving in Java and another 10 or so in Vietnam. The Sumatran rhino is an elusive animal, rarely seen; the world's population is estimated to be between 250 and 500. There may be up to 2,000 great Indian one-horned rhinos in India and Nepal. Chitwan National Park in Nepal has seen an increase during the past decade and the current population could be as high as 500; problems exist, however, between local farmers living next to the national park and the rhinos which forage at night amongst the cultivated crops.

iv. Grand Canyon

America's Grand Canyon National Park is world famous, with some 5 million visitors each year. Wildlife here must surely be safe from human activity. Wrong. In 1996, two dozen mule deer were shot by park rangers. Appalling? They thought so, too. The rangers didn't want to do it. The mule deer were sickly, weakened, and starving. Why? Because tourists were feeding them, despite signs and leaflets asking them not to. These deer became habituated to human food and consumed plastic bags, food wrappers, and plastic twine along with the biscuits and potato crisps.

Autopsies revealed that the deer's stomachs were clogged with ingested rubbish. In some cases an astonishing

3–5lbs of plastic obstructed the animal's digestive system. Food could not be absorbed and the deer were starving even while they ate. The park rangers pleaded with visitors for help, saying: "Don't make us do a job we hate doing."

Mule deer, admittedly, are not endangered. But this small and sickening example nonetheless illustrates the current limitations of so-called "environmental awareness" within a generally educated human population. Though obviously motivated to visit places of great natural beauty, and usually thrilled to see wildlife such as mule deer, many people are still ignorant of their own behaviour and its impact on nature.

LESSON 1: THE DANGERS OF A WINDY DAY

"Going for a walk on a windy day isn't what it used to be."

v. Rainforests

Tropical rainforests used to cover about 14% of the land around the equator. More than half of this has been destroyed in the past 30 years or so and the clearance is continuing – at an alarming rate of 2% per year. 150,000 square kilometres are being cleared annually – equivalent to the size of Florida – with an area as large again being

28

severely altered or disrupted through excessive logging. There is a real danger that most of our tropical rainforests will disappear during the next few decades.

The destruction of natural habitat also means the loss of animal species. Tropical rainforests provide a home for approximately two-thirds of all the world's species of plants and animals. As well as causing the extinction of unique species and a reduction in biodiversity, destroying these huge areas of forest threatens to disrupt the future of the whole planet. The leaves of trees and other plants absorb carbon dioxide and release oxygen during the process of photosynthesis; tropical rainforests have been described as being the world's "lungs". Rainforests also help stabilise global weather patterns and they remove excess carbon dioxide which plays an important part in regulating the greenhouse effect.

The majority of primates live in tropical rainforests. One of the best-known is the orang-utan. Originally found throughout South-east Asia, the orang-utan now survives as two sub-species on the islands of Borneo and Sumatra. Numbers of this great ape have seriously declined to no more than 30,000 due to destruction of their forest habitat by permanent agriculture, mining, and mechanised logging. There is also illegal trafficking for the pet trade and to supply circuses and zoos. Orang-utans have one of the slowest reproduction rates of all primates; a new mother will not give birth again for up to eight years. They are intelligent and gentle, with individuals displaying unique personalities. If the fight to save the orang-utan's habitat is lost, thousands of other species are likely to perish as well; what is home to one, is home to many.

vi. Seas

More than two-thirds of the world's surface is covered by seas and oceans. These huge areas of water contain an amazing variety of life. The oceans help to regulate our global climate, and the algae they contain produce over half of the oxygen which we and other animals breathe.

And yet we use the seas and oceans as an apparently never-ending dump. Every day, ships throw more than 5 million items of waste into the sea. Annually, an estimated one million sea birds and 100,000 marine mammals and sea turtles suffer cruel deaths as a result of being entangled in, or through ingesting, plastic garbage. I have personally seen, for example, a young penguin helplessly caught up in the discarded plastic rings once used to hold together a six-pack of beer cans; fortunately, this particular animal was rescued and the potentially lethal rubbish cut away. Every year, three times as much rubbish is dumped into the world's oceans as the weight of fish caught.

"We're saved! Civilisation must be near."

Each year, about 80–100 million tonnes of fish – which are amongst the last wild animals to be extensively hunted across the world – are caught and killed. Those caught in trawl nets are often crushed to death under the weight of the catch. Fish that are still alive by the time they reach the decks of the fishing boat either suffocate or are disembowelled with a gutting knife. The fishing nets also catch dolphins, porpoises, small whales, sharks, diving sea birds, shellfish, crabs, starfish, and many other creatures – as well as other species of fish which are unwanted. Thousands of miles of drift gill nets are still set, for example, which kill an estimated 1,000 dolphins and 3,000 sharks every day. 70% of the world's fisheries are now officially in a state of collapse due to over-exploitation.

vii. Coral reefs

Coral reefs are the most biologically diverse marine ecosystems on Earth. 93,000 species have so far been identified living on and around coral reefs, but there are probably many more. Reefs are home to a third of all known species of fish, with a density 100 times greater than the ocean average. The rate for coral growth is very slow, about one centimetre per year; human hair typically grows 30 times as fast.

At least 10% of the world's coral reefs have already been destroyed and a further 30% are heading towards being irreversibly damaged. Specific problems include fishing with explosives and cyanide, the dumping of sewage and other pollutants, sediment runoff from land development which smothers the reefs, tourist boats dropping anchors together with visitors trampling on the reefs, and collection of coral for souvenirs and aquarium decorations.

3

Myth vs. reality

i. Are you following like sheep?

Be prepared to do your own thinking. This is one of several messages I hope you will get from this book. The alternative to doing your own thinking is to follow like sheep.

Most people like to think that they do think for themselves and may resent being referred to as sheep-like. Those who strongly identify with being "green" might be especially offended; after all, haven't such individuals already challenged conventional wisdom and switched to an alternative way of thinking? Perhaps contrary to what many like to believe, the reality is that very few people actually choose or know how to do their own thinking. Human beings are vulnerable to mass conditioning.

There is a strong tendency to conform and identify with one group or another. People generally feel most comfortable by taking sides on an issue. There is safety and companionship in numbers. Someone is usually "for" or "against" a particular idea – unless, of course, they can't be bothered. Most human beings are irrational to a surprisingly high degree. They often fail to take into account all the relevant factors, especially when making complex decisions. Instead, it is common for them to be influenced by what makes the deepest impression at the time or perhaps by what first comes to mind. They go on what knowledge, suggestions, or suspicions are available – frequently failing to seek out additional information. There is a knee-jerk reaction.....an inability to suspend judgement. Existing biases are almost always perpetuated. It is comparatively rare to find an individual who is consistently doing his or her own thinking, instead of merely following the herd.

It is therefore common to find that large numbers of people believe something which might be a myth rather than reality. We are encouraged to conform to what is "supposed to be". Assumptions are thereby rarely challenged and so become accepted as "truth". People generally cling to their existing beliefs and opinions, sometimes desperately, rather than facing the fact that they might be wrong.

ii. One movement or many?

The general public usually assume that the conservation movement is united, with everyone more or less in agreement against a common enemy. Actually, this is not the case. The various environmental organisations differ enormously in their aims, in what they accept as true or relevant, and in their tactical approach.

To begin with, there is a wide range of motivations. Many wish to preserve wild places for human recreation. As places of beauty for relaxation. As places to be physical – perhaps to hike, ride a bicycle, or go rock climbing. As places to photograph or paint. As places in which to go fishing, hunt an elephant or lion, or perhaps shoot a few ducks. As places to enjoy their bird-watching hobby. Others might want to restrict human access, declaring an area of wilderness solely for use as a scientific reserve for study and research. Some believe that human development has gone too far and wish to see special areas set aside for nature itself, regardless of human loss or gain. Still others may be motivated by money, aware that certain regions have a high appeal to tourism and therefore represent a lucrative financial opportunity.

Additional motivations are common closer to home. A growing number of people and groups are sparked into action by what is happening in their neighbourhood, perhaps as a reaction to their personal misfortune. It could be the threat of having a new rubbish dump or motorway in their own backyard. Or people's environmental concern might be triggered by their children suffering from asthma, blaming increased rates of local traffic pollution. Others could be scared by technology which they do not fully understand, such as the perceived threat of a nearby nuclear power station or the genetic engineering of food.

Many people have become active in the conservation movement as a means to develop their own careers. Environmental consultants have sprung up in recent years as fast as daffodils in spring, realising that "green" concerns represent a profitable business opportunity. Other commercial ventures have focused on the marketing of "green" products. Scientific researchers eagerly looking for their next grant have been quick to corner a significant part of the conservation pound or dollar, usually motivated by personal ambition rather than an altruistic passion for establishing factual objectivity. Zoos have likewise jumped on the bandwagon, under criticism and thus desperate to update their old public image of being a place to visit for light entertainment; their new face is supposedly as a modern Noah's ark, offering captive-breeding and educational facilities. Various charitable organisations have emerged, not least as a way for those who run them to enjoy a paid career in conservation. Even politicians have seen the benefits to be gained via media coverage and increased votes by establishing themselves as being apparently pro-environmental.

So motivation within the various parts of the conservation movement differs greatly. What each accepts as true and relevant likewise widely differs. There are those whose concern extends only as far as stopping a new road proposal from going ahead, because it will interrupt their quiet countryside existence (and no doubt lower the value of their property). Others perceive that nothing short of a radical change of lifestyle is necessary. At one extreme of the debate, it is seen as enough to merely legislate a bit more and tighten up on existing regulations. The other side argues this will achieve very little and that a major re-think of modern economic development is required. The many groups and organisations therefore each have a particular environmental philosophy – which might range from being shallow to deep, narrow in concern to broad, light green to dark green.

Tactical approach also varies considerably. There are those who take a confrontational stance, whilst others choose to work in closer partnership with the perpetrators of environmental damage – i.e. "the opposition". Some will concentrate on campaigns which appear to be clear-cut and dramatic, so as to grab the headlines. Others rarely or never attempt to get media exposure. Most organisations by and large play it safe, wishing to appeal for support to the bland majority. The larger groups often seek to win approval from the establishment and thereby, it is hoped, eventually influence policy-making. Other groups – usually more sceptical, impatient, and/or frustrated – take to the streets or woods in bursts of direct action against what they see to be wrong. Still others pick up their banners, lobby their MPs, and collect thousands of signatures as petitions. A few have adopted violent tactics, targeting and destroying property belonging to a perceived enemy – sometimes even threatening human life.

It has often been said that variety is the spice of life. A range of tactics could and sometimes do complement each other. Although this is true to a degree, the differences of approach between the various environmentalists go much further than is generally understood. Certain views are fundamentally irreconcilable.

Those who believe a deeper approach is necessary argue that it is a waste of time and effort to merely modify the current system which they identify as being a large part of the problem. Mainstream "green" thinking, the radicals insist, is misconceived. It is weak and any victories are likely to be cosmetic, involving token compromises. Most mainstream conservationists disassociate themselves from such a radical view. They seek wide public acceptance and therefore must be cautious; their sources of funding could be jeopardised if they threaten to rock the boat too much.

So those playing the game of nature conservation do not all agree on the rules, nor on the size of the pitch, and they differ in their perception of where the goal posts are. Factions and cliquish associations have thus been formed according to an organisation's philosophy and approach. Whereas there are a number of environmental coalitions between various groups which give the impression of at least some unity, huge chasms nevertheless exist within the movement; these need to be addressed and understood before real progress can be expected.

iii. Chief Seattle's speech

During the past 25 years, many in the environmental and spiritual movements have quoted the speech of an American Indian, Chief Seattle. His words have become legendary – repeatedly printed on posters and in leaflets, magazines, and books.

The speech is inspirational: "What is man without the beasts? If all the beasts were gone, man would die from a great loneliness of spirit. For whatever happens to the beasts, soon happens to man. All things are connected.... Man did not weave the web of life; he is merely a strand in it. Whatever he does to the web, he does to himself." And so on.

The reality, however, is very different from the myth. Almost all of the chief's best-known and best-loved quotations are fictional. They are actually the words of a scriptwriter from a 1971 film, which have since been further embellished by others.

An ageing Chief Seattle (who spoke no English) did apparently make a speech in 1854, before signing away the tribal lands on which the city of Seattle now stands. But this was not written down until over 30 years later – and then by someone who used poetic Victorian language and who was not fluent in the chief's native Duwamish tongue, making even the "original" of questionable authenticity. This initial written account was itself modified twice in the early 1930s and again in 1969.

Then, in 1971, Ted Perry decided "to do a new version, inspired by rather than based on the original" as part of a film on pollution and ecology. In its first limited showing, the speech was clearly accredited to him. But the producers subsequently revised Perry's script and removed the credit line without his knowledge when the film was re-shown on one of the television networks. Viewers wrote in for transcripts and 18,000 posters were sent out in quick response.

Parts of the speech are historically inaccurate. For example: "I have seen a thousand rotting buffaloes on the prairies left by the white man who shot them from a passing train." There were no buffalo anywhere near the chief's tribal homeland; he lived a thousand miles from the prairies. And he spoke 15 years before the Union and Central Pacific railroads were built across the plains. Perry has honestly admitted such historical bloomers as "pure ignorance on my part". He tried to set the record straight about his fictitious writing, but the modern-day legend had already taken on a life of its own. He believes "on reflection, it was ethically wrong on my part" to present even a fictionalised version of a long-dead native American.

Organisations such as Friends of the Earth have since used the speech time after time. So have the organisers of Earth Day. The US vice-president, Al Gore, quoted Chief Seattle in his book on the environment. Dan Fogelberg, one of my favourite singer/songwriters, included some of the chief's wise words within the packaging of a CD released in 1990. And a best-selling children's book has recently "adapted" Chief Seattle's message.

So what? Does it really matter if these words were actually spoken or merely made up? Isn't it the message itself which is important? This is the occasional postscript of semi-embarrassed environmentalists. But would hundreds of thousands of people continue to buy the posters and books if these inspirational sayings were clearly stated to be the words of a film scriptwriter? No. And (perhaps more importantly) why are people so eager to believe a romanticised image of some native American, rather than the naked reality?

If we are to find a genuine solution to our environmental crisis, we must learn to face the facts – however sobering they might be. Idealism based on fantasy will not help. We need to replace this dubious and superficial attitude with a deeper approach based on realism.

iv. Recycling

Recycling has widespread support. Environmental groups promote it. Governments give them grants to keep promoting it, enjoying the rewards of being seen to be doing something "green". And the general public, quick to adopt a good idea, is increasingly doing it. It doesn't seem to cost people anything and they don't have to make any major lifestyle changes; it is simple and easy, taking only a few minutes. But does recycling really work or is it a myth?

Before continuing, I want to make clear that recycling is a good idea. It's just that the actual practical realities are not clear cut. Aluminium drink cans, for example, seem to be worthwhile items for recycling. It is financially viable to recycle aluminium and only takes about 5% of the energy compared to making it from bauxite ore, (excluding all the transportation considerations); large amounts of energy are needed to convert the ore into metal, making the production of new aluminium very expensive and therefore an ideal material to recycle.

But other things made of steel, paper, plastic, and glass are much less straightforward when recycling is seriously considered as an option. These are common, low cost materials and the demand for them has been depressed or limited on many occasions. Accordingly, street collections of old newspapers – for example – have been discontinued for months at a time when it was not worth doing. Waste paper collected in Germany, where there is stricter legislation, has been dumped in other countries such as Italy and Spain. Questions also exist about potential markets for recycled goods following processing and re-manufacture; in the case of paper and plastics, products are of a lower quality and this is not always desired or best.

A lot of recycling projects appear to work because they are heavily subsidised and perhaps mandated by government regulations. Millions of pounds are given each year as grants to recycling initiatives – money which could be better spent in other ways to help the environment. Local authorities are pushed into recycling by laws and financial penalties via the landfill tax. Whilst people seem happy to put out their "suitable" rubbish in plastic blue boxes (or similar) provided by the council for recycling, along with the rest of the garbage in the usual bins or bags, they are mainly unaware that this adds approximately 15% or more to the cost of kerb-side waste collection; in short, such recycling is an additional burden on tax payers and a strain on local services.

Some people are trying to question the sense of indiscriminate recycling. Professor Andrew Porteous of the Open University, for example, has said: "You can get over enthusiastic. It can cost a lot of money to achieve very little. You might end up spending £100 a tonne to collect, say, waste paper for which you may have to hand over a £5 note before the paper mill will take it. You might spend another £100 a tonne collecting plastic bottles, hauling an awful lot of air around the country."

Financial costs of collecting materials for recycling will obviously be greater in rural areas, which have a small and widespread population, as compared to a densely populated city. Furthermore, a lot of energy is used to collect waste materials for recycling; in many instances, once all the factors are calculated, it actually takes more

"I'm convinced! Recycling's a good idea!"

energy to recycle than to use virgin or renewed resources. So who is really benefiting? You, because you get a good feeling about being "environmentally friendly"? Or the environment?

The high (and escalating) cost of salaries in industrialised countries is often ignored – and yet this single factor threatens to make most recycling efforts prohibitively expensive because recycling is typically a labour-intensive activity. In the poorer countries, recycling is still commonly practised as a way of making small amounts of money; it works because wages are low, together with the lower cost of living. In Britain, earlier in the 1900s, the rag-and-bone man – together with his horse and cart – was a common sight. And during the late 1960s as a youngster, I earned pocket money collecting empty glass fizzy drink bottles on the beaches of Clacton-on-Sea. Today, standards of wealth are higher, even for children who think nothing of spending £100 on a pair of fashionable trainers (and who would

RECYCLING FACTORY

"On second thoughts, I'm not so sure!"

probably dismiss bottle collecting for pennies – if still possible – as "uncool"). So, instead of leaving recycling in the hands of market forces and entrepreneurs to either succeed or fail, an artificial situation has been created with subsidies, taxes, and compulsory directives from government. But is this worthwhile or just a waste of money and effort, considering that the basis for recycling is looking increasingly unsound?

When people are blinded with the soft option of recycling and all its accompanying propaganda, this distracts attention away from the basic issues (which we will be considering in the next few chapters). Better ideas on how to deal with waste disposal are also ignored, due to insufficient interest and support. One of these alternatives is energy-from-waste incineration (as opposed to simple incineration). A lot of energy can be reclaimed or recovered during the process of incineration (up to 500 kilowatt hours per tonne of waste), then re-used in the form of either electricity or heating from hot water – a system which would be reasonably easy to apply in city and industrial areas. A substantial reduction in the volume of waste is achieved by this method – thereby satisfying one of the major criticisms of using landfill sites to get rid of our rubbish; the remaining ash could be used for road foundations and other construction purposes. Yet how many of you have heard of this idea, compared to recycling? Beware of myths. Learn to do your own thinking, instead of following like sheep.

SECTION TWO:
BASIC ISSUES

4

The fundamental problem:
"me, me, me"

i. Selfishness

Human beings have so far developed one basic psychology: "me, me, me". People mainly put themselves – or themselves and their family – first, before the needs and interests of others. There are degrees and occasional exceptions, of course, but this "me before you" attitude generally dominates day-to-day life. From childhood onwards, everyone is psychologically conditioned into self-orientated behaviour – by their parents, their friends, and society in general. It is regarded as being "normal" and "acceptable", apart from certain excesses which are labelled as "selfish".

The word "selfish" is actually commonly misused; its meaning and scope needs to be widened. People who call others selfish are almost always hypocrites, simply because the vast majority of their own behaviour is also self-orientated or selfish. The problem is that most people do not like to think about what the problem with them is – and so they are unlikely to recognise or admit their own basic selfishness.

Through being primarily concerned about what you want for you or your family, there is usually little time left to think about the needs of others. Self-preoccupation produces a strong tendency to avoid what is difficult, inconvenient, and/or uncomfortable. It seems easier to ignore or forget than to fully face the reality of what is happening in the wider world. Complacency and apathy help maintain this pattern of avoidance, together with the various "I can't, because....." excuses. People become less responsive to the suffering of others – although psychological avoidance might result in the denial of this fact.

"Why doesn't somebody do something about it?!"

ii. Limitations

Self-orientated behaviour has many disadvantages and it results in a wide range of global and personal suffering: murder, rape, child abuse, robbery, fraud, drink driving, vandalism, drug abuse, torture, corruption, famine, war, terrorism, persecution, greed, indifference, boredom, prejudice, jealousy, hatred, loneliness, insecurity, etc. And destruction of natural habitat, extinction of species, pollution, cruelty to animals, and overpopulation.

The "me, me, me" psychology is not a complete failure; it has also produced many advantages, though not for everyone. We can perform complex medical operations, involving highly technical and expensive equipment – albeit whilst millions of our fellow human beings in poorer countries still suffer and die each year from the lack of basic health care. Those who can afford the price of international travel are able to fly around the world for holidays and business – whilst countless others have to walk miles each day just to get sufficient water for their primary needs. People in the affluent developed countries buy one cookery book after another to satisfy their craving for different tastes and indulge themselves at expensive restaurants – seemingly indifferent to the fact that a large percentage of the human population continues to be threatened with starvation or endures ill-health caused by malnutrition. Our technological advancement gives us astonishingly sophisticated weapons as we continue to kill one another in war after war; television allows the rest of the world to watch it happening, perhaps even "live" via satellite. There can be no doubt that self-motivation – be it on an individual, institutional, or national level – has produced a great deal of progress. But where is the balance? And where is our humanity?

The psychology and culture of selfishness is inherently dysfunctional and problematic. It produces "winners" and "losers" – the "have's" and the "have-not's". Its usefulness is limited and it causes unfairness, resulting in widespread suffering. This "me, me, me" mentality is the number one fundamental problem in the world.

iii. Are humans inherently selfish?

As a trained biologist, I understand that we are intelligent animals. There is no doubt that we are biologically programmed for survival and self-preservation. Nature has evolved through survival of the fittest, and humans are no exception. But, uniquely on our planet, we human beings have also developed a complex psychological/cultural aspect to our being. Unlike other animals, we are not primarily motivated by elementary factors such as the need to eat, drink, and find the safety of shelter. Life is no longer usually just a matter of survival and our concerns have developed far beyond the basic essentials: "Why do young people take drugs?" "And will my own children do so?" "What is going to happen in the next episode of my favourite television programme?" "Which football team do you support?" "Can I afford a new car?" "What occurs inside a black hole?" Most of our behaviour is now psychologically or culturally based, instead of merely stimulated through biological instinct.

It would be a mistake to assume that just because we are biologically conditioned for self-preservation, this therefore means that human nature is inherently selfish. Rather, it is the "me, me, me" psychology which causes all the problems – not the physical drive to simply stay alive. Survival is central and absolutely essential to existence, whereas our psychology and culture can be questioned and changed through re-education if a better alternative becomes available.

The balance of nature is being seriously upset by the current human psychology. The natural world is clearly not "nice" nor like some romantic fairy tale; lions chase, catch, and tear apart the flesh of zebras and other prey species, for example. But even though nature is hard and unforgiving, the bottom line is that it has successfully worked for millions of years. The comparatively recent development of human intelligence, combined with our corresponding ability to create technology, has added a new dimension to life on our planet. The human species now has the ability to significantly control, change, and/or destroy the environment in which we all live. And this is more a reflection of our psychological capability – which makes us different from other lifeforms on Earth – not merely a response to our biological urge to survive.

Selfishness – as opposed to basic biological self-preservation – is actually a poor strategy for survival. As we have already briefly seen, it causes a huge amount of suffering in the form of wars, crime, and personal unhappiness. And it is leading to the rapid extinction of other species, together with the destruction of natural habitat, and possibly even threatening our own future existence. We need to clearly understand that this dysfunctional self-orientated psychology is at the root of our problems. Once this is accepted, our main task must be to evolve further.....towards an alternative non-selfish psychological strategy.

In Chapter 13, I will discuss this alternative psychology and explain how it offers a solution to the environmental crisis. It is enough to say here that a radically different psychological strategy does exist – one which is real and an evolutionary potential waiting to be fulfilled.

iv. A key factor

The selfishness factor is rarely, if at all, considered by the majority of environmentalists. Perhaps it is seen as too big, too obvious a problem, to merit discussion. They apparently choose to ignore it as the main cause of our environmental crisis, blindly hoping that this fundamental issue will somehow go away. And/or they might be reluctant to risk alienating their supporters with such straightforward education, no matter how urgently it is needed. Maybe they are unwilling to admit, and then have to do something about, their own hypocrisy if this particular can of worms is opened up? It is hardly surprising, therefore, that many of the numerous "solutions" so far – invariably based on a shallow approach – have failed to properly work.

Most of the general public, whilst endorsing nature conservation, are nevertheless in favour of promoting human interests over those which are of benefit to wildlife.

They insist that human beings matter more. But if this belief is sincere, why do such people aggressively defend their own affluent lifestyles over that of a poor African villager who is also human? No, such an argument is really a defence of the "me, me, me" attitude.

To summarise, it is our mental abilities which have allowed us to dominate nature and accomplish our many achievements to date. Humans are physically weaker than gorillas, chimpanzees, tigers, wildebeest, and many other animals; our strength comes instead from an increased brain capacity, allowing us the powerful skill of complex thought and reasoning. However, the "me, me, me" perspective is limited and flawed. Human beings have become intelligent baboons, but it is questionable if we have yet become truly civilised. We now need to evolve further, changing our perspective from "me, me, me" to a more healthy and mature "you and me" outlook – broadened to include everyone and everything. This basic psychological factor is surely at the heart of the environmental issue.

5

Too many people

"Population growth is the creed of the cancer cell."
                                        Edward Abbey

i. The numbers

The world population is 5.9 billion and rising. It is growing by over 80 million people per year – nearly three people every second or 225,000 every day. The number of human beings has doubled since I was born in 1957. It is set to roughly double again by the time today's teenagers become grey-haired. These are staggering statistics that should get you thinking.

In the days of the Roman Empire and Jesus of Nazareth, the world population was probably about 250 million. It was not until the mid-17th century that it increased to half a billion. There were 1 billion people by the year 1800 or thereabouts. The 2 billion mark was reached in the 1930s. Exponential growth then more quickly resulted in there being 3 billion people by 1960, 4 billion by 1975, and 5 billion in 1987.

Population growth has not just happened because of more births. Generally improving living conditions – including better housing, sanitation, and nutrition, together with cleaner drinking water and modern medical care – have led to a decline in death rates, especially amongst infants and young children. And people have been living longer; life expectancy has significantly risen during the 20th century. All of which, generally, are welcome improvements.

The United Nations has tried to predict future growth trends, using alternative scenarios. Their medium variant (and most likely) projection suggests a world population of over 8 billion by the year 2025 and nearly 10 billion by 2050; it might then level out at 11.5 billion in 2150. This forecast could prove to be inaccurate, of course, with the growth rate being less or a lot more; according to the high variant projection, for example, there might be as many as 28 billion human beings alive by 2150.

Whatever the future growth rate, there are already too many people. More people means using more natural resources – and more space for human activity, with less space for nature. One million extra people is a lot of new people, an increase happening every four days or so. This addition requires more houses, schools, factories, hospitals, roads, car parks, and shops to be built. More food must be grown. And these added people will want to buy clothes, cars, furniture, electrical goods, gifts, and go on holiday.

ii. A third world problem?

Most, but not all, of the population increase is now happening in the developing countries. Africa has the highest annual growth rate, but Asia has by far the biggest number of people. China with over 1.2 billion and India with 970 million (1997 figures) have the world's largest national populations.

A common opinion held by many of those who live in the developed countries is that overpopulation is a third world issue; it is not "our" problem. Official government views of these affluent nations seem to support such thinking. France (with 59 million), Germany (with 82 million), and Japan (with 125 million) are three examples who think that their birth rates are "too low". The United Kingdom (with 59 million) and the United States of America (with 268 million) are among those who consider theirs to be "satisfactory". It is easy to conclude that such governments appear to be more intent on preserving their own economic growth than being concerned about the environmental impact of so many human beings.

The fact is that the richest 20% of people – largely those in the industrialised countries – are using 80% of the world's resources. An average family in Europe consumes approximately 25 times as many natural resources as an average family in one of the least developed countries; the average American family uses up 50 times as much.

Population scientist Paul Ehrlich has suggested the equation $I = P \times A \times T$ in which I is the impact of any group or country on the environment, P is the population size, A is the affluence, and T is the technology used in supplying the goods and services for consumption. Using this formula, a simple calculation makes the point that the population problem is very much the responsibility of people in the richer countries. The industrialised nations contain a fifth of the world's population or 1.18 billion people (as opposed to four-fifths in the developing countries or 4.72 billion people) and have an income 17 times higher, with an energy use – one of the easiest measurements of technology – 9 times higher. According to Ehrlich's equation, the impact of the developed countries is therefore nearly 40 times ($1.18 \times 17 \times 9$ as opposed to $4.72 \times 1 \times 1$) that of the poorer developing nations. So our population size, even if it is a relatively small part of the total, is an important factor.

Our behaviour in the industrialised countries is doubly important. We surely need to start acting more responsibly and, by doing so, set a new example for those in the developing countries to follow. If we do not change and they continue to want to copy our "more, more, more" lifestyle, then what state will the planet be in when half, two-thirds, or all of the world's population progresses to a high consumption way of life? Such widespread reckless activity would quickly deplete many natural resources and perhaps push us beyond Earth's carrying capacity. Serious disruption in the future or catastrophic upheaval is a worrying possibility. Whereas I have never believed it likely that the human race would end with a bang, a series of whimpers could cause significant setbacks to our advancement. If we are sensible, the time to change is now; it is easier, cheaper, and less disruptive to act before the situation gets worse.

iii. What kind of population control?

China realised its population was growing alarmingly out of control and that something had to be done.....fast. Their approach to the problem was state-led, in keeping with their political system. Whereas the country's partial successes have often been overlooked, the negative elements of China's efforts have become commonly known. Coerced abortions and sterilisations have sometimes taken place. Families have practised female infanticide due to their desire to have a son within the one-child-per-family limit. These are not just the consequences of a state dictatorship; they are also the effects of crisis and alarm. A better way, which we should all accept as our personal and international responsibility *before the eleventh hour*, must be voluntary consideration of the problem and agreement to do something about it.

For those in the developing countries, a combination of actions is needed to reduce family size: adequate nutrition, good hygiene and sanitation, basic health care, access to contraception, and improved education for girls and women. Better nutrition, hygiene, and sanitation are necessary to minimise ill-health. Parents must be sure of reliable medical care for when their children get ill. (The mortality rate for babies and children under the age of five years is more than 20 times greater in the least developed countries as compared to the industrialised nations.) People enjoy sex, so contraception is essential for family planning. With at least a few years of secondary education, a woman is 10 times more likely to use family planning; she will have fewer children and greater freedom of opportunity. Although usually better educated, men must learn to take more responsibility with regard to contraception and family planning.

Attitudes in the industrialised countries generally ignore the global impact of overpopulation. Governments are greatly influenced by economists, who are usually strongly in favour of population growth. They argue that a reduction in population size would cause major economic and social problems. For example, as there would be proportionately fewer younger people and more old people, (at least in the short term), it would become burdensome or impossible for those still working to generate enough wealth for the old to be taken care of without a major drop in living standards. More to the point, it is claimed, a large number of consumers is necessary for economic growth to continue. However, economists have largely ignored ecological considerations, believing natural resources to be free or cheap and presumably unending.

Individuals in Britain and similar rich countries also have a tendency to ignore the wider and long-term global picture. Most people believe they have a right to parenthood. Many are primarily influenced by their personal finances, their attitude towards a career, by social/cultural/religious/family pressures, or they realise in advance that having children isn't all fun. Unfortunately, very few decide to voluntarily restrict themselves for altruistic reasons. Regrettably, just talking about a guideline of "two children or less" is enough to get some people angry.

Some countries or policy makers hide behind the population density issue – i.e. the number of people per square mile or kilometre. Australia, for example, has a density of only 6 people per square mile (compared to 632 people per square mile in the UK). But although Australia has the fourth lowest density in the world, it is a big country and almost all of its 18 million people live in cities and urban sprawl along the coast. Such figures also disregard factors such as fertility of land and rainfall. Australia has already been significantly changed since European settlement over 200 years ago, and some Australians are beginning to think that their large but mainly arid country cannot properly sustain more than six million people – a third of its current (and growing) population. The United States of America also has a relatively low (or low to medium) density with 76 people per square mile. In addition to the fact that large areas of land have low fertility and low rainfall (similar to Australia), we have already seen that the average American is by far the highest consumer of natural resources; they are fast using up their own resources and buying those of other countries as well.

iv. Mass starvation?

Paul Ehrlich and others predicted in the 1960s that there were already too many people and warned of massive famines likely to happen in the 1970s and 1980s; the world's capacity for food production could not provide for a much larger human population. Whereas millions unfortunately did die – I personally saw and got involved in helping with the Ethiopian famine of 1984/1985 – the worst predictions have not yet proved correct. In the mid-1980s, Ethiopia and other African countries were principally affected by prolonged drought; the majority of Africans normally struggle as poor subsistence farmers, with very limited reserves available for times of severe hardship.

Ehrlich and others might be forgiven for not having foreseen significant advances in modern agriculture. Yields have increased greatly since the 1960s due to research into farming methods, improved crop varieties, and widespread use of agrochemicals in the form of fertilisers, insecticides, and herbicides.

Mass starvation has also been put off by other changes in human activity. Growing populations have led to environmentally damaging practices such as overgrazing and shortened fallow periods. Huge numbers of people have left their family farms for the increasingly overcrowded cities, broadening the economic structure of poorer countries but introducing new problems such as unemployment and high crime levels. And humans have spread outwards from the more fertile areas to also make use of marginal farmland.

The earlier predictions might not have been wrong, but merely delayed by technological progress and the tough determination to survive as shown by millions of poor people. But now almost half of the world's poorest people – more than 500 million by the most conservative estimate – live on marginal lands in the Sahel and in the upper watersheds of the Himalayas and Andes. And this number will probably rise to 800 million by the year 2020. The livelihoods of all these people are directly and acutely affected by natural resource degradation; they live and depend upon lands which are extremely fragile. Landslides, prolonged droughts, floods, erosion, increasing salination, and dwindling surface ground water supplies are some of the man-made disasters now waiting to happen as never before.

v. Interactive factors

The $I = P \times A \times T$ equation helps us to understand the role of population size in the environmental crisis. We have already seen above how the rich nations have such serious population problems because the A and T multipliers for each person are so large; (their citizens proportionately consume a lot more than people in the third world). It also shows us that countries with the largest national populations, such as China and India, will have an enormous impact on the planet with even a little extra development (because the P multiplier on the A and T factors is so large).

Unfortunately, many environmentalists appear to ignore or even deny this reasonably straightforward mathematical relationship – seemingly unwilling to acknowledge that population size interacts with every other factor. Instead, they overly stress the problem of pollution and cry out for cleaner technology. They recognise that there is a limit to most natural resources, but naively rely on a solution involving recycling, re-using, repairing, and the reduction of waste. Whereas cleaner technology is needed and will help, together with the four "R"s, it will simply not be enough. We cannot continue to take and take, more and more – the subject of the next chapter – nor can we afford such a high human population, especially if everyone is to enjoy a good standard of living.

To further illustrate how this interaction works, consider the following example. Suppose that recycling, re-using, and the reduction of waste manages to reduce overall global consumption of resources by 5%; (the A factor). And also suppose that cleaner technology led to 5% less damage; (the T factor). This would reduce the total impact (I) of humanity by about 10%. However, unless population growth (P) was restrained so that it did not rise further, any increase would nullify the 10% improvement and bring the amount of negative impact back to the previous level within less than 10 years (calculated at the current annual rate of population increase).

vi. Stability

Realistically, there is no possibility that zero population growth will be achieved in the immediate future (unless there is a sudden, huge rise in the death rate). This is because of "demographic momentum" – which is the technical term to explain that a previously growing population will probably keep expanding long after reproductive rates have been reduced. Demographic momentum occurs due to the youth of a rapidly increasing population. In 1997, 38% of people in the developing countries (excluding China) were under the age of 15 – yet to enter their prime reproductive years and have their own children. It will be roughly half a century before they reach old age and therefore become part of the death rate.

So population control is not a "quick fix". It is a long-term policy from which our children, grandchildren, and great-grandchildren will benefit rather than ourselves. We must think of the future generations – of humanity, but also the wild animal and plant species which are part of life on Earth.

When the average couple has slightly more than two children – statistically that is! – a population has reached replacement reproduction or stability. (The "slightly more" than two is to compensate for the deaths of infants and children.) For this to be practically meaningful, it needs to be as a global average. At present, almost every country in the world still has an increasing national population.

Although our first target must be to stop the number of human beings increasing any further, we then have to all decide what might be a desirable total population size. We do not just need numerical stability; we should rather think in terms of *ecological* stability – i.e. what is best for everyone and everything. I think it is almost certain that people in the future will want to reduce the human population in size, probably significantly. Such a decision will ultimately bring benefits for all.

vii. Who wants overpopulation?

We are a gregarious, social animal; few humans would wish to be completely solitary. But large numbers of people do not just upset the balance of nature, they also cause lots of problems for themselves. Who enjoys sitting in a traffic jam on a national holiday or even on the way to work in the morning? Or standing on a bus or train, unable to find a seat? Overcrowding might suit flamingos or a large shoal of fish which gather together for safety against predators, but people generally find it stressful and unpleasant.

Overpopulation also tends to overstimulate demand for both essential and popular goods and services. House prices get higher and higher, whilst the houses themselves get proportionately smaller in size. Anything which is in short supply but high in demand is likely to push up the price, causing the headache of inflation – whether it be food at a time of scarcity or famine, or tickets for a sporting cup final where there is a limited number of seats available.

Greedy business people – and not all business owners are greedy – might benefit economically from over-population if they are selling a popular product or service. Economists are needed to make sense of an unstable situation and so welcome an ever-increasing population. Also dictators usually want large populations to keep their workforce and armies strong. But the vast majority of us, if we stop and think, have little or nothing to gain and a lot to lose. And nature, if you care about wildlife or just the peace and safety of your own environment, is already losing. The world in which we live today, I suggest, has too many people. Who wants overpopulation?

6

"I want more"

i. The American dream

"Buffalo Bill" Cody killed 4,280 buffalo in just 17 months for a railroad company. President Theodore Roosevelt, whilst expressing minor personal reservations, greeted the mass slaughter as something necessary for the advancement of white civilisation westwards across America. Out of an estimated 60 million buffalo in the American "wild" west, less than 500 survived to see the beginning of the 20th century.

In 1908, Henry Ford brought out the Model T and aimed to make the automobile available to any American earning an average salary. He famously offered his car "in any colour, so long as it's black". Mass production started shortly afterwards, in 1913.

During the first half of the 20th century, the USA's population grew by 100% – whereas mineral production grew by 500%, oil consumption by 5,600%, and electricity consumption by 6,000%. The number of motor vehicles increased by 600,000%. Between 1900 and 1950, people consumed more non-renewable natural resources than in all of the human race's previous time on Earth.

If the American dream got well under way in the first half of the 20th century, it carried on charging ahead during the second half. As the chairman of President Eisenhower's Council of Economic Advisers said, the American economy's "ultimate purpose is to produce more consumer goods." And the chief executive of an advertising company remarked in the 1950s: "It's our job to make women unhappy with what they have."

The consumer culture has rapidly spread and grown during recent decades, even affecting the majority of young people who tend to be more idealistic at that age. 44% of American students entering college in 1967 believed it was essential to be "very well-off financially"; this had changed to 74% by 1990. During the same period, the number of college students who thought it was important to develop a meaningful philosophy of life dropped from 83% to 43%.

The American dream is epitomised by phrases such as "bigger, better, and faster." America's cars are certainly bigger (and now genuinely available in any colour). And the range of US military weapons is frighteningly better than that of any other country. But, perhaps most famously of all, it was America who introduced the "fast food" industry to the rest of the world. In a nation where half of its people claim to be religious and still believe in the idea of biblical creation (i.e. disbelieving the evidence for evolution), it seems that money has become the new god. Furthermore, the American lifestyle is envied by many people and countries throughout the world; it has become a model for successful development.

ii. Global land use

As the human population has dramatically increased, our activity has expanded almost everywhere. 11% of the planet's land surface is now used to grow crops; a further 25% (or one quarter of the total) serves as grazing for domestic livestock; approximately 2% is paved over as roads or covered by cities and towns. Most of the 30% that is still forested is either exploited to some degree by people, has been converted into tree farms with only limited benefit to wildlife, or is still being destroyed at an alarming rate. The remaining third is in the Arctic and Antarctic regions, or is harsh desert, or is too mountainous to be of much use for human exploitation; a small amount is allocated as national parks or other nature reserves.

The USA is annually losing 35,000 square kilometres of land – wilderness or agriculture – to houses, offices, factories,

"Watch out! There's a size 10 problem coming our way!"

shopping malls, roads, and other forms of urban expansion. Again, many other countries admire the American lifestyle and seek to follow the same development path.

With the number of human beings still increasing at 5.9 billion and probably set to double again, the pressure on land use will continue to escalate. There is already very little wilderness left for nature. And many of the popular national parks are becoming so overcrowded with tourists at certain peak periods of the year that additional restrictions are now having to be introduced; too many people walking about at particular locations is causing erosion, for example, and too many cars carrying the endless streams of visiting tourists are jamming access roads and overstretching available car parks.

Buying a home (at least in the developed countries) is the most expensive purchase most of us are ever likely to make – a basic necessity made considerably more difficult by the high premium paid for limited space with building permission, caused by overpopulation. In the developing countries where the majority of those who are poor survive as subsistence farmers, a growing number of people are either landless or else have insufficient space to produce enough food for themselves just to exist. In the search for something better, many turn to city life where they are forced to dwell in the makeshift squalor of squatter camps and slums.

iii. The water bomb

Worldwide demand for water is doubling every 21 years, (and more so in some regions). Supply cannot keep pace with this increased demand, as populations and living standards soar. Water is absolutely essential to life; we cannot survive without it. Not surprisingly then, there is even a risk that wars of the next century will be fought over water.

Parts of Africa could shortly experience a "drying out". As demand escalates, supplies may decline faster than ever. Egypt's water supply per person is expected to shrink by .30%, Nigeria's by 40%, and Kenya's by 50% in under a decade. By the year 2025, the amount of water available to each person in the Middle East and North Africa will have dropped by 80% in a single lifetime.

Rivers carry water regardless of national boundaries. The potential for insecurity is great. Botswana, Cambodia, Gambia, Sudan, Syria, and many other countries receive 75% or more of their fresh water from the river flows of (often hostile) upstream neighbours. Four out of every ten people in the world live in the 250 river basins whose water is competed for by more than one nation. Great rivers like the Nile, Niger, Tigris, Me Kong, Brahmaputra, and Indus each flow through several countries – all of which want to extract as much water as possible for their own use. All have been the subject of recent international disputes. For example, the Nile flows through a number of volatile countries. It provides 97% of Egypt's fresh water. But water developments upstream in Sudan, Ethiopia, Kenya, Rwanda, Burundi, Uganda, Tanzania, or Zaire (now called The

Democratic Republic Of The Congo) would add to existing tensions. Only Sudan and Egypt have so far signed a water-use treaty.

Similar disputes over who can use what water are happening locally within nations. Numerous examples exist, ranging from the fruit-growing areas of the Western Cape in South Africa to the farmlands here in the south and east of England. And as tensions grow even more within society between farmers, industry, and individuals over water use, agriculture will generally suffer shortages if preference is given to the industrial and urban areas which tend to generate more wealth. Eventually, we will be forced to ask "Where's the food going to come from?"

The sayings "money makes the world go around" and "money talks" are unfortunately true indicators of who presently holds the power over our natural resources. As shortages develop, water will be no exception. And the well-off (which includes almost everyone in the industrialised countries) continuing to overconsume will just make matters worse. According to the Food and Agriculture Organisation, an average of 15,000 cubic metres of water is enough to irrigate one hectare of high-yielding modern rice or sufficient for 100 rural families for three years. Yet the same amount of water will supply 100 luxury hotel guests for just 55 days.

iv. Looking good?

The Iwia was one of New Zealand's most remarkable birds. It had long black tail feathers with distinctive white tips. The feathers were worn only by tribal chieftains as a symbol of their authority. Hunting was strictly limited by traditional law.

Then, a hundred years ago, the Duke of York – the future King George V – made a royal trip to New Zealand. During his visit, a Maori chieftain presented him with the elegant black-and-white feathers of an Iwia. The Duke stuck the feathers in his hat and, by so doing, unknowingly condemned the Iwia to extinction. A fashion craze for Iwia feathers followed the Duke's return to England. By 1907, the last Iwia had been shot.

A better-known example of such fashion-related greed is the killing of rare cats for fur coats. Millions of wild animals are slaughtered each year to supply the fur trade – including leopards, ocelots, cheetahs, snow leopards, and jaguars, as well as non-cat species such as arctic foxes and mink (often, but not always, farmed). Germany, Italy, the USA, and Japan have been amongst the biggest buyers of furs, but many other countries including Britain have contributed to the mass suffering.

Department stores in Japan, for example, were still openly selling full-length tiger and clouded leopard coats well into the 1980s – despite CITES banning such trade in endangered species. The coats were for sale at prices greater than US$100,000 each, just part of this billion dollar industry. (After 14 years of work, CITES officials admitted during the 1987 convention that they were only about 17% effective in controlling the illegal wildlife trade! Yet the general public are often under the impression – wrongly – that CITES has more or less put an end to such activities. Interpol – the international alliance of police, exchanging intelligence and information regarding criminal matters – estimates that the worldwide trade in endangered species is worth US$5 billion every year; this is second only to the illegal trade in drugs, in terms of its cash value.)

The Miss USA and Miss Universe beauty contests were presented for years by American TV personality Bob Barker. Barker resigned, in 1987, much to the shock of the organisers; those in charge had insisted on presenting the winners with fur coats. "It isn't necessary to torture and kill animals to show how much money you have," Barker told reporters. "You can buy a nice cloth coat and pin money to it."

Lynx, the anti-fur campaigning organisation, made several effective adverts which shocked the general public into thinking about the fur trade. Their best short piece of film showed three models, each wearing a fur coat, parading up and down the cat-walk. Suddenly, those viewing the fashion show – presumably designers, trade buyers, reporters, and rich clients – start getting splattered by blood from the fur coats. As one of the models walks off the stage, the fur coat leaves a trail of blood behind it. The advert finishes with the powerful slogan: "It takes up to 40 dumb animals to make a fur coat. But only one to wear it."

v. Are you a poacher?

Most people are against the poaching of elephants for their ivory or rhinos for their horn. And let's be honest, the poachers have no excuse. It is true that they get little of the money in comparison to the middle men and end traders. It is also true that most of the poachers are relatively poor. But they don't have to poach. Millions of other poor people in Africa and Asia survive without poaching. No, it is simply a matter of greed and opportunity.

If we really think about it, isn't almost everyone a poacher? Especially in the high consumption societies like ours? Are you honestly that much different to the men who poach elephants, rhinos, tigers, etc?

The dictionary defines a poacher as someone who intrudes on another's preserve in order to kill game or upon another's fishing to catch fish. But is this definition too narrow? And do we really have the right to "own" nature? The dictionary definition goes on to describe poaching as seeking an unfair advantage, trampling or stirring up, and as a one-sided encroachment. These additional explanations help to clarify my point, suggesting a wider meaning that people are generally abusing the environment.

Fishermen kill seals "because they are eating *our* fish ." Yet from the seals' perspective, it is humans who are the intruders. Through learning how to build and sail boats, we have been able to leave the land on which we walk and so exploit the seas. And why eat fish anyway? Millions of

healthy, fit vegetarians all over the world demonstrate that it is not necessary. Even if you do not accept the case for being a vegetarian, the basic problem surely is that human beings have become greedy.....wanting more and more. In 1950, according to the United Nations, the total world fish catch was 20 million tonnes. By 1990, there had been a 500% increase to 100 million tonnes. But the human population had just doubled during the same period.

The vast majority of human beings are now taking more from nature than they are giving back – usually much more. This is one-sided encroachment or poaching. Our intelligence has made us the dominant species and we are thoughtlessly using this advantage. You have poached from the seas, from the forests, from the meadows, from the mountains to the valleys. Although you might not kill elephants or rhinos, nevertheless you are a poacher. Think about it.

vi. Nature fights back

The prickly saguaro cactus of the Sonoran Desert symbolises the American southwest. It is Arizona's state plant and a protected species. It has been described as a plant with a personality due to its variety of odd, almost human-like shapes. The growth of this green giant is extremely slow. After 15 years, the saguaro cactus may be barely a foot tall; at about 50 years, the saguaro can be seven feet high and only after 75 years does it start sprouting its first branches or "arms". By 100 years, these cacti could have reached 25 feet; saguaros that live 150 years or more might tower as high as 50 feet, weighing eight tonnes or more. The saguaro is like a multi-storey apartment; many of the desert birds make their homes inside holes made in the trunk and large branches.

Unfortunately, there has been widespread destruction of this important plant. Cactus-rustling to supply collectors and garden landscapers is big business, both within America and for people overseas. Vandalism is also a major problem. The state authorities have fined and even jailed serious offenders. In 1980, Arizona set up a small team of "cactus cops".

In February 1982, David Grundman from Phoenix went out into the desert and fired shotgun blasts into a giant saguaro cactus. Grundman's target was 27 feet tall, but he concentrated his aim about four feet up from the base of the plant. As he shot for the third time, the trunk gave way; the 23 foot upper section of the heavy and prickly cactus toppled down on him. Grundman was pronounced dead on arrival at hospital.

vii. Getting what you might not even want

In England, less than 2% of ancient woodland remains. Globally, wilderness is shrinking by an estimated 5,000 acres every hour. Everything we buy or get given has to come from somewhere. And with billions of people consuming more and more, this is producing a big hole in nature. Our landscapes are being raped.

The newspapers produced in the UK during a single year are enough to wrap around the Earth 270 times. Most of these newspapers are purchased by people because they want them. They want to check out the latest sports results, ogle at bare breasts on page three, study the financial news, find out what is happening at home and overseas, and/or read about the latest gossip or scandal. But other newspapers are pushed through the letterbox in your door whether you want them or not. Many are not even opened, going straight into the rubbish bin. Here in Sussex, two "free" newspapers are delivered to most homes each week. One of these contains an additional 32-page free paper, advertising local properties for sale. Yet how many people are considering moving house at any one time? As all newspapers rely heavily on income from advertisers, readers are constantly being urged to buy this or "save money" on that.

Then there is all the junk mail which buries the rest of your letters. And aren't some environmental groups (and other charities) just as pushy and wasteful by sending out countless appeals for your money?

viii. Need before want

During a regular field trip to South Africa, I talked with two nature conservation students one evening. They were just finishing a two-year college course and were genuinely enthusiastic – keen to get out there and make a difference. But one thing was blatantly missing: neither had any concept of putting need before want. Indeed, they were both full of what they wanted to do; the young woman, for example, had a dream of working with the Masai people in Kenya. In two years, nobody had mentioned or discussed the idea that placing need before want is necessary if we are to prioritise what conservation actions are required. They were obviously startled by what I was saying – but, due to years of conditioning, were nevertheless unlikely to change or downgrade their "I want" ambitions.

Earlier this year, I gave a talk as part of Brighton and

Hove's "environment week". The subject I chose was the same as this book's: a deeper approach to nature conservation. Towards the end, during questions from the audience, one woman made a very good point. Telling us her job had been as a teacher for the past 30 years, she then self-honestly commented that my talk had made her realise her emphasis had been wrong. She had always believed it was best to encourage the children to express what they wanted. Now she suddenly and clearly could see that it was more important to focus their attention first on need (and, secondly, on want).

ix. When is "enough" enough?

Admit it: you're greedy. Not as greedy as some people, perhaps, but you still want more. (Like the "me, me, me" issue, I appreciate that it might be difficult to initially acknowledge this.) We all take – and take, and take. It is literally impossible not to take, unless you're a corpse. However, the real question is "How much do you take and how much do you give?"

I think that most environmentalists are spineless and hypocritical – and they don't seem willing to work out basic mathematics. They constantly tell you to recycle and reduce your waste, conveniently ignoring this matter of greed. Yet greed is a central factor. It is not going to magically disappear without discussion and re-education. Focusing on waste reduction whilst avoiding the greed of overconsumption is like pretending that a pair of gloves will keep a naked man warm in the freezing snow; it might help a little bit, but the problem essentially remains unsolved.

We have got to stop blaming the oil companies, the logging industry, and other business giants. They are only the more obvious part of the problem. The real opponent to a healthy, balanced environment is the day-to-day greed of the man and woman in the street. It is the total sum of all human activity which most threatens nature. And if you are taking more than you are giving back, this is greed.

Your own greedy behaviour will most probably never make headline news – unlike a shipwrecked tanker spilling oil into the sea, with the accompanying pictures of countless dead sea birds. But multiply all the materials and energy you consume by nearly sixty million in the UK or six billion worldwide and you will begin to understand what is happening. There *are* those who are cynically and knowingly exploiting the environment as fast as they can, but this is just the tip of the iceberg. Most of the problem is hidden in the form of "normal" behaviour. Do you keep up with the Joneses? Or how about the Smiths, Patels, or Williamses? People avoid facing their own greed and so make scapegoats out of the oil and logging companies, etc. Whilst wriggling off the hook, they leave responsibility up to the government to do something or else somehow expect environmentalists to solve the problem. Many people just bury their heads in the proverbial sand. And carry on being greedy.

7

Who can you trust?

i. The Brent Spar

Greenpeace is best known for making waves. As a pressure group, it has campaigned against the slaughter of whales and seals, the exploitation of the Antarctic, and the dumping of toxic waste into the seas. Their direct action tactics have often required personal bravery and have been tailored for capturing media attention. Their skill has been to market protest and outrage. Public donations have followed the dramatic images of Greenpeace's high-profile stunts.

In 1995, Greenpeace saw an opportunity to campaign against the deepwater disposal of the Brent Spar. German Greenpeace activists hatched their plan in a Hamburg bar on 10th April; Greenpeace International gave approval the next day. On 30th April, Greenpeace climbed their way aboard the unoccupied Brent Spar anchored in the North Sea – bringing with them a lot of high-tech broadcasting equipment and news-hungry journalists.

The Brent Spar was taken out of operation in September 1991 after 15 years of service. An unusual installation, it had acted as a giant floating oil storage and loading buoy. New pipe-based technology had eventually rendered it obsolete. Shell UK then took over three years to evaluate a range of options for disposal. At first, Shell hoped to return the Spar to land and break it up there – but the problem was more complex. There was an assessed risk to human health and to the environmentally-sensitive shallow coastal waters. After numerous studies carried out by various experts including independent scientific institutions, it was decided that the Best Practicable Environmental Option was to dispose of the Brent Spar in the deep ocean where risks to both humans and the environment were considered minimal. The British government agreed, satisfied that Shell's plans complied with national and international regulations; they granted the necessary licence.

And so the battle for people's hearts and minds over the Brent Spar began. Greenpeace quickly used expensive broadcasting equipment to send out edited video images to TV news networks around the world, supported by a temporary press office on the Shetlands to bombard the media with their message. Many of the general public no doubt saw Greenpeace as the brave, adventurous "good guys" – and, by contrast, Shell UK as the greedy multi-national corporation which was prepared to pollute the seas yet again in the pursuit of even more profit.

After considering the options, a large mobile platform was sent out and on 23rd May Shell staff, backed by police observers, reclaimed the occupied Brent Spar. During this action, Greenpeace threw smoke bombs – a questionable tactic in a potentially dangerous situation, which some considered to be at odds with their peaceful public image.

Within a few days of being evicted, Greenpeace was back at sea – this time trying to slow down the moving of the Brent Spar from the North Sea to its planned disposal site in the Atlantic. The world's press were of course there; this was a news story easy to present as a modern-day David versus Goliath. Greenpeace repeatedly stage-managed a number of incidents, whilst video cameras rolled into action and still cameras clicked. The activists would even deliberately place their lives in danger, relying on the conscience of Shell's workers to save them. On one occasion when a Greenpeace inflatable got into trouble and Shell sent out a rescue dinghy, pictures portrayed the rescue as a ramming. Greenpeace began to win the propaganda war due to such daring visual stunts and media-friendly images.....regardless of the whole truth.

Meanwhile, several independent UK scientists were making their views known to the TV, radio, and news-papers. They objected to Greenpeace's campaign of emotive misinformation and exaggeration of the dangers; instead, they insisted that Shell's plan for deepwater disposal was correct and best for the environment. Marine biologists such as Tony Rice and Martin Angel from the Institute of Oceanographic Sciences tried to make clear that even if Shell's calculations were wrong by as much as ten times, the danger to deep-sea life would still be negligible.

During the campaign, Greenpeace got at least one thing spectacularly wrong. In early June, they placed adverts in national British newspapers such as *The Guardian*. Using the slogans "Back Again" and "You can be sure of Greenpeace" (above their appeal for donations), they claimed that Shell was going to "dump 14,500 tonnes of toxic litter in the North Sea." This statement was factually inaccurate. Firstly, Brent Spar's total weight was 14,500 tonnes – the vast majority being clean steel and ballast. Secondly, it was going to be dumped in the North Atlantic.....not the North Sea.

In Germany and other parts of continental northern Europe, Greenpeace's propaganda went even further. Jochen Vorfelder of Greenpeace Germany later admitted on television that they were prepared to blatantly mislead the public and "be naughty", as the end justified the means. People were emotionally stirred up and encouraged to boycott Shell garages. Subsequently, 50 of Shell's service stations were damaged by persons unknown; two of these were fire-bombed and one was shot at with bullets.

On June 20th, just a few days before the Brent Spar was due to be sunk, and with Greenpeace activists expecting imminent defeat, Shell decided to abort the operation. Chris Fay, chairman and chief executive of Shell UK, was summoned to a board meeting with his continental colleagues; they believed that Shell's position had become untenable due to public opposition and pressure from some European governments. Later that day, Greenpeace staff were filmed for TV celebrating with champagne and wine; they had won a famous victory.

But what kind of victory? Many informed onlookers could see that it was a victory for emotional propaganda based on fear and ignorance – and some publicly said so. The following weekend, I was representing The Wildlife For All Trust at an agricultural/country show. Asking several dozen people what they thought about the Brent Spar episode, I was amazed that almost everyone was on Greenpeace's side; only a few people remained unsure of who was correct. A month after the Shell versus Greenpeace battle, MORI asked more than 2000 British adults nationwide: "Who won the argument? Shell and the government? Or Greenpeace?" The verdict was ten to one in favour of Greenpeace; 63% said Greenpeace, 6% Shell and the government, 11% neither, and 20% "don't know."

As director of a British registered environmental charity, I was appalled by Greenpeace's dubious pressure tactics. Immediately after their "victory", I wrote to the Prime Minister expressing my reservations. I stated the need for clearer thinking and less emphasis on emotional hype; in short, a more mature approach.

In August, UK television executives admitted to a lack of objectivity and balance in their coverage of the Brent Spar story, and to using dramatic video footage supplied by Greenpeace which might have misrepresented the facts. Then, in early September, Greenpeace publicly apologised to Shell UK for their earlier claim that the Brent Spar had contained 5,000 tonnes of oil, which had subsequently been proved false. Their often repeated allegation that the Brent Spar was "a considerable threat" now clearly seemed hollow. In response to this climbdown, the pressure group was quick to emphasis the "littering of the seas" argument, rather than the toxic and dangerous contents claim.

But were they being hypocritical about "littering the seas"? Ten years earlier in 1985, the *Rainbow Warrior* had been sabotaged in Auckland, New Zealand, by French secret agents. The incident got a lot of media coverage and many outraged members of the public came rushing forward to join Greenpeace; the organisation was quickly getting richer. A number of activists wanted the *Rainbow Warrior* repaired to sail again, but Greenpeace officials decided to re-sink her off the New Zealand coast – with the world's media present, generating more publicity – and then to buy a new ship.

Greenpeace spent approximately £1.4 million on the Brent Spar campaign. Just recording and transmitting video images for television cost them hundreds of thousands of pounds. A lot of money. I, for one, think it could have been used much more efficiently to safeguard the seas and oceans. And this is not the first time that a Greenpeace campaign has been accused of being misleading or factually incorrect. Who do *you* trust?

ii. Tiger crisis

Project Tiger began in 1973 to rescue the Indian tiger; numbers had declined from an estimated population of 40,000 at the beginning of the century to about 2,000 or so. India's Prime Minister at the time, Indira Gandhi, took a personal interest. WWF donated US$1 million for the project.

The Indian authorities quickly established a number of tiger reserves. Some of the individual reserve directors, such as Fateh Singh Rathore, were committed to their task. For the next few years, the situation looked hopeful and everyone began talking of a success story. Project Tiger became the flagship of the international conservation movement. WWF, in one of their newsletters of 1983, described it as "one of the most successful conservation programmes ever undertaken." They went on to report that the endangered tiger was "on a course of assured recovery." By 1989, the official number of tigers in India was announced to be 4,334. But was it true?

Over the next few years, the reality of what was happening became known. The world famous tigers of Ranthambhore National Park – including Laxmi, Noon, and Genghis – had been poached. These tigers had previously featured in a number of books, articles, and natural history films. I saw Noon myself during my first visit to Ranthambhore in 1988, as she preyed on a young sambar deer at the edge of the lake. One poacher was caught in June 1992; he admitted killing eight tigers, six leopards, and about a thousand other animals in the past three years. Ashok Kumar, a businessman and committed conservationist based in Delhi, had collected enough evidence by the end of 1993 to suggest that 500 tigers or more had been recently killed by poachers throughout India.

A few independently-minded people had tried to sound the alarm. But WWF and other organisations, although quick to claim earlier success, seemed reluctant to accept what was going wrong. Environmentalist Jonathon Porritt later commented that they were guilty of "astonishing complacency". Warnings were ignored and maintaining diplomatic relations appeared to be more important than blowing the whistle. In India, government officials likewise were unwilling to admit the problems – perhaps because this would mean that they, too, had been failing in their job.

Significant poaching of India's tigers probably got worse in the mid-1980s. China had hunted its own tiger population in the south of the country to near extinction during the 1960s and 1970s. Their stockpile of tiger bones, penises, and other parts for use in Chinese medicine then began to run low. Demand for new supplies undoubtedly encouraged an increase of this illegal trade in and from India. The bones of just one tiger can be worth US$10,000.

Other difficulties were also mounting. People were cutting down the trees that make up the tiger's forest habitat. Some were doing this as part of subsistence living, needing firewood to cook the family meals. But many were cutting trees for money. And the poaching of non-cat species – deer in particular – was reducing the amount of prey animals available to support a healthy number of tigers.

Ullas Karanth, one of India's tiger biologists, has been critical of the method Project Tiger staff use to "count" the number of tigers. Based on the mistaken belief that every tiger can be identified by its footprints, project personnel copy the outline of pugmarks onto glass, transfer these to paper, and then compare all the drawings within an area. Karanth thinks the system is seriously flawed: "just a bunch of tracings." To demonstrate this, he got 33 tracings from four captive tigers under differing substrate conditions. Six experienced Project Tiger staff (including a field director) examined the footprints and estimated that the marks were made by between 6 and 23 different tigers; nobody could even sort out all of a single tiger's marks correctly. This simple test suggests that the census numbers have been exaggerated for years. Ullas Karanth prefers using "camera traps" which photograph a tiger, allowing accurate identification through comparison of their unique stripe markings. As a wider method for assessing tiger populations, he recommends counting prey; research has indicated a direct relationship exists between the number of animals such as deer and the number of tigers an area can support.

The danger of having to confront armed poachers is a constant risk and the following is merely a tiny glimpse of this occupational hazard. On 10th April 1993, in the Ranthambhore area, two guards of the Forest and Wildlife Department were killed by a gang of poachers. Two other guards were injured; one of these was shot in the head, face, and shoulder. Three days later, two forest guards were shot at and injured in Corbett National Park – another of India's famous wildlife reserves.

A poaching incident occurred when I was working at Ranthambhore during my second visit in January 1994 – not of a tiger, but a female nilgai (a large antelope) pregnant with two calves. As part of my work, I met Gopal Singh Panwar, the forest guard who had risked his life in arresting the poacher. This brave officer had literally faced death through a loaded rifle being pointed towards him at close range; undaunted, he tackled the offender.....grabbing the barrel of the gun and then beating the man unconscious.

When a colleague arrived on the scene, they carried the poacher four kilometres out of the forest on foot. Such devotion to duty, I was told, had been inspired during earlier years under the strong and committed leadership of Fateh Singh Rathore when he was the park director.

Findings of a survey in 1995 revealed that 80% of park directors lacked an armed anti-poaching force; 87% were short of guns and communication equipment; 63% had no money for gathering intelligence. Furthermore, 37% admitted having no appropriate management plan for their reserves. Of the reserves themselves, 60% had villages inside their core areas in addition to the surrounding human populations. Valmik Thapar, author and conservationist, remarked: "That's why we are not saving the tiger."

What I have briefly outlined about Project Tiger in India is just a fraction of the problem. The situation is just as bad, or worse, in other countries where the tiger still survives. Environmental organisations have now woken up to the crisis. They have been energetically fundraising, claiming that with perhaps two tigers being poached each day, this well-known and majestic animal could be extinct in the wild by the year 2000. Whether or not WWF and others have learned their lesson remains to be seen.

iii. Scientists are not always unbiased

The scientific method has given us a reliable way to work out, sooner or later, what is objective fact. This helps to reduce ignorance and makes decisions less reliant on belief and/or opinion. It is based on testing an idea or hypothesis through careful experimentation. Results are then analysed and discussed, with cautious conclusions helping to formulate theories. Repeatability exposes mistakes, accidental or otherwise, as well as strengthening our understanding of the accumulated data. Worldwide debate by fellow scientists allows critical comment and suggestions for additional research.

As I will make clear in a later chapter, I am not anti-science. The human race has greatly benefited from science and will undoubtedly continue to do so in the future. Environmentalists should embrace science as an important tool to help us find out exactly what is happening. If our knowledge is soundly based, our response can be appropriate and precise.

Scientists should be reliably objective. Unfortunately, this is frequently not the case. Their scientific integrity is often compromised by a range of personal and social psychological factors. Scientists are commonly just as concerned for their own careers as they are for pure objectivity; climbing up the ladder is regarded as important, which usually involves being seen to be saying and doing the "right" thing (regardless of whether it actually is or not). Researchers might also be influenced by the viewpoint or goal of those who provide funding for their work or by whoever directly employs them. Scientific caution can easily be misused and the data modified and made to look as if it supports a particular biased position.

In addition to the "ladder climbers", you also get the "shiny bums". Within the biological sciences, field work is often crucial for a proper understanding of how a species behaves or an ecosystem functions. Certain field trips involve periods of time spent in harsh environmental conditions, perhaps well away from many of the home comforts one might be accustomed to enjoying. Danger, such as the risk of encountering poisonous snakes, might be involved. Not everyone accepts or adapts to this part of being a scientist. As soon as they begin to climb up the ladder, such people are keen to minimise or even avoid time spent in the field observing and learning. Perhaps they also realise that such effort is not as helpful in career-building as presenting a well-written paper or report. So they spend too much time sitting on their chairs in the office and in front of their computer screens. Losing touch with the real world of nature, these individuals quickly become "shiny bums".

iv. Trading on ideals

The Body Shop is perhaps the best-known example of a major business supposedly based on environmentally-friendly principles and concern for people in the poorer countries of our world. Anita Roddick, the businesswoman who started the company, is frequently interviewed by the media for her views. She is intelligent and self-assured, and comes across as a sincere person.

Prior to 1994, The Body Shop used the "Trade, not aid" slogan. Some of the ingredients for their beauty care products were purchased overseas from tribal people of the rainforests and such like. They presented an attractive and powerful advertising message: buy our cosmetics and at the same time help the native people of the rainforests preserve their simple lifestyle and environment. Many people, especially girls and young women, soaked it up. But what is wrong with aid? As rich countries like Britain have exploited many of the poorer countries in the past, surely we have a duty to now help by assisting with relief and development? There is a lot wrong with how the aid is given, and the aid agencies themselves are dreadfully inefficient and ineffective (as I have outlined in Chapter 8 of my previous book *Actions Speak Louder Than Words* and in reports specifically written for the organisations) – but the concept of aid is good and just. Thankfully, the company has more recently dropped the "Trade, not aid" slogan to publicise its work with indigenous peoples, and it now uses the less derogatory "fair trade" catch-phrase.

Journalists have repeatedly challenged The Body Shop's image. They have pointed out that the company seems to trade as much on making the most of its apparent virtue as on the cosmetics it actually sells. And there have been serious doubts as to the reality of this "ideal" trade arrangement. For example, in 1992 The Body Shop launched a new product made from Brazil nuts purchased from the Kayapo tribe. Yet within months, allegations were being made about a leading member of the tribe, Paiakan, whom

The Body Shop had been keen to promote as a partner in their work. A leading Brazilian magazine announced during the Earth Summit at Rio that Paiakan was facing a charge of rape. Paiakan's lifestyle was subsequently shown to be anything but the model of simple tribal existence and sustainability that The Body Shop had portrayed. He enjoyed homes in the city, cars, and alcohol. It was even alleged that he was one of the beneficiaries in the Kayapo tribe receiving millions of dollars a year in royalties from gold mining and logging. Whether or not The Body Shop knew all of this is not the issue; the point is that they were too quick to present a romantic ideal and promote themselves as an exemplary, high-principled business.

v. African elephants

The history of killing elephants for their ivory goes back a very long time. Poaching is not new. As an example, pianos became popular in the 1800s and remained so into the 20th century. In 1910, the United States of America alone manufactured 350,000 pianos. It took 700 tonnes of elephant tusks to provide the ivory for the piano keys – which represents about 13,000 dead elephants for just that one year of production. Nobody seemed to care.

In the 1970s, the problem started to escalate. By the 1980s, ivory poaching was common and widespread. Iain Douglas-Hamilton, a leading expert on elephants, estimated that 500,000 were slaughtered within this single decade.

The main economic force behind this ivory rush was the increased wealth of ordinary people in Japan. More Japanese could now afford to buy ivory Hanko seals, prized status symbols in their society, with which they signed their letters. But many other countries were also to blame. The USA was importing 25% of the world's ivory as bracelets, necklaces, and carved ornaments (ironically including elephants); 97% of these products were carved in Hong Kong, a place known to be the recipient of mainly illegal ivory.

Somali poachers were amongst the toughest and most determined. Accustomed to living in harsh conditions, they easily infiltrated Kenya's national parks. Armed with an AK-47, a poacher could gun down a whole family of elephants. But the Somalis were by no means alone. Throughout Africa, many people became involved in the ivory business; senior government officials were often implicated. An elephant with ivory was seen to be like a paper bag full of money left lying under a bush.

Iain Douglas-Hamilton – together with Oria, his wife – repeatedly tried to get the conservation movement to take notice of what was happening. A number of other individuals shared the couple's concern. Even as evidence of both the slaughter and illegal trade grew, key organisations were reluctant to act.

One central issue of disagreement was whether or not to continue trying to regulate a legal trading of ivory. Throughout much of the 1980s, the influential WWF was amongst those organisations which (perhaps surprisingly) opposed a ban. In favour of continuing a regulated trade, they claimed that a ban would merely drive the trafficking underground. The Douglas-Hamiltons and others (with whom I agree) said such an argument was absurd; 90% of all ivory on the market had been obtained illegally anyway.

Increasing publicity during the late 1980s coincided with a mushrooming of new organisations and campaigns dedicated to saving the elephant. On the positive side, there was a lot of heartfelt concern – a refreshing change from the apparent indifference within parts of the conservation establishment – and this was helpful in motivating the support of governments. But on the negative side, highly emotional appeals tended to misrepresent the true state of what was happening to the African elephant. One organisation after another started saying that the species would be "extinct within 10 years."

Although huge numbers of elephants had been poached across much of Africa, there was another side to the story. In Zimbabwe and Botswana, there had been an *increase* of

50,000 elephants – despite regular culling by the park authorities as part of their management policy. And South African conservationists thought that people in Europe and North America were ruled by their emotions, unable to rationally think; in the famous Kruger National Park, hundreds of elephants were annually culled by the park staff due to overabundance. In total, there was still an African elephant population of 600,000.

Nevertheless, something had to be done to reduce the widespread poaching in many parts of the continent. Perhaps the symbolic turning point was on 18th July 1989. Richard Leakey, the famous palaeontologist, had recently been appointed as director of Kenya's national parks and wildlife; his style of leadership was straightforward and decisive. A giant pile of ivory – more than 2,000 tusks worth about US$3 million at the time – was constructed in the Nairobi National Park and set ablaze in front of VIPs and media representatives. This was Leakey's way of announcing to Kenya and the world that the poaching had to stop. The burning of ivory and its clear message was followed up by strong anti-poaching measures.

Although it was important to act, the way in which many of the "ele" organisations and campaigns chose to inform the general public must be questioned. It was blatantly untrue to say that the African elephant was in serious danger of becoming extinct within 10 years. Yet they did this time after time. The situation in southern Africa made the idea of the elephant facing extinction simply ridiculous. Educate, yes. Urgently appeal for help, yes. But to "cry wolf" is a dangerous tactic that often backfires in the long-term. It also has the effect of distracting attention and funds away from genuinely endangered species.

vi. A comment about zoos

I am not an anti-zoo person. However, there are still a lot of improvements, some involving radical change, that I believe need to be achieved before zoos can be fully accepted as being ethically responsible. But zoos have their place, especially with regard to education. I have photographed and filmed wildlife as part of a range of educational initiatives; however good and inspiring, these images cannot replace the experience of actually encountering a living animal face-to-face. As not everyone is fortunate enough to be able to travel the world and view wildlife in the wild, captive groups of animals (properly looked after) provide an alternative.

Zoos today have inherited their past function of being a source of entertainment as well as places of curiosity and interest. Conservation has become a worldwide issue, changing the public's perception; the old idea of wild animals as something to merely look at with a mixture of amazement and amusement is outdated. People are now more interested in the natural world.

So zoos today present themselves as some kind of modern Noah's ark – with "an important role" in conservation. And this propaganda has succeeded in fooling many people. Captive-breeding of endangered animals for release to the wild is the most common myth. The fact is that it very rarely happens. Such an exercise is harder to achieve than generally realised; it is also usually expensive. (The breeding is comparatively easy, but successful release into the wild is more complicated.) It is much better to concentrate efforts on improving the situation in the wild. Then, if required, translocation – moving wild animals from one place to another – is a more sensible method for aiding recovery. Captive-breeding for release to the wild is little more than a desperate "last chance" option, and is only really necessary when all else has failed.

The quality of education that zoos currently offer to the public continues to be poor. Much of this is still of the "how-many-vertebrae-in-a-giraffe's-neck?" variety. Newspaper and magazine articles, and natural history and current affairs programmes on television, offer better information than does a visit to most zoos. Part of a zoo's "educational" message is little more than a series of internal fundraising appeals and propaganda to justify its own existence.

If zoos are really serious about making a significant contribution to conservation, they should begin by reducing the huge costs incurred through maintaining extensive animal collections and a large staff requirement. By offering a greatly slimmed-down range of captive animals – enhanced through much bigger enclosures, together with better quality education for the public – large amounts of money could then be re-directed towards genuine conservation requirements. Instead, zoos are currently competing with other organisations for funding. I suggest they should have a major re-think: to become fund-raisers, rather than fund-wasters.

vii. Empire building

Former US President Ronald Reagan once said: "I sometimes suspect that the lobbyists for the environmental interest feel that they have to keep their constituents stirred up or they might not have jobs anymore." Whereas this might have been uttered as an excuse for US government inaction, there is also truth in the statement. The conservation movement is increasingly far from pure in its motivation. All kinds of hidden agendas – emanating from career-driven individuals to a wealthy complex of small and large organisations – commonly confuse the picture.

Five years ago, in 1993, the Organisation for Economic Co-operation and Development stated that the annual world market in environmental goods and services was worth at least £170 billion and growing at a rate of 5–8% per year. Helping the environment has become big business.

Charities and pressure groups heavily rely on public support. As these organisations have grown, so has the size of people's salaries (individually and as a whole). Money is equated with power. Paying wages to staff becomes a regular on-going commitment; the money has to keep pouring in or people start losing their jobs. Imaginative campaigns and encouraging newsletters are churned out to keep members and other donors interested. But you can't easily combine the imagination and mind of an environmental (or social) reformer with the job of being a fundraiser; the two are effectively at odds with each other, because it is the majority view which is the problem in need of reform. Criteria for getting government funding and other grants will also reflect the prevailing opinion, which is likely to conflict with radical and progressive ideas.

The various organisations heavily compete for your money. Overcompetitiveness leads to bitter rivalry, disregard for a balanced presentation of facts, glossing over (or even denying) failure, and use of emotional hype. Coalitions emerge from time to time, based just as much (if not more) on cliques and self-interest than on caring and genuine mutual concern for nature. People and organisations begin to get illusions of power. The heart of the matter can be lost.

Whatever the group, organisation, institution, or department, it is likely to overstate its role to the exclusion of others. In an overcompetitive environment, people are quick to claim credit for any victory. And these "victories" themselves are usually exaggerated and easily undone. The claims and counter-claims about which organisation is doing what and who is "leading the fight" can be very confusing, amusing, or just plain sad (depending on how you look at it).

Empire building is inefficient and distracts effort away from the cause, especially when more and more start competing in the same game. So-called "free" gifts are commonly offered by charities to help tempt your support. These can range from key rings, Christmas cards, pens, and posters, to car stickers (usually with no educational message, but always with the organisation's name), T-shirts, badges, and bird-feeders. (Ironically, it seems that these organisations are trying to encourage consumerism, rather than question it!) And then there are the clever marketing slogans; "running out of time" was one which caught my attention the other day – the catch-phrase of a save-the-cheetah group.

Qualities such as integrity and straightforwardness are amongst the casualties of this empire building approach. It becomes hard to work out fact from fairy tale. The language of public relations takes over. Image becomes more important than substance. Public relations is preoccupied with reputation – the result of what you are seen to do and say, and what others say about you. It creates a shallowness. It is a waste of time, energy, and money. Open dialogue suffers because it threatens to spoil that well-rehearsed, cut-and-dried line and so must be avoided. The slick presentation of the public relations game is only needed when you get into trouble. Then it obsessively feeds off itself. I suggest that empire building gets you into more and more of a dilemma.

8

Examining "sustainable development"

i. A missed opportunity?

The term "sustainable development" has been one of the key environmental phrases in recent years. It became commonly used after the 1992 United Nations Conference on Environment and Development in Rio de Janeiro – the Earth Summit. But what does it mean?

If anything was achieved at Rio in 1992, it was this: the governments of the world formally acknowledged that something was going wrong with the environment. But, as certain countries have already industrialised and others are still poor and in the process of catching up, the subject of development needed to be included in any debate. And so development – not the environment – dominated the proceedings. Poorer countries understandably demanded the right to develop. President George Bush, at the other extreme, stubbornly declared that the lifestyle of the United States of America was not a matter for discussion.

The overall composition and thrust of development in the world was not seriously questioned. Indeed, it was endorsed. The environmental factor was merely added on. History may see it as an important step forward. Or future generations might regard the international meeting as nothing more than an enormously expensive waste of time – spent on talk and compromise – a side-stepping of the crucial issues. (There were more than 40,000 participants. Over 100,000,000 sheets of paper represented the views of those attending the summit.)

ii. A flawed concept?

The vast majority of people do not seem to have a problem with "sustainable development". In theory, neither do I. But in practice, considering today's mind-set, I think it currently means little more than a token consideration to environmental concerns. People have been fooled by clever words, made possible by the usual lack of both clear and deep thinking; it sounds good, so they presume it must be good.

The fundamental difficulty is with whatever we mean by the word "development". It is generally understood as being economic growth, bringing a higher standard of living. But for almost everyone – individuals, businesses, governments, whoever – development effectively means the right to continue being selfish. "Me, me, me." "Money, money, money." "I want more." Human beings willing to carry on exploiting nature.

Development isn't just a matter of technology or economics. Essentially, it is driven by our psychology – a reflection of our perceptions, thoughts, feelings, and ambitions. So those numerous, perhaps well-intentioned environmentalists who believe that a solution is mainly to do with cleaning up existing technology are deluding themselves. We also need to look inwardly and change ourselves.

People are quick to insist on their rights – such as the right to develop or keep on developing. But how about the balancing responsibilities? It isn't that humans are irresponsible; they're just not responsible enough. It isn't that they don't care; they simply don't care enough. "Me first." "Me and my family first." "My country before yours."

The self-orientated psychology is dysfunctional and limited. It currently exists side by side with what we call development. So whilst humans remain within this selfish frame of mind, they cannot be relied upon to sustain anything other than themselves. There is a blind spot. There is greed. Taking outweighs or outstrips giving. Therefore, "sustainable development" is presently a flawed concept. It is a contradiction in terms. Unless human psychology radically changes – or, at very least, people learn to be genuinely sensitive to this dilemma – the idea of sustainably developing will not work.

iii. "Sustainable use"

In the context of a selfish psychology, "sustainability" is an unreliable ideal and a dangerous distraction from what really needs to be done. "Sustainable use" of natural resources is a licence to keep on destroying, rather than to call a halt to the devastation and thereby let live.

There is little evidence which shows that "sustainable use" actually works. When there might be some possible benefit to nature conservation – such as increased revenue through "harvesting" wildlife – it is linked to a commercial advantage. If an animal, plant, or area of wilderness offers an attractive economic opportunity, it might be saved so it can be exploited or utilised. But when there is no longer a good enough financial incentive, the will to conserve is lost. Meanwhile, there is the real risk of over-exploitation when markets are involved.

We have had more than 20 years of CITES. Theoretically, this should be able to regulate trade according to the abundance or scarcity of a species; scientists and other specialists investigate and make recommendations, approved by international agreement. Yet, in reality, time after time the laws are disregarded by those who want to sell and own. (We have seen several examples of this in earlier chapters.) The fact is that selfishness corrupts. It cannot be trusted. Greed spoils the possibility of "sustainable use" being taken seriously. And life's increasing pressures will heighten the overall trend to want more.

The concept, as well as being flawed, is limited. Not every species or habitat in need of protection has commercial potential. So when there is no financial incentive, how will it be saved? The answer, very simply, is through altruistic caring. Human beings are capable of looking beyond their own self-interest, appreciating nature for its own sake – realising that we can all exist together. This caring just needs to be cultivated. If this solution is required in cases where the possibility of monetary gain is absent, we should be able to apply the same solution in *all* circumstances. And whereas financial benefits might fluctuate, lessen, or even eventually disappear, a love of nature (once gained) is more likely to remain strong.

iv. Do people really think globally when acting locally?

One potentially good initiative which emerged from the Earth Summit in 1992 was Agenda 21. The idea was to get people involved at a local level – looking towards creating an action plan for the 21st century, including better ways for how we live our lives, reducing our impact on both the local and global environment, and ensuring that future generations can continue to enjoy a good quality of life. Agenda 21 recognises that environmental, social, and economic issues are inherently linked.

Here in Britain, each local authority was asked to consult with the community. A partnership between local government and residents, businesses, schools, environmentalists and other special interest groups within the area should work together to draw up an action plan to ensure that we move towards more sustainable lifestyles – a Local Agenda 21.

Unfortunately, however, this opportunity seems likely to be wasted. The majority of district councils appear to be more or less copying each other's approach to what is actually a huge, complex, and potentially radical undertaking. They are not addressing the most important issues, although the publication of their documents indicate that they seem to recognise the existence of these problems. The actions suggested do not tackle the root of the problems; basic topics such as greed and overpopulation are being conveniently ignored. What they are doing is repeating the same rhetoric and concentrating on the promotion of superficial actions which promise to deliver little or no change to the overall situation. Instead of rising to the challenge "think globally, act locally", the thinking still appears to be narrow-minded and self-orientated.

v. An example of international fudge

Fudge is a sugary sweet. It is also another word for evasiveness, to dodge, to deceive, or to cheat. Fudging the issue, but coating it in words of compromise and superficial agreement, is common in politics.

In 1990, an international gathering of leaders met at the Second World Climate Conference. Our climate seems to be changing and sea levels are rising. A number of island states in the Pacific exist only about two metres above sea level. They could be the first nations in history to disappear completely due to an environmental disaster. They would simply be drowned. Action was (and is) needed, not the hot air of rhetoric. Yet hollow words prevailed.

And so the Prime Minister of Tuvalu spoke out: "I am not happy with the commitments made by a number of industrialised countries, which has resulted in what I regard as a weak declaration. It appears that science is being ignored by a number of decision makers. If science is being deliberately ignored, then I will regard such an attitude as one of total selfishness. We in Tuvalu contribute little or nothing to the problem, and yet we will be first to suffer. Our survival is at stake."

vi. Priorities

A lot of the current conservation effort is being directed to try to make "sustainable development" work. Environmental activists and lobbyists have succeeded in getting their subject international recognition. Businesses are more or less willing to adapt, so long as they can keep on making money. And governments are pleased to be able to accommodate most people's views and get some of the credit. But all this ignores the fact that the "sustainable development" concept means different things to different people. A general, superficial, and cleverly-worded agreement might explain the concept's popularity – but it ignores a mountain of disagreement which arises when specifics are considered, with the risk of exposing fundamentally opposing perspectives.

Much of the argument in favour of pursuing this strategy depends on management improvements – such as minimising pollution, better energy efficiency, recycling and the reduction of waste, etc. However, whilst efficient distribution of cargo within a ship is helpful and can significantly increase carrying capacity, there is still a maximum weight beyond which the ship will sink. And if you don't know or understand this, you might be shuffling the load around.....only to be suddenly caught out by the ship beginning to sink, as one more bit of weight is added.

For a practical example of this, look at cars. (I'm not an anti-car person; overall, they have provided many benefits and greatly enhanced personal freedom.) Looking back over the past few decades, motor vehicles have gradually become more fuel efficient; a better designed engine means more miles or kilometres to every gallon or litre of fuel. Additionally, the fuel itself has probably been made safer (e.g. unleaded petrol) and exhaust emissions are being reduced. However, these gains are being undone by the production of more cars and an increase of car usage or vehicle miles/kilometres driven. Furthermore, models with unnecessarily large engines have become more and more popular – in comparison with those at the economy end of the range – typically advertised by how quickly the car can accelerate from zero to 60 miles per hour. The most obvious result of all these changes is more traffic jams and delays, despite more road building; the system is simply being overloaded.

Some environmentalists have seen through the bland promise of "sustainable development". They see it as being more about the conservation of economic development, rather than the conservation of nature. They claim that mainstream organisations have compromised the basic principles which motivated many of the early pioneers into action. Instead, they insist (and I agree) that the priorities are wrong. We must first concentrate our aim on achieving *ecological* sustainability – solving existing problems, before rushing ahead and thereby creating more difficulties.

At this point, I disagree with the future vision of many of these so-called deep ecologists. They are usually anti-industry and they dream of some kind of a simple existence with nature, heavily dependent upon self-sufficiency at a local community level. I think this notion of the good life is over-romantic, backward, and unnecessary. I see nothing inherently wrong – and much to gain from – modern medicine, television, etc. I am sure that once we have stopped our heavy-handed approach and helped restore ecological sustainability, we can *then* maturely consider how to develop further without threatening the environment.

9

Poverty

i. Shameful facts and figures

Although poverty has been reduced in many parts of the world, a quarter of all human beings still remain in severe poverty. In a global economy of US$25 trillion, this is shameful. It represents an unacceptable level of inequality and a dismal failure of international policy.

About 1.3 billion people in the developing countries live on incomes of less than US$1 a day. Over half a million women die each year in childbirth – at rates 10 to 100 times higher than those in industrialised countries; in Somalia, for example, 1 woman in 7 will die in childbirth – compared to 1 in 5,100 in the UK. Over 350,000 children die every day from illnesses which are easy and cheap to cure. Nearly a billion people are illiterate. More than 1.2 billion lack access to safe water. Some 840 million go hungry, are chronically malnourished, or face food insecurity. And nearly a third of the people in the least developed countries – most of which are in sub-Saharan Africa – are not expected to survive to the age of 40.

ii. A widening gap

There are 447 billionaires in the world (1996 figures). Their wealth is greater than the combined annual incomes of half the human population. That's 447 people on one side of the scale and about 2,950,000,000 on the other. The wealth of the single richest Mexican in 1995 was US$6.6 billion – an amount equal to the total earnings of the 17 million poorest Mexicans.

A number of multinational corporations command more wealth and economic power than most states do. Indeed, of the world's 100 largest economies, 50 are megacorporations. General Motors, Ford, Toyota, Exxon, Royal Dutch/Shell, IBM, Unilever, Nestlé, and Sony each have corporate sales bigger than the combined GDP (gross domestic product) of Ethiopia, Rwanda, Burundi, Nepal, Madagascar, Kenya, Sierra Leone, Niger, Mali, Uganda, Mozambique, Gambia, Chad, Malawi, Senegal, Tanzania, and Ghana. That's one of the above companies having a greater annual turnover than all 17 of the developing countries listed put together. Most of these multinational corporations actually have a greater income than the combined GDP of all 48 of the least developed countries.

The total cost of running a medical clinic in Sudan – which I have done for the past 14 years, working non-paid – is roughly equivalent to the average salary of one paid British charity worker. This amount includes enough money for purchasing medicine, equipment, and laboratory materials here in the UK for 35,000 patients a year, shipping it overseas and transporting it by lorry to where we work, constructing and maintaining all necessary buildings, employing 12 medically-trained and other local staff, running a vehicle/ambulance and generator, supporting patients who need referrals for specialist hospital treatment, and the essential administration costs of such a project. There are only two differences between how we and other charities operate: (1) we are acutely aware of the problematic and deceptive nature of the "me, me, me" psychology, and (2) we clearly remember who the poor people are and that it is they who need the help, not us.

And then there's you. Whatever your level of income – whether you are "poor", average, or rich by British standards – you are still effectively a "millionaire" in many respects, compared to large numbers of other people in the world. Can you imagine living on an income of just US$1 a day? Even if you were able to grow some of your own food, such a small amount of money doesn't buy very much. This is the difference between absolute or severe poverty and the so-called "poverty" in a country such as Britain.

iii. The poor are getting poorer

In addition to a widening gap between the rich and poor, many of those suffering from poverty are getting poorer. During the past 20 years, more than 100 developing and transitional countries have suffered disastrous failures in economic growth, causing drastic cuts in living standards. As a result of these setbacks, the incomes of more than a billion people have fallen below levels first reached 20 or even 30 years ago.

The least developed countries, with 10% of the human population, have only 0.3% of the world's trade – half their share of two decades ago. The poorest 20% of people now live on a miserable 1.1% of the global income. This is down from 1.4% in 1991 and 2.3% in 1960. After many years of development aid to help the poor, we surely should have been able to expect the opposite?

iv. A change of policy

Poverty means the denial of choices and opportunities for a tolerable or better life. The poorest of the poor are severely disadvantaged.

Whereas the economic growth of a country can be a way of reducing poverty, this does not automatically trickle down to help everybody at the bottom end of the income scale. The reason for this is due to the wide variations of individual ability to take advantage of any such opportunity. The rich and moderately rich are generally better at exploiting promising situations – due to having more education, information, and money to invest – whereas the poor do not know how to benefit or are otherwise unable to do so. Individuals and nations generally try to get the best deal for themselves – "looking after number one" – and habitually exploit their fellow human beings in a similar manner to their abuse of nature.

This increasing inequality is heightening envy and other forms of dissatisfaction. People have rising expectations as they see around them the material benefits of others being rich. (There are, for example, more than 1.2 billion televisions worldwide.) Sadly, however, most people have plummeting prospects as we have seen. This will add a new dimension to the overall situation. The World Health Organisation is predicting that stress-related illness will be the biggest problem of the developing countries by the year 2020. It is easy to understand why and how.

If poverty is to be reduced, policy makers must avoid "ruthless" growth that just seems to help the rich get richer. We somehow need policies which are pro-poor. The United Nations, governments, and other institutions are considering how to achieve this, but a definite solution seems far from clear. Affluent countries consistently demonstrate that they are unwilling to give even a small percentage of their wealth – as opposed to a tiny token amount – necessary to begin amending the unfairness in lifestyles. And what little is given each year, quickly gets wasted by the empire building aid agencies and career-driven aid workers. (Many people usually believe that it is the overseas politicians and businessmen who are stealing money intended to help the poor. This happens, of course. But remember that it is the aid organisations which receive most of the funding and therefore have the easiest means of misspending what is available.)

v. A radical re-think

It is probable that the absolute poverty of the third world – which most people in the rich countries never get to see, hear, smell, taste, or touch (other than through television pictures or perhaps during a sanitised holiday taken somewhere like India) – will be gradually solved. Huge numbers of children who today die of measles or diarrhoea might hopefully one day not do so. In my opinion, increasing global business activity is sooner or later likely to bring this change about – rather than through help from the aid organisations. But other problems will no doubt remain and new ones are certain to occur. A billion people might jump out of the frying pan of absolute poverty into the fire of emotional and communal poverty – still facing a life of general insecurity, albeit in a different way.

If the psychology and culture of selfishness is indeed the fundamental cause of our problems, then there is unlikely to be any major overall improvement until a radical re-think takes place. I suggest this is needed as much with regard to the issue of human poverty as it is with the environmental crisis. If we are prepared to examine our basic attitude and approach to life, making changes at root level, only then can we hope to genuinely succeed.

Greed must be replaced with altruism. International peace, human rights, compassion for animals, as well as poverty and nature conservation, all currently take second place to the lust for wealth, power, and material gain. These priorities should be reversed. Too many people still believe that money can buy happiness. Although money can undoubtedly make some things easier, this advantage is usually overestimated. The "me, me, me" psychology produces certain limited benefits, especially for the "winners" – but a "you and me" way of being would bring about a far wider range of gains for everyone.

vi. Environmental considerations

As the poorer countries and their citizens develop, they are going to spend their increased wealth on a variety of goods. These will range from materials essential for basic infrastructure and services – such as roads, sewage systems, hospitals, schools, and all associated equipment – to better housing and an improved general living standard. Significant amounts of extra energy will be needed both to produce and operate these new material benefits. All of which have to come from somewhere; they are, of course, natural resources.

The poor have a right to develop. We cannot – should not – ignore severe poverty. It is vitally important that we care for people who are in desperate need, as well as for wildlife and the environment. Both issues require a solution. Caring is caring.....and it should not be limited.

If we accept this right to develop – and we must – then today's least developed countries will consequently consume more natural resources in the future. Unless somehow balanced, this developmental change for the better will inevitably produce an increased pressure on nature. If we believe in fairness, those of us who live in the more affluent countries need to restrict our consumerism so as to compensate for others catching up with the basic standard of living which we enjoy and usually take for granted. Otherwise, our planet's wildlife and environment will continue to suffer and decline – probably at an even faster rate than is presently the case.

vii. A comment about poverty in Britain

There are many people in Britain and other industrialised countries who will insist that they are poor. I do not disagree, relatively speaking – if you are only comparing upwards. But in comparison with the poorest of the world's poor, they actually have little to complain about. Yet they often do. The so-called poor within affluent countries have generally produced a culture of moaning and feeling sorry for themselves. Some seem addicted to their "victim" mentality. They demand rights, but conveniently overlook the associated responsibilities. There is always someone else to blame for their less-than-ideal situation.

I have personally known what it is to be poor, living in Britain, (and I am not without sympathy towards others, where it is deserved). But this is very different from the life of someone living in a mud hut in Ethiopia or Sudan, with little or no access to basic modern infrastructure such as health care. Those who are less well-off in the rich countries should ask when is "enough" enough? If they do not, they will continue to get caught up in a self-indulgent cycle of greed and discontentment. Meanwhile, the absolute poor urgently need our help – as does nature.

10

The beast that kills for kicks

i. A royal tradition

In the early 1960s, Queen Elizabeth II and Prince Philip – together with British government officials, including the foreign secretary of the time – hunted and shot tigers at Ranthambhore in India, as well as in Nepal.

Earlier, in 1924, the then Duke and Duchess of York – later King George VI and Queen Elizabeth (the Queen Mother) – enjoyed a hunting holiday in Kenya, killing a range of wild animals. One photograph shows the couple standing proudly beside a black rhino they had just killed; in another photo, they are shown casually sitting on top of a dead elephant.

Probably the biggest safari of all time, however, took place in 1909. The US President Theodore Roosevelt went hunting in East Africa, supposedly collecting for the Washington Museum as well as for his own private collection. Roosevelt is nowadays often considered to have been a pioneer of conservation, but Frederick Jackson – then acting governor of Kenya – noted in his diary: "He was utterly reckless in the expenditure of ammunition, and exceeded reasonable limits, in particular with the white rhino of which he and his son Kermit killed nine!" By the end of his expedition, 2,500 animals and birds had been shot.

These examples of the privileged elite hunting for pleasure are only a tiny fraction of what went on. Such "sport" was considered to be highly fashionable amongst the rich, famous, and those who had gone to live in far-off countries like Kenya seeking adventure or their fortune.

ii. Trophy hunting today

There has been a growing interest in trophy hunting during recent years. In Africa, it is legal in a number of countries to shoot big game - including rhino, leopard, and elephant. Exotic game ranches have sprung up in places such as Texas, USA; a variety of species from around the world are offered for sale, without the hunter having to afford the much higher costs involved in travelling overseas. Safari Club International holds a large annual show in America at locations such as Las Vegas and Reno to attract hunting clients and offer rare (and consequently endangered) species available to shoot. It is big business, with individuals willing to pay more than US$75,000 to get that next prized trophy. In countries where hunting certain wild animals is illegal, the trade nevertheless still flourishes when officials are open to bribery.

In my previous book, *Actions Speak Louder Than Words*, I briefly mentioned the following case. A wealthy client staying at a private game ranch in Zimbabwe already had many trophies hanging on his wall back home. But he didn't have a giraffe and so he wanted to shoot one. At first, the ranch owner was reluctant to co-operate as he only had six giraffes on his property. However, the money offered went up and up until it was "too good an opportunity to miss." A member of staff was told to select one of the giraffes for the client. He found a giraffe which was blind in one eye – but the incident sickened him so much that the man left his job shortly afterwards in disgust at both men's greed.

Shooting an elephant is considered by many to be the ultimate in trophy hunting. Yet elephants are highly intelligent, social animals. They are sensitive and enjoy family relationships – apparently capable of humour and grief, according to those who have spent years studying them. After being killed, a chainsaw is usually used to cut off the head and ears which are then re-created by a taxidermist; the elephant's feet are severed for use as waste bins or umbrella stands.

iii. Motivation

Trophy hunting is basically a matter of greed and showing off. A person wants something and has the power/money to get it. There is, of course, the thrill (and even, perhaps, the skill) of the chase. But, ultimately, the wild animal has no chance against a hunter with the might of a modern rifle. This is not sport in the real sense of the word. Humans who hunt are, on one level, undeniably demonstrating their dominance over nature – but does this mask individual insecurity or some other psychological inadequacy?

One well-known absurdity involved an American trophy hunter who had a whole elephant stuffed and painted pink; he then proudly displayed it next to the bar in his New York apartment. Such sick humour clearly illustrates a total lack of regard for wildlife. In another case, multi-millionaire Aristotle Onassis had the bar stools aboard his yacht, the *Christina*, made from the penises of sperm whales.

iv. Helping conservation?

It is claimed by the trophy hunters – and those environmental organisations (such as WWF) who support them – that the big game industry helps conservation. Superficially, there is an argument in favour of this view. Advocates usually point towards Zimbabwe's Campfire Programme in which regional communities get a share of the money spent by rich foreign hunters. Local people, supposedly, are therefore encouraged to regard wildlife as a valuable resource to be conserved. "Use it or lose it" is the motto. Money is also gained for environmental management and research; funding is always needed, by organisations especially, for staff wages.

Regulations which aim to control hunting, however, have been and will continue to be broken. If greed is accepted, it will flourish – together with corruption.

Furthermore, many wild animals roam or migrate across large distances which inevitably leads to problems where hunting areas are allowed. For example, in 1995, a number of the famous Amboseli elephants wandered across the Kenyan border and were promptly shot in a Tanzanian hunting block.

Hunters and their supporters stress that they only kill the old males of a species, leaving the way clear for younger males to take their turn at breeding. And where culling is considered part of management, the pro-hunting lobby argues that they help execute this aim and pay a lot of money for the right to do so. But what they conveniently overlook is the threat to a healthy genetic stock. Some fear that trophy hunters will take out the best bulls, thereby adversely affecting the gene pool. This has already happened as a result of hunting and poaching in the past. A century ago, for example, the average elephant tusk weighed about 30 kg.....whereas today it is just 7 kg.

Perhaps most importantly, the offer of money from hunting towards conservation has blinded those environmentalists who go along with it to the need for education and ethics. Television documentaries show us the wonder of nature. Wildlife organisations (including WWF) remind us about the horrors of poaching. But surely big game hunting is only a form of sanctioned or legalised poaching? Most of the people who marvel at wildlife documentaries and financially contribute towards anti-poaching projects will be appalled at the idea of killing an elephant, rhino, lion, or leopard for kicks. Educationally, it is superficial and contradictory to believe that conservation and hunting can lie comfortably together in the same bed. Ethically, the concept of trophy hunting is selfish and immature; if human beings (and the conservation movement in particular) wish to grow up, caring needs to replace the greed for money and the power of the gun. If hunters want a real challenge, they should try shooting with a camera – aiming to get top quality photographic images.....

v. Poachers

Some conservationists disagree with the activities of rich trophy hunters, then make allowances for poor people who "survive" through poaching. But there is no excuse for poaching. This is misplaced sympathy, perhaps tinged with guilt and embarrassment at being faced with the prospect of having to criticise someone less well-off. Millions of poor people throughout Africa and elsewhere do not turn to poaching; they work hard by farming or other jobs.

Poachers in the developing countries remain comparatively poor by western standards. (It is the middle men and end traders who make by far the most money from this illegal pursuit.) Nevertheless, they are only selfishly thinking of themselves and poaching is seen as an easy or quick way to get money. Whereas there are widely differing levels of greed in the world, greed is still greed – and it should be recognised as such if we are to genuinely progress.

vi. Other kicks.....

Big game hunting is not the only abuse of animals which has to be considered. Fox hunting, deer stalking, pheasant shooting, and bullfighting are just a few of the other "sporting" ways in which the human beast kills for kicks. If it is believed necessary to control the number of foxes and deer, is it ethical to get pleasure from the killing? We must re-think these (and other) traditional forms of recreation, questioning whether they might in fact be barbaric and demeaning as well as cruel.

But the most common practice involving cruelty to animals is that of meat-eating. Millions of farm-bred animals and wild-caught fish are slaughtered every day because people enjoy eating their flesh. Yet millions of healthy and fit vegetarians prove that eating meat is unnecessary. (In fact, from a physiological perspective, humans and the other great apes are frugivores. This means that our bodies are adapted for a diet of fruit, root vegetables, nuts and seeds – not for eating meat. If you doubt this, why not try jumping on the back of a cow and biting it?)

The various ways in which farm animals and fish suffer is well documented, with information readily available in countries like Great Britain. (The Human Potential Trust, for example, has produced a booklet titled *Vegetarianism: food for thought* – obtainable free-of-charge on request.) The mass cruelty is often associated with factory farming methods, but not always. Transportation to and slaughter at the abattoir also results in countless incidents of maltreatment and distress.

It is hypocritical to be against such things as the poaching of elephants for ivory, trophy hunting, bullfighting, fox hunting, etc, if you eat meat. All these activities are based on selfish gratification and a disregard for another creature's life. Meat-eating continues to be accepted as "normal" only because of widespread social conditioning – in which the issue is usually psychologically avoided and the hypocrisy conveniently ignored. Butchers prepare (and increasingly disguise) the slaughtered carcasses for the consumer, so that the product offered for sale looks less like a dead pig and more like a piece of bacon (or whatever). It is surely time for everyone to think more and care more, whatever the issue.....

SECTION THREE:
TOWARDS
A GENUINE SOLUTION

11

What is "nature conservation"?

i. Recognising the problems

*If you don't know where you're going – what your goal is –
you might have worked hard climbing up the ladder, only
to finally discover that it is leaning against the wrong wall.*

Nature conservation has come about through the
recognition that something is wrong and needs to be
corrected. But, as we saw in Chapter 3, there is not one
united environmental movement; there are many factions,
with widely differing aims and motivations. This reflects
how the problems are perceived. Is nature conservation
about saving species from extinction? Has it anything to do
with animal welfare? Is it about preserving beautiful places
so that people can enjoy leisure activities, away from the
noise and stress of everyday life? Or is it about clean air and
water, free from pollution? Or perhaps too many cars? Or
not wanting a waste dump next to where someone lives?

It is just as important to clearly recognise, accept, and
understand the nature of a problem as it is to know the
solution to it; these are actually two sides of the same coin.
If a problem is misunderstood due to narrow-mindedness,

the proposed solution will also likely be limited and therefore lacking to some degree. So, before pushing ahead to make things better, we must first identify what is going wrong and why.

ii. What is causing the problems?

The various causes of our environmental problems exist on several levels. They have occurred due to a combination of changing physical factors (such as technological progress and overpopulation), together with a mixture of psychological attitudes or worldviews (including "I want more" and "go forth and multiply"). Therefore, it is probably naive to think we can solve all our pollution problems – for example – just by making certain technological adjustments, without also considering the issue of greed.

Governments and non-government organisations frequently talk about having to "manage" nature. A national park or private game ranch in Africa which has a healthy elephant population faces a dilemma. One elephant will destroy three trees every day in its quest for food. Park officials and researchers say that a growing number of elephants will eventually destroy or severely alter a reserve's ecosystem, and so they usually recommend culling as part of a management or control policy. But this situation is really a human factor problem, not a natural one. We have artificially boxed wildlife into comparatively small areas, which then require some sort of management. Standing back and seeking a broader perspective, should we not instead be working towards managing humans rather than trying to manage nature?

For every paid conservationist in a rich country like Great Britain, the USA, or Australia, the same amount of money could be spent employing up to 30 local staff in any of the least developed countries – for example, as anti-poaching guards. Year after year, wildlife organisations have been moaning about the shortage of anti-poaching staff in African or Asian national parks and/or the lack of essential equipment for them to do their job.....yet these western conservationists continue to gobble up large amounts of available funding by paying themselves generous salaries (not to mention how much it costs for all the associated trimmings, such as attending conferences and organisational "flag-flying" promotions). Self-serving hidden agendas commonly get in the way of caring, reasoning, integrity, etc.

How we see a problem – together with how we decide to solve it – is therefore determined by the way in which we understand the situation. Generally, a person's perspective is restricted or even distorted by some degree of psychological avoidance. Our views about the environment are linked with (and reflect) how we look at life. And this inner state of being is just as important when trying to appreciate both the cause of and solution to our environmental crisis as, say, the outer reality of an oil spill or a bulldozer stripping the land of its natural vegetation.

iii. Science, technology, and industry

Greenies are often anti-science, anti-technology, and anti-industry. Indeed, they can seem to be anti-progress – as there is a lot of talk about returning to a more natural and harmonious lifestyle in which industry is the banished evil enemy. Their heart is usually in the right place.....but their head must surely have a screw loose or missing.

It is misleading and potentially dangerous nonsense to believe in such a romantic dream. The growth of science, technology, and industry has provided the comfortable lifestyle we all enjoy to one degree or another in the industrialised countries.....a wide range of things which people are quick to take for granted. Science and technology have given us the television, for example, allowing people to watch and learn from natural history documentaries; industry has mass-produced over a billion television sets so far at a cheaper and cheaper cost. Science, technology, and industry have increased agricultural output – allowing more food to be produced from the same space. Medicines have been developed and made widely available, together with increasingly sophisticated surgical techniques – giving us better health and prolonging our lifespan.

So the anti-progress environmentalists are confused. It is true that the rise in technological progress and mass-production of industry has caused countless environmentally damaging incidents. But technology and industry are only guilty by association; they are not, in themselves, the main or real cause. It is the greed and selfishness of people which is actually at fault – and this has been given more opportunities to flourish as material progress has increased.

The scientific method has given us an invaluable tool to go beyond belief and superstition. The knowledge from science is sooner or later available for everyone to use, exploitatively or wisely. Technology is the means to find ways of applying this pure knowledge in everyday or specialised practical areas of life. Industry supplies the market demand for this technology, making the achievements widely obtainable to society. To repeat from above: if there is anything wrong, (which there is), it is the usual psychological factor of greed and other forms of selfishness.

Those who claim to want to revert back to a simpler lifestyle more or less free of technology and materialism can be very petty. Take bananas, for instance. Here in Britain, we all laughed in disbelief when the European Union made specifications about the "correct" shape of bananas which could be allowed in trade. But the greenies, obsessed with a (hazy?) vision of how we might live more harmoniously with nature, would stop us importing and therefore eating bananas altogether! They consider such international trade to be indulgent and wasteful, insisting instead that it would be better if we just traded within our own region and lived on local produce. Personally, I enjoy bananas and I intend to carry on eating them. (I also happen to grow almost all the vegetables I eat.) To me, what really matters is how much you give and take overall – and petty distractions merely divert attention from the need for such a basic assessment.

Embracing science, technology, and industry is not incompatible with a deeper approach to nature conservation. Those environmentalists who believe the opposite simply do not understand the underlying causes; they are not thinking clearly enough. They are also often ignorant of science and perhaps, therefore, feel intimidated. We need to progress even further and make the benefits of development available to everyone. To believe otherwise is daft and elitist – probably even racist – and such people would quickly change their minds or dreams in the cold light of day. The words of Joni Mitchell's song *Big Yellow Taxi* are again true (in a different sense): "You don't know what you've got till it's gone."

iv. Live and let live

Through the work of our wildlife charity, I have helped to secure, establish, and improve nature reserves both locally and internationally. In the short-term, we have no choice but to use such reserves to protect endangered species and threatened habitat. Having said this, I think that the idea of nature reserves – be they national parks or local sanctuaries – is fundamentally flawed. By concentrating so much attention onto these reserved areas for wildlife, people automatically give themselves the right to exploit or destroy the rest of the natural world.

Human activity has spread more and more; we have largely dominated nature and pushed much of the planet's wildlife into small remnants of habitat. This mass human intrusion is halted (or at least reduced) through the creation of national parks and similar havens, but major problems nevertheless still exist. As we have already briefly seen, for example, elephants do not have enough space to exist without being "managed" through culling when their numbers get too high. More commonly, there might be conflict between the interests of people living next to a national park (or similar) and the wild animals being protected within it; an increasing human population will often demand more land or the right to cut wood from the reserved area, and the wildlife might graze upon the people's crops around the border of a national park.

But aside from a variety of problems and other tensions like the examples above, the concept of national parks is worrying from a longer-term perspective. By severely limiting the space of a reserved area – and therefore the number of individual animals or plants living within this restricted zone – it is likely that we are preventing the possibility of further evolution. The existing assortment of protected wilderness and natural habitats might, perhaps, be just enough to preserve a reasonably wide range of unique species. But really these areas are too small and disconnected, with a few exceptions. Much more space will be required if there is to be the potential for continued evolution. This protection of the evolutionary process must surely be an essential component of true wildlife conservation.

The capacity for further evolution is undeniably a basic biological consideration and should be recognised as such by all policy makers – just as the importance of ecosystems has already been understood to be crucial to conserving individual species. Healthy-minded parents do not just want a baby or child to safeguard; they wish to see the youngster grow and mature into his or her full adult potential. Similarly, conservationists and society in general should realise that wildlife is not something to keep in small living museums to be visited for a holiday or studied to get a PhD. As our planet's most intelligent species, we are effectively now in the position of destroyer or guardian. If we choose to be guardians, we must look after (by keeping safe *and* open) the future of non-human species as well as the future of our children and grandchildren.

In time, if given enough space and freedom, we might be privileged to see an existing species develop further as the evolutionary factors continue. Imagine, for example, how chimpanzees – our nearest relatives – could be in a few thousand or million years from now. It would be the ultimate form of selfishness if our species denied the opportunity for other species to grow and flourish further through the evolutionary process. Life on earth has been developing for many millions of years. Charles Darwin's book on the origin of species was only published some 150 years ago – so it is ironic that as we begin to understand how life in all its forms has evolved, human beings are simultaneously bringing to a halt and effectively denying this basic process of development.

A radical change is therefore necessary. Our thinking ought to be reversed. Restrict the majority of human activity to limited areas and let nature once again have the rest. Beyond these boundaries, people would have to respect the natural habitats as being primarily the home of wildlife – leaving only footprints and taking only photographs and memories, as is currently the advice when visiting today's reserves. In deciding to take less space for our own activities, we will give back to nature its fundamental freedom of wildness.

It will obviously be impossible to achieve such a dramatic turn-around overnight. First, through education, there needs to be understanding. Then we can begin to take the steps of giving back. More and more space can be recovered for nature, but only as humanity decides to voluntarily limit its own population and self-regulate its level of consumption. A great amount of space is especially necessary for the larger mammals that we seem to particularly marvel at and care for. To repeat, the present national parks and other areas are too small and inadequate for nature to properly thrive.

v. Ecological sustainability

The balance of nature is not some romantic state of harmony in which everything lives happily ever after. In reality, nature is often hard and chaotic. It is an ongoing fight for survival in which the fittest individuals or species do best or at least adapt the quickest to fill a particular ecological niche. There have been catastrophic events in pre-history causing mass extinctions, but nature has always had the freedom of space to bounce back. Until the recent domination and spread of *Homo sapiens*.

As discussed in Chapter 8, the current idea of "sustainable development" is muddled and unlikely to significantly help towards solving our environmental crisis. Indeed, it seems to guarantee that development will more or less continue as before – with economic considerations dominating. A better and safer way forward would be to make *ecological* sustainability the top priority, with development options only being considered if this crucial condition was satisfied first and foremost.

We do not know what the Earth's carrying capacity is or what future effect billions of people wanting more and more is going to produce. Such an experiment, if we wish to think of human activity in this way, is taking place at a rapid and still increasing speed. Species are going extinct every day and what little wilderness remains is being lost as each year goes by. It is possible that the ship might sink – or at least begin to sink – before we realise it is overloaded. For our own future safety, as well as respecting the basic right of other species to co-exist with us on planet Earth, an approach based on ecological sustainability is surely the wisest. If the present interpretations of so-called "sustainable development" are allowed to persist, then further species extinction is certain – despite the theoretical recognition of the need for biodiversity etc and all the politically correct words.

vi. Let's get serious!

People haven't yet thought rationally enough and/or cared enough to solve the problem of human beings elsewhere in the world starving and dying due to absolute poverty. So what chance has nature conservation got?

Tokenism can never be enough. It might possibly achieve the winning of a battle or two, but the war will surely be lost. It might deceive some conservationists who want to believe that their efforts are not in vain. Meanwhile, the problems continue and even get worse.

We must embrace all aspects of nature conservation, facing the whole reality of what is going wrong and what needs to be changed. We should not be intimidated nor put off by what looks like a huge problem. It is crucial that we care about wildlife and also human beings. Nature conservation must include the long-overdue need for a wider ethic of social justice, especially towards the poorest people and countries in the world.

The task ahead is daunting and genuine progress will take time to achieve. The environment is seriously in crisis and human activity spiralled dangerously out of control several decades ago. There really isn't any choice: we *must* act.....it is just a question of how, where, and when.

A deeper approach to this environmental situation has to include a broader understanding of the nature conservation concept. We have to clearly recognise all the problems and appreciate what causes them, level by level. So, for example, human attitudes and values are just as important to look at as industrial pollution. We also have to realise that science, technology, and industry are not the real enemies; indeed, they offer us a better life. And conservationists cannot be small-minded if we accept that the evolution of nature is (or ought to be) a continuing process. A radical re-think is required with regard to how much space should be left for wildlife as wilderness, largely free from human interference. One of the key factors towards achieving this future goal must be to concentrate first and foremost on ecological sustainability, rather than so-called "sustainable development" as currently talked about.

12

"What can I do?"

"For every thousand hacking at the leaves of evil, there is one striking at the root."

Henry David Thoreau

i. Compromise or extremism?

As already stated, environmentalists differ enormously in their attitude and approach. Many believe in compromise, whereas a few take an extremist and uncompromising stand. I am convinced that both ways are lacking, yet partly correct.

Extremist activism is usually unsuccessful. Individuals holding such controversial views alienate themselves and invariably refuse to work with others of a different perspective; they are angry and to co-operate would be considered as a betrayal of their principles. However, the extremists do often generate interest and debate. By contrast, the majority who believe in compromise and gaining acceptance from the establishment (the attitudes of which they are trying to change) usually end up with little or no conviction. They are gradually lured into the fold – eventually deciding that if you can't beat them, join them. Careers often matter more than the cause.

In considering this issue of "compromise or extremism?", it is essential to understand exactly what is making change difficult. With nature conservation, it is the current selfishness of human behaviour – whether it be the indifference of the average man and woman in the street or the more obvious greed of some powerful industrialist. Six billion human beings have been psychologically and sociologically conditioned to want more for themselves rather than to care about what happens to the environment. The latter, at best, comes a poor second. Extremists are more or less aware of this mass cultural hypnosis and how difficult it has so far been to change it, and so they understandably turn to drastic measures and shock tactics. (The American group Earth First! are a well-known example of what I mean by extremists – whereas Greenpeace, although seemingly outrageous, are not.....due to being forever eager to win widespread sympathy and support from the general public using sound-bites and media-friendly images.)

The way forward, I suggest, is to be a flexible and realistic extremist. There can be no doubt that our environmental problems are huge and call for urgent attention, so we ought to think big and be prepared for serious action. Significant or radical changes are needed, not just minor adjustments. But we need to be practical and realistic, accepting that genuine progress will not be gained immediately. There is a need for flexibility, as opposed to the compromising of principles. When accepting a staged or partial goal, it is crucially important to remember that a battle won is not the same as winning the war. We should always look beyond it, towards the much higher and more distant objective.

ii. One brain, one body

There is no point in feeling helpless or inadequate; we can all learn to be powerful. We all have one brain and one body – and therefore basically the same potential. As an individual, you have freedom of choice, including freedom of speech and action. To gain real individuality, you have to be true to yourself. Accepting personal responsibility, for yourself and others, produces healthy individuality.

We can choose to go along with the crowd and play the supposed-to-be games. Or else we can stop being sheep-like and do our own living. The choice is always ours. We make

119

a particular decision – then have to be prepared to pay the price, one way or another.

It is frequently those individuals who are prepared to be true to themselves – to stand up and if necessary go against the general trend – who end up doing the most good. What the conservation movement needs is more individuals who are prepared to be true to themselves.....to know themselves and the problems we face.

To learn, you have to listen – which involves patience, openness, and the motivation to understand. Courage and self-honesty are also required; initially, before being able to say "I am responsible", you might have to admit "I am irresponsible". Usually, most people react negatively to situations, out of conditioning and defensiveness; learning how to be proactive, instead of reactive, is another necessary ability. A reactive person is likely to give up when faced with a major problem or set-back – whereas a proactive person will look for a way through, around, or up and over the obstacle.

It is pointless to believe that politicians are going to solve everything. As you wait for others to act, the problems will undoubtedly continue and get worse. Unfortunately, politicians are often self-serving and scared of taking controversial decisions in case they lose the next election. Always remember that the most famous people (politicians or otherwise) also only have one brain and one body. Don't underestimate the power of responsible individuality.

In doing your own thinking, don't be scared to ask questions and make your views known. Some environmental ideas, like society's norms, might not be valid. The suggestion of eco-taxes, for example, is currently fashionable. In my opinion, it will fail to achieve its goal and is just another distraction. If you take the greens' idea of putting extra tax on petrol, for instance, which has now been adopted by government, this is highly unlikely to persuade affluent people to use their cars less; but it will penalise those who are poorer, which cannot be fair.

iii. "Two or less"

Perhaps the most important thing you can do to help the environment is to think carefully about overpopulation. This major problem could be solved if couples were to have *two children or less.* Many will consider that two children per family is reasonable, as it replaces the older generation with the next. A decision not to have children should also be encouraged, which will help stabilise and then reduce the current excessively high population.

Every child that you have (apart from those rare cases in which the baby or youngster unfortunately fails to survive) significantly adds to the amount of natural resources being consumed. If a couple choose to have two children, this doubles the rate of consumption whilst everyone is alive. As we are already in environmental crisis, with huge increases in worldwide materialism still occurring, there is therefore a good argument for considering not having children. Plenty of couples demonstrate that this childless option can still lead to a fulfilling and enjoyable life.

If this suggestion comes too late and you are already a parent or grandparent, you can still talk with your children and/or grandchildren about the "two or less" issue. Education and advice about overpopulation is surely just as important as learning good manners, keeping safe, and other basic lessons of upbringing.

iv. Lifestyle assessment

There are a number of organisations offering leaflets and other forms of advice on what you can do for the environment. Much of this is just common sense and has long been practised by people who do not have money to waste. Turn off lights and other appliances when not using them; draught-proof doors and windows; only heat water when you need it; re-use margarine containers etc for food storage or other uses; don't fill the kettle with more water than you are going to use; start a compost heap in your garden with kitchen waste and weeds; don't drive too fast as this uses more fuel; buy a fuel-efficient car; walk or cycle when you can; use public transport if possible. These suggestions are repeated over and over again – together with the usual simplistic recycling message – as if this is all that is needed.

The flaws and limitations within such advice are seriously worrying, and indicate ignorance or avoidance of the overall situation. There is hardly ever any guidance on the basic issue of overpopulation and family planning. You are constantly asked to re-use, repair, and recycle – even to reduce waste through buying items free of unnecessary packaging – but you are rarely asked to reduce your overall level of consumption, which is surely of fundamental importance. As the cost of wages goes up and up, the idea of repairing everything becomes a very expensive option. It is nowadays usually much cheaper to buy and fit a new spare part, rather than repair and re-use the existing component, simply because it is quicker when paying a car mechanic or plumber by the hour. Indeed, with items such as washing machines, televisions, and video cassette recorders, it can be cheaper to buy a completely new model than attempt to fix the old one. Other campaigns such as "car-free day" and similar initiatives have so far made little or no impression on escalating road use.

I think many environmentalists become feeble and wobbly at the knees when giving educational advice to the public. Perhaps they fear getting a bad reaction, which might affect their cherished reputation, funding, and career prospects? Individually, they might steer away from any kind of confrontation – whether it be constructive or not. Perhaps they also underestimate the public's intelligence and ability to accept the facts. And so they settle for the idea that doing a little bit is better than nothing. This may be true but it is not enough. If there was only a small problem, then a small effort would be sufficient. But the environmental problems are huge, so surely we must do whatever is needed to solve them? Imagine that someone you love had just been seriously injured in a car accident and he or she had been rushed to hospital; would you be impressed if the emergency doctor merely gave the patient a band-aid and aspirin, when major surgery was needed, then went off to have a cup of tea or play golf announcing that he or she had "done a little bit" to help.....?

v. Take less

Most people take far too much. Our society is addicted to over-spending and over-eating. People increasingly go shopping or do some other activity to get a buzz or relief from the stress and boredom of their everyday existence. They usually work in jobs that lack meaning, other than getting paid at the end of the week or month. They get what they can, whilst those above them get more. The rat-race has been accepted.

The word "need" has become confused with "want" and so there is no real sense of perspective or scale. People are always wanting more and more, comparing up to what they haven't yet got. Dissatisfaction, encouraged by advertising and the "keeping up with the Joneses" effect, holds them trapped in an upward spiral. At some level, aware of shame and hypocrisy through acting selfishly, people avoid too much self-honesty – busying themselves, even perhaps believing that they are succeeding, only to forget what matters deeply to us all.

If we are genuinely concerned for the environment, we must take less. This involves reducing our level of overall consumption. Spend less and buy less. Learn to appreciate what you have already got. Delight in the simple joys of life, which usually cost little or nothing. Understand what your essential needs are and make sure they are met. Additionally, take pleasure in a limited amount of what you want – a few occasional luxuries, as opposed to unrestrained indulgence.

vi. Eat less meat or become a vegetarian

Using huge areas of land for grazing as a means of producing food is inefficient and destructive. Fertile land is capable of producing much more vegetarian foodstuff than meat on a per acre/hectare basis. Cows and sheep waste approximately 90% of the plant material needed to feed them – as they use up large amounts of energy through growing, moving about, reproducing, defecating, and so on – making meat production a highly inefficient system of generating food for humans. The same land used for grazing could thus be better utilised for growing fruit, vegetables, pulses, nuts, wheat and other cereals, etc for direct consumption.

The current level of meat-eating is causing the destruction and alteration of natural habitats. A slash-and-burn policy clears millions of acres of South American rainforest, making way for the grazing of cattle to produce cheap beef at a high environmental cost. In Queensland, Australia, the native brigalow vegetation has been extensively "pulled" – again to facilitate cattle grazing – contributing to the severe decline of the now critically endangered bridled nailtail wallaby. Numerous similar examples are occurring all over the world.

A significant reduction in the amount of meat-eating – or, better still, adopting an ethically responsible vegetarian diet – would greatly help solve this problem of excessive land use. The less fertile land presently exploited for grazing would largely be freed by such a change of consumer behaviour, which could then be re-allocated as nature reserves and wild places.

vii. Give more

Taking less by reducing the amount you consume is important. So is giving more. As you take less, you should have spare money or spare time. What do you do with it?

Use this excess time and money to help do something useful. There are many things you can do to benefit the environment, either on your own or by joining a group of others. Get ideas from local and national organisations, but most importantly look around for yourself and use your own brain. Alternatively, give your time and money to another much-needed cause other than the environment. Sacrifice and altruism can be personally rewarding and even fun. As with switching to a vegetarian diet, you are only giving up what causes suffering or other problems.

Earlier in this book, especially in Chapter 7 "Who can you trust?" – and in Chapter 8 of my previous book, *Actions Speak Louder Than Words* – I have explained how charities are not as they should or could be. There is widespread ineffectiveness and inefficiency, along with much flag-flying and empire building. So I would caution the reader to be very careful in giving time or money to an organisation without a great deal of scepticism and thought. Ask if the director gets paid and, if so, how much. Ask what the total cost of salaries is per year. This might indicate if your giving of time or money is likely to be exploited by hidden agendas.

If you want to help the charitable work we are doing, an invitation to get involved is included at the end of the book. We work non-paid – and our approach is straightforward, with no hidden agendas.

viii. A sense of purpose

> *"I know of no more encouraging fact than the unquestionable ability of man to elevate his life by conscious endeavour."*
>
> Henry David Thoreau

The majority of people in our society live and work in crowded towns and cities. They have become divorced from nature. They drive through the countryside in heated or air-conditioned cars. There is little direct contact with wildlife, except perhaps the blackbirds and robins encountered in the garden. If there is an appreciation of nature, it is usually through the natural history documentaries shown on television.

It would be helpful, I am sure, if we all spent more time outside in the wild. This could be done through walking, climbing up hills and mountains, or just by sitting and watching. It does not really matter whether we learn to admire the beauty of a butterfly or the hard work of an ant colony, or travel further to gaze in awe at seeing a tiger or the wildebeest migration. We will benefit from discovering a shared unity – from the recognition that all our differing species exist together within complex, interconnected ecosystems. There is wonder and admiration to be gained through contact with nature, which can lead to a basic respect for all forms of life.

In addition to gaining (or re-gaining) a feeling of affinity with nature, we need to *do* something about what is going wrong in our world. We cannot stand aloof or bury our heads in the sand without suffering further alienation ourselves. We need to act – to care and give help. Nature conservation requires a lot of assistance. So do animal welfare concerns. And those people who live in the poorest countries have suffered too much already. There are many victims of abuse in our own country, whether it be someone who has been raped or suffered neglect. Older and disabled people may need more assistance than most of us. The list is almost endless. By taking less and giving more, we can find a sense of purpose or meaning in life. And this will help towards bringing about a better society, better individual psychological health, and a better environment.

13

A fundamental change

i. Shifting paradigms

> *"The significant problems we face cannot be solved at the same level of thinking we were at when we created them."*
> Albert Einstein

> *"Insanity is continuing to do the same thing over and over and expecting different results."*
> Albert Einstein

It is unrealistic to hope that we could solve all our environmental, personal, and social problems by focusing on the symptoms. Instead, we need to concentrate our attention and effort on the fundamental cause of what is going wrong. This will require a different or deeper approach, rather than merely continuing or adapting the same old superficial attitude which presently dominates people's thinking. In short, a fundamental shift of paradigms is needed.

A paradigm is the basic pattern of perceiving, thinking, feeling, valuing, and acting. In the widest sense, it can be thought of as a psychological or behavioural map for living. If you have the wrong map (or an inaccurate map), it will be unhelpful and even misleading. Trying harder won't help if you don't know where it is you have to go. What you need is a change of maps.

The history of science has a number of instances in which there has been a revolution or shift in paradigms. For example, people used to believe that the Earth was the centre of the universe – that the sun and stars all revolved around us. Then Copernicus worked out that our planet and moon (together with all the other planets and moons in our solar system) actually moved around the sun. This created a paradigm shift.....and a lot of resistance and hostility; once apparently at the centre of creation, we no longer seemed so absolutely important. Darwin likewise shook established thinking with his ideas about the origin of species. Einstein revolutionised physics and our understanding of the universe with his relativity theory. Quantum physics, originated by Max Planck but developed further by others, brought about a fundamental shift in our understanding of the sub-atomic world. And Pasteur founded the science of microbiology and developed the technique of vaccination; prior to this, there was little or no understanding of micro-organisms, how they killed millions of people, nor knowledge about what preventative measures could be taken.

ii. Questioning the self-orientated paradigm

The prevailing paradigm is currently one of selfishness or self-orientated behaviour. This psychological mind-set results in global and personal suffering: murder, rape, child abuse, robbery, fraud, drink driving, vandalism, drug abuse, torture, corruption, famine and other forms of absolute poverty, war, cruelty to animals, pollution, destruction of natural habitats, extinction of species, terrorism, persecution, greed, depression, indifference, avoidance, boredom, prejudice, jealousy, hatred, insecurity, etc etc. The old habitual psychology which produces this dysfunction and suffering needs to be questioned, unlearned, and dumped – and replaced with a new non-selfish paradigm.

To unlearn our basic selfish mentality and replace it with a radical alternative psychology is a huge undertaking. In *Actions Speak Louder Than Words*, I describe it as an "almost impossible task".....going on to state "But it can be done." The "me first" conditioning is a response people have repeatedly learned throughout childhood and adult life. This "acceptable" selfishness is at the root of almost all motivation and behaviour, dominating human existence. So the resulting psychology is both incredibly complex yet also simple; the symptoms or expressions are intricate and individually unique, but the core or foundation is predictably evident: "me, me, me".

There are many people who already appreciate the good sense and attractiveness of such an alternative. They frequently use words like "holistic" and "wholeness" as if this superficial lip-service was enough. The reality, however, is that these people are usually a million miles away from properly understanding a non-selfish human potential – let alone personally demonstrating it as an actual "to-be-lived" reality. Whilst dominant selfish tendencies remain, there is always the danger of self-deception and hypocrisy. Words come easy, especially within an educated society. To begin with, the scale of genuine non-selfishness will probably be underestimated.

Hypocrisy – and its friend, avoidance – are amongst the major difficulties to overcome. These factors alone can cause irrational reactions and limitations, making even an intelligent person seem stupid. There needs to be a willing-ness to learn and to be open-minded, together with an awareness that this is unlikely to happen unless a lot of psychological baggage which gets in the way is first put aside.

The unspoken acceptance of general selfishness helps to perpetuate this cultural hypnosis. Wanting to belong, together with the shallow face of conformity, brings a degree of respectability and inclusion – but at the terrible expense of losing integrity, straightforwardness, self-honesty, and other similarly important qualities. Hypocrisy and psychological avoidance or denial then becomes inevitable to some degree. Even within those groups of people seemingly interested in a better way of living, there has been the absence of an anti-hypocrisy test such as "actions speak louder than words".

iii. Is non-selfishness possible?

> *"I am completely convinced that Iain Scott's rare experience is likely a part of the evolutionary destiny of Homo sapiens."*
>
> Edgar D. Mitchell
> – the sixth astronaut to walk on the moon.

Evidence of an alternative psychology or consciousness has been provided by the testimony of thousands of people from all parts of the world throughout recorded history. Best known of these individuals are the founders of the major religions, such as Buddha, Jesus, and Mohammed. The concept of a greater understanding, love, and unity is basic to all the great spiritual teachings. (Clearly, numerous differences and disagreements have since occurred on all sides – probably due to the difficulty of interpreting what the founders meant, made worse by conflicting personal and institutional agendas.) Many others have experienced a mystical vision or glimpse of this better way, including some of the world's most famous poets. Obvious and significant similarities are apparent from their accounts when studied. The potential of a "new" psychology is clearly suggested.

I personally experienced a spontaneous change of awareness between 1975 and 1978, repeatedly being "catapulted" into a different and greatly expanded consciousness. The insights and feelings were powerful and profound, presenting an alternative choice to that of normal or ordinary behaviour. Since 1978, the resulting trans-formation has consistently and constantly remained.

Leading researchers are suggesting that such experiences might be due to or associated with "coherent whole brain activity" – whereas most people, most of the time, are polarised towards a strong dependency upon one or the other hemisphere of the brain as the dominant organiser of their inner experience. The well-known psychologist Abraham Maslow, who died in 1970, was especially interested in the expanded consciousness of peak experiences and what he called "self-actualisation". Maslow was sure that the majority of people had not yet achieved their potential of becoming fully human, as the following quotations show:

> *"Certainly a visitor from Mars descending upon a colony of birth-injured cripples, dwarfs, [and] hunchbacks...could not deduce what they should have been. But then let us not study cripples, but the closest thing we can get to whole, healthy men. In them, we find qualitative differences, a different system of motivation, emotion, value, thinking, and perceiving. In a certain sense, only the saints are mankind. All the rest are cripples."*

And again:

> *"The notion I am working towards is of some ideal of human nature, closely approximated in reality by a few 'self-actualised' people. Everybody else is sick [to] a greater or lesser degree, it is true, but these degrees are much less important than we have thought...There seems no intrinsic reason why everyone shouldn't be this way [i.e. self-actualised]. Apparently, every baby has possibilities for self-actualisation, but most get it knocked out of them...I think of the self-actualising man not as an ordinary man with something added, but rather as the ordinary man with nothing taken away."*

The study of ecology shows us that interconnectedness is a basic principle of nature. Unique individual specimens and species exist, but within a wider framework or ecosystem which is interrelated and interdependent. Individual parts might change and be replaced, but the interconnected relationships of the whole remain essential. We cannot exist in isolation.

Another basic principle of nature is survival of the fittest. But this primary biological factor should not be confused with the human psychological conditioning of selfishness. The latter has developed from the former. Biological self-defence is necessary so as to exist in a world of complex diversity. If a rhino charges at us – or, to use a more frequently encountered modern example, if a car accidentally threatens to knock us down – we immediately respond. When danger is perceived, the biochemical adrenalin is released and we are able to accelerate into a heightened defensive action. This is obviously a necessary and helpful strategy; it is a matter of survival or existence, not selfishness. On the other hand, psychological self-defence is inherently problematic and based on dysfunction. It might seem to be possibly useful, but only because others are playing the same supposed-to-be game. Widespread evidence demonstrates that the self-orientated psychological strategy is flawed, contradictory, and likely to cause suffering. A non-selfish worldview, by contrast, would be non-divisive – accepting the uniqueness of individuality as part of the whole.

iv. An evolutionary step forward

Humankind is now at the beginning of a new form of evolution. As an intelligent species, we have the capacity to be responsible for our own future development. In the past, evolution has been a matter of biology. Now, it is our psychological evolution which is necessary for us to progress towards becoming fully human and genuinely civilised. Our emotional health needs to drastically improve and mature. The shift from selfishness to non-selfishness would be an enormous improvement, undoubtedly recognised as an evolutionary step forward. Such a massive psychological change would solve almost all of our personal, social, and environmental problems – at a fundamental or causal level – as well as bringing untold positive benefits.

Non-selfishness is a tremendous human potential waiting to be developed. It seems to exist already in people as something which is buried, neglected, misunderstood, denied, or suppressed. When it is searched for and attempts made to unfold it, this potential appears to be fragile and easily distorted. It is probably something deep within our nature at a pre-conditioned, pre-moral, and pre-cultural level. The latent brain capacity for this alternative, expanded psychology has already physiologically evolved – perhaps thousands of years ago – so it just needs to be developed in actual use.

Several psychological and biological triggers have already been identified as causing (or helping to cause) the rare glimpses of this "new" consciousness. But, however profound and overwhelming these spontaneous experiences are, they quickly fade apart from a lasting memory. What is surely most needed is a way for people to achieve a constant and complete transformation, instead of just a brief glimpse.

Education is required: precise and relevant knowledge – not some "new age" mumbo-jumbo, nor belief. Learning about the non-selfish psychology and how to apply it is not enough. An even more difficult and complex task is the unlearning of all the selfish conditioning already acquired since birth.

The radical alternative of non-selfishness has no basis in the self-orientated strategy and current range of human activity. The shift from selfishness to non-selfishness is not a continuum. There are two completely different starting points. Each is a fundamentally different option. There is a naked choice: selfishness or non-selfishness?

Several thousand years of confusion, misinformation, and hypocrisy have not helped to make this subject clear or straightforward. Belief systems are obviously limited and therefore inadequate from a practical perspective. The selfish conditioning is immense and on-going, certain to cause self-deception. Occasional experiences of non-selfishness are rare and usually go no further. Reliable and exact information on how to proceed is hard to find. The Human Potential Trust, a British registered charity, has accordingly been established to advance the education of the general public and to promote research into non-selfish consciousness. For further details, begin by reading *Actions Speak Louder Than Words* which provides an overview of the subject, including a description of the difficulties which commonly frustrate change and an outline of how to achieve a successful shift of consciousness.

v. Psychology and the environmental crisis

Human activity is causing our environmental problems and most of this behaviour is determined by our psychology. A few Americans have made this link between psychology and the environmental crisis, inventing terms such as eco-psychology and transpersonal ecology to express how they see the two academic disciplines being linked. They are generally correct in what they are saying, of course, but do not go far enough. There is too much soft philosophical content and insufficient emphasis on the harder aspects of human psychology.

We must be practical and down-to-earth. Realism is called for – not speculative idealism, whether true or not. Ecological psychology will only become relevant if and when it helps produce actual change. And if it is going to stand any chance of doing this, it cannot underestimate the difficulties involved in attempting to alter behaviour. A cosmetic or shallow approach will not work. The usual American-style "pop" psychology will only fool the believers; it won't be deep or solid enough to influence people sufficiently so as to prevent further habitat loss or species extinction.

A better understanding of our psychology is, however, urgently required. The initial goal should be to heighten sensitivity and increase awareness of all aspects of the current selfish strategy. If people then more clearly appreciated the scale and nature of the core problem, they could choose to voluntarily minimise their selfish behaviour without necessarily deciding to fundamentally change overall. This would be a valid first stage target for individual and general public education. Such a goal in itself is ambitious and would represent a big improvement in understanding. If successful, there should be a noticeably large impact on the environmental situation. Encouraged by real progress, a shift in psychological strategies – from selfishness to non-selfishness – could then be attempted.

Everyone concerned for the environment must take a long look at their own psychology, behaviour, and lifestyle.

They should learn to recognise and observe selfishness in all its forms – not just the extreme selfish actions which are already acknowledged by society in general. Self-honesty is not always encouraged and it can be emotionally painful to face reality until you get used to doing so. A reliance on avoidance, together with a fear of admitting hypocrisy, has to be overcome. But the alternative is worse: more of the same and a declining environmental situation.

As I have repeatedly stated, all our major problems are related – be they environmental, personal, or social. By facing this fundamental issue of selfishness, we open the way forward in many ways. The urgent need for nature conservation is also an opportunity for humanity to take another important step in its own evolution. As researchers have shown, individual happiness only goes so far – regardless of increasing wealth and material comfort; a radical shift of paradigms offers the prospect of greater personal well-being, in addition to solving most of the world's troubles.

We cannot ignore today's "acceptable" selfish psychology. In the short term, it might be easier for people to fool themselves that a bit of recycling and the occasional donation to WWF or Greenpeace will make a real difference. But in the long term, if we get it wrong, our children and grandchildren will suffer – along with nature – and be faced with an even more disastrous mess to clear up.

In the previous chapter "What can I do?", I suggested that a sense of purpose was important. Knowing yourself and changing yourself, together with helping to reverse our environmental crisis, is undoubtedly the task of a lifetime. Real progress involves a lot of hard work and takes time. Truly significant change, environmentally, might not be achieved during the course of a person's life. But we must start, once sure of our goal and map, and keep going when obstacles are encountered. If you lack the ethic of hard work and the toughness of determination, spend time watching the behaviour of ants – I did as a boy; they never give up.

Conclusion

"A human being is a part of the whole, called by us 'universe', a part limited in time and space. We experience ourselves, our thoughts and feelings as something separate from the rest – a kind of optical delusion of consciousness. This delusion is a prison for us, restricting us to our personal desires and to affection for a few persons nearest to us. Our task must be to free ourselves from this prison by widening our circle of compassion to embrace all living creatures, and the whole of nature in its beauty."

Albert Einstein

Life on Earth is an astonishing thing. Millions of species have evolved into uniquely different forms. From tree-frogs to tigers, kingfishers to kangaroos, the animal world never ceases to amaze us. The giraffes with their long necks and the porcupines with their pin-sharp quills are just two examples of nature's unusual adaptations. Fish of the tropical seas and coral reefs are coloured so brightly, they almost seem unreal. Other species, such as the chameleon family, can change their colour at will – as an emotional response or for camouflage. The wildebeest migration across East Africa's Serengeti and Masai Mara is spectacular by the huge number of individual animals involved. The great apes remind us that we are closely related. Butterflies, with their delicate and graceful wings, can travel long distances – even crossing oceans.

The plant world, too, is impressive and incredibly varied. Beautifully coloured flowers range in size and shape from tiny mountain alpines to the large king proteas of South Africa's Cape fynbos. Unforgettable trees range from the giant redwoods of California to the smaller but very old bristlecone pines found high up in the White Mountains of the same state. During autumn, many trees produce a dazzling display of colour – from butter yellow to deep red –

as their leaves prepare to fall for the winter. Cacti amaze us with an ability to withstand drought, usually protected by thousands of menacing spikes – yet made attractive to pollinating insects through their bright yellow, orange, pink, or red flowers which quickly open after a brief season of rainfall.

Our planet, itself, may not be "alive" in the biological sense. But the more we learn about its activity and geology, it seems to be a living entity in a different sense. Over time, continents heave and shift. Volcanoes erupt, their molten lava rapidly changing the surrounding landscape. Wind, rain, snow, and ice erode mountains – sometimes forming natural arches or bridges in their wake. The more we look and understand, the more we see that nature is full of wonder.

We, ourselves, are part of this astonishing complexity of life and existence. Our brains are especially incredible when we stop to think what such an organ allows us to do and become. We have developed intelligence and culture, unique on our planet (though probably not in the universe, which is surely full of life – including beings far more advanced than us). Through this development, humanity has set itself aside from nature in certain ways. Medical science keeps us alive longer, by counteracting dangers such as harmful bacteria and viruses. Agriculture has stabilised and intensified food production, allowing us to remain in one place and giving us the luxury of extra time to pursue non-essential interests. We live in houses which usually keep us safe from extremes of weather and dangerous animals.

Although this progress has been largely beneficial, we have also lost something in our modern concrete and plastic jungles. Most people have now become too isolated from nature. They have forgotten their connection with it – that we are part of our environment. It is not just something "out there" that we watch on TV natural history documentaries. Occasionally, some people are reminded of this in a drastic manner – such as at times of a hurricane, flood, drought, or similar upheaval – their arrogance temporarily shattered by a more powerful force of nature.

We should be proud of humanity's achievements so far. But we also need humility. Rather than it being forced upon us through a rare catastrophe (when we will react mainly negatively), we can experience a sense of awe and humbleness by having more contact with the natural world. This can range from watching wildlife in any of its forms to walking through a forest or up a mountain – or just looking up at the stars on a cloudless night. Such experiences help to remind us of our place in the overall picture. Each of us is no more and no less than a tiny part of life. We are important.....but so is an ant, an elephant, a sparrow, and an eagle – and a forest, a flower, a desert, a lake, a mountain, and a stream or river.

Now that people have learned to live more or less secure from the threatening aspects of nature, we must concentrate on learning to live together with our fellow human beings and other forms of life. Our intelligence should no longer be used to dominate and exploit, but rather to live safely and harmoniously as part of life on planet Earth. In voluntarily limiting human activity, the wildness of nature will once again expand. To successfully co-exist, we need to develop the qualities of appreciation and respect.

The selfish psychology can be no more than a mistaken wrong turn down a dead-end road when viewed in the context of humanity's evolutionary journey. It is time to wake up to this blindness or limitation – to retrace our steps and head towards a better way. Most human suffering is unnecessary; it is self-inflicted. Likewise, cruelty to animals and our environmental problems are due to the dysfunctional selfish mentality. Humankind urgently needs to emotionally mature and really use its intelligence. Nothing less than a fundamental shift of paradigms will do. The unhealthy self-obsession of today's normal or ordinary consciousness has to be replaced with a non-selfish psychology. Whereas this is certainly a desirable goal and a real potential, it would meanwhile be foolish to underestimate the hurdles to be overcome – such as hypocrisy, avoidance, and self-deception.

The nature conservation movement has already started and taken an important step or two forward. But most of the problems still remain. A deeper approach must replace the current shallow messages. We should ask "Who can we trust?" Basic issues including overpopulation and overconsumption cannot be ignored. Our concerns for wildlife and the environment have to be matched with greater caring for the poorest people in the world and a heightened desire for social justice. Individually, we need to develop responsibility and get on with putting our aspirations for a better world into action. Collectively, we should encourage straightforwardness.

We are obviously capable of great love. We can dream and be creative. And we are clever enough to invent marvels of technology. We care and want to help – just look at the best examples of ambulance drivers, doctors, and nurses. So it shouldn't be difficult to put an end to the human-caused extinction of species and destruction of ecosystems if we really put our minds and hearts together. During the lifetime of today's young people, it is possible that human beings will successfully walk on Mars. We have already made it to the moon. So big challenges are well within our grasp. We just need the motivation, to begin and then keep going, and to be exact. This is what it will take.

An invitation to get involved

In addition to the suggestions outlined in Chapter 12 "What can I do?", you can help in one or more of the following ways:

- Financially support The Wildlife For All Trust, preferably with regular donations; (please write for further details). Projects include working to save "forgotten" endangered species and their habitats, and educational initiatives to promote awareness of the need for a deeper approach to nature conservation. (The Wildlife For All Trust is a British registered charity, number 1006174.)

- Financially support You And Me, preferably with regular donations; (please write for further details). Humanitarian projects include a medical clinic in Sudan, helping Ethiopian and Eritrean refugees as well as thousands of poor Sudanese villagers, and an educational centre and school in Nepal. You And Me also has a long record of raising the issue of aid agency ineffectiveness and inefficiency. (You And Me is a British registered charity, number 296169.)

- Organise a sponsored or fundraising event for either or both of the two charities above.

- Buy extra copies of *What Will It Take? A Deeper Approach To Nature Conservation* and give them as presents to friends and family, etc. The book is an important educational tool and resource. (My author's royalties and other profits are automatically donated for charitable use.)

- Following on from the above, assist with Wildlife For All's educational activities – such as distributing leaflets and posters in the local area where you live and work.

- If you are especially sincere, down-to-earth, and serious – willing to change and capable of self-honesty – write for details of workshops organised by The Human Potential Trust (British registered charity, number 1044200). Meanwhile, read my previous book *Actions Speak Louder Than Words* (available from all good bookshops, priced £6.99 – ISBN: 1-899131-02-7) for further details of how to shift from selfishness to non-selfishness.

The postal address for Wildlife For All, You And Me, and The Human Potential Trust is:

The Oasis
Highbrook Lane
West Hoathly
Sussex RH19 4PL
England

Please enclose a stamped addressed envelope with all enquiries.

What will it take? A summary

A brief summary of the main points may be helpful, both to individuals and teachers.

- The environmental movement is still in its infancy. A deeper approach to nature conservation is urgently required. The current shallow approach cannot succeed with regard to its core objectives.

- Many examples, year after year, all over the world, have demonstrated that something is wrong. This is a continuing – and possibly worsening – situation.

- Don't follow like sheep. Do your own thinking.

- The environmental organisations are not united in a single movement. There are many differences and disagreements with regard to motivation, area of concern, and approach.

- There is myth and there is reality – e.g. Chief Seattle's speech.

- The benefits of recycling are overemphasised; its impact so far has been negligible.

- The fundamental problem is the "me, me, me" psychology.

- Overpopulation is a basic issue which cannot be ignored.

- Greed and the overconsumption of "I want more" is also a crucially important issue.

- Who can you trust? Most organisations, individuals, zoos, and government departments have hidden agendas which get in the way. Remember the Brent Spar and Project Tiger.

- "Sustainable development" is a flawed concept. What we need is ecological sustainability.

- The problem of severe poverty must also be solved. As

poorer countries develop, this will have huge environmental implications.

- Hunting and conservation do not easily mix.

- It is misleading to be anti-progress. Science, technology, and industry are advantageous if used wisely.

- More space is required for nature. Wildlife should be able to survive and evolve further.

- Be true to yourself. An approach based on flexible and realistic extremism might be best. Be responsible.

- Have two children or less to help stabilise and then reduce the human population.

- Assess your lifestyle. Don't be fooled into thinking that "doing a little bit" is enough; it isn't.

- Take less. Spend less, buy less, and appreciate the simple joys of life.

- Eat less meat or, preferably, become a vegetarian. This will help ease the stress on land use.

- Give more.

- Develop a sense of purpose, including an affinity with nature. Do something useful with your life.

- A fundamental change must involve a shift of paradigms. There is a basic choice: selfishness or non-selfishness? Non-selfishness is a real alternative – but factors such as hypocrisy, avoidance, and self-deception make changing difficult. But it can be done.